WANAMAKER'S TEMPLE

Wanamaker's Temple

*The Business of Religion in an
Iconic Department Store*

Nicole C. Kirk

NEW YORK UNIVERSITY PRESS
New York

NEW YORK UNIVERSITY PRESS
New York
www.nyupress.org

References to Internet websites (URLs) were accurate at the time of writing. Neither the author nor New York University Press is responsible for URLs that may have expired or changed since the manuscript was prepared.

Library of Congress Cataloging-in-Publication Data
Names: Kirk, Nicole C., author.
Title: Wanamaker's temple : the business of religion in an iconic department store / Nicole C. Kirk.
Description: New York : NYU Press, 2018. | Includes bibliographical references and index.
Identifiers: LCCN 2018011910 | ISBN 9781479835935 (hardcover) | ISBN 9781479827237 (paperback) | ISBN 9781479807314 (ebook) | ISBN 9781479893928 (ebook other)
Subjects: LCSH: John Wanamaker (Firm)—History. | Department stores—Pennsylvania—Philadelphia—History. | Social responsibility of business—Pennsylvania—Philadelphia—History.
Classification: LCC HF5465.U64 W365 2018 | DDC 381/.1410974811—dc23
LC record available at https://lccn.loc.gov/2018011910

New York University Press books are printed on acid-free paper, and their binding materials are chosen for strength and durability. We strive to use environmentally responsible suppliers and materials to the greatest extent possible in publishing our books.

Manufactured in the United States of America

10 9 8 7 6 5 4 3 2

Also available as an ebook

To Kirk Brauer and the other JW

CONTENTS

LIST OF FIGURES

Introduction

A cold rain poured on the crowds making their way to the old railroad freight depot at Thirteenth and Market Streets on the edge of Philadelphia. It was Sunday, November 21, 1875, and revivalists Dwight L. Moody and Ira Sankey were finally in Philadelphia for the first in a series of 250 revival meetings after years of petitions to visit the city by religious and civic leaders.

Tickets were issued, and extra policemen circulated to help control the throng. Despite the rain, thousands squeezed into the improvised freight depot tabernacle to hear the words and music of Moody and Sankey. The *Philadelphia Times* noted that "it looked as though the whole city had turned out before breakfast on the muddy, dreary morning" to attend the revival.[1] Many were turned away. The *Times* reported without a hint of irony that as the bells of the nearby Catholic churches rang to announce Mass, the Moody revival began. The congregation stirred when Moody and Sankey mounted the stage and "two snow-white pigeons roosting in the rafters above the pulpit" took flight, circling over the gathered multitude. Soon the combined voices of the choir and congregation drowned out the rival church bells.[2]

Ample press coverage breathlessly detailed the religious spectacle as thousands congregated nightly in what was dubbed the "Tabernacle Depot" by the media.[3] Moody's advertising machine, assisted by local Protestant business leaders and newspaper owners, whipped up demand for tickets.[4] Special reserved streetcars and trolleys brought scores of Philadelphians to the site, filling the twelve thousand seats day after day. People continued to stream to the far side of town for twelve consecutive weeks, making the once remote location a well-known landmark.[5]

The improvised tabernacle was meticulously organized. Inside, attendees found a well-lit space with thousands of chairs in neat lines. Nearly three hundred "blue-badged" ushers, many of them employees of a local department store, rushed to seat the demanding crowd. Once all the seats were occupied, the latecomers had to stand at the back and along the sides of the room.

Revival organizers cast the gatherings as disciplined and orderly affairs and asked audience members to sit "perfectly still." The instruction served a twofold purpose: to help make it possible to hear the speaker throughout the cavernous space, and to demonstrate the respectability and decency of the revival proceedings.

On the second night, Moody stressed that his revival meetings kept to a tight schedule by dramatically declaring that "the doors will be closed and locked, if the house is only half full, and the other half outside." Emphasizing the seriousness of his declaration, he announced, "If the President of the United States himself should come, . . . he wouldn't get in."[6] In fact, President Grant would attend the revival a month later, along with his entire cabinet and the U.S. Supreme Court after touring the yet unfinished Centennial Exhibition grounds and buildings.

On the fourth night of the revival, the hordes continued to prove greater than the space could accommodate. One disappointed man exclaimed, "It's as hard to get into heaven as it is to get into this depot," and another worried about the structure's safety if a fire broke out.[7] Every night following Moody's preaching and Sankey's heart-stirring singing, Moody's friend John Wanamaker, the owner of Philadelphia's leading men's wear store and provider of the revival's ushers, led postrevival meetings at a nearby Methodist church. Wanamaker also owned the freight depot sanctuary. A little more than a year after the last night of the revival, Wanamaker transformed the temporary tabernacle into one of the first American department stores.

The Problem with Business

Eight months after the revival, Moody wrote to his old friend, urging him to sell his successful stores. "I cannot get you out of my mind for the last few days and nights. I must set down & write you & make one more effort to get you out of your business."[8] It was not a new tension in their relationship. Moody had shared his concerns with Wanamaker before. In this letter, he worried for his friend's salvation, telling him, "It seems to me as if the devil wanted to cheat you out of your *Crown* and I was a fraid you will lose it the way you are goin–on." Moody coaxed further, "You can recover all you lost & gain your heart and the hearts of the people."[9]

Moody and Wanamaker's friendship had developed out of a shared past. They both came from working-class backgrounds and discovered evangelical Christianity as store clerks. They both served as paid secretaries for the Young Men's Christian Association (YMCA) and worked with the U.S. Christian Commission during the Civil War. Both men started Sunday schools in major American cities that became the megachurches of their day. And they both feared the influence of the developing urban environment on young Christian men and women. However, their perspectives on the moral nature of business were at odds.

Wanamaker and Moody took different directions in their ministries. Moody became a revivalist and educator while Wanamaker became a successful retailer and church layman. Although Wanamaker's success funded and supported Moody's evangelism—for instance, Wanamaker purchased the property for Moody's seminary in Northfields, Massachusetts—Moody remained unenthusiastic about the rapid expansion of Wanamaker's dry goods store. In Moody's mind, business was not equal to ministry and business could corrupt—a paradoxical stance, given Moody's reliance on business techniques, advertising, and businessmen for the success of his revivals. He believed that a high commitment to Christian service demonstrated faithfulness.[10] Moody wanted Wanamaker at his side "to look after the business [of ministry]" and to be fully committed to Christian work. By closing his growing store and devoting himself to full-time ministry, Moody claimed, Wanamaker would "be a free man again."[11]

Wanamaker disagreed. He neither abandoned his store nor left ministry behind. Instead, he built one of the largest retailing businesses in the world and helped to develop the American retail shopping experience, creating one of the early American department stores. The freedom to browse without purchase, one price for each product clearly labeled for all customers, generous return policies, and annual white sales—these retailing conventions that he helped to implement continue to define American retail to this day. A stint as the U.S. postmaster general stimulated an interest in political office, only to be thwarted by a series of defeats. His introduction of Rural Free Delivery (RFD) expanded mail service to rural customers and supported his growing catalog business and that of other mail-order stores. Seeing the opportunity for ready-to-wear clothing, Wanamaker embraced changes in production, later developing his own line of products under the Wanamaker store label. He fashioned his stores as regional enterprises and special destinations, drawing customers from across the eastern United States with promises of more than shopping; his stores offered a full cultural education, including art galleries and concert music, under one roof. His store advertisements offered shopping advice and homespun wisdom in addition to marketing goods and educating consumers. Wanamaker's massive stores in Philadelphia and later New York City and his active mail-order business, along with his enormous buying and production power, put him in a league with the other American merchant princes: A. T. Stewart, Marshall Field, Edward Filene, Aaron Montgomery Ward, and Julius Rosenwald. Wanamaker helped to create American retail. But business was not his sole occupation.

Wanamaker was also a prominent Christian lay leader. From his youth in the 1850s until his death in 1922 Wanamaker participated in the major Protestant moral reform movements that gained momentum during the second half of the nineteenth century to address concerns over the effects of immigration and the rapid growth of cities. Like many urban young men, he ignored sectarian differences and threw himself into more than one reform movement.[12] He began as a local leader in the Philadelphia outbreak of the Businessmen's Revival of 1857–1858. That same year, he started a Sunday school mission that later became Bethany Church, one of the largest institutional churches on the East Coast. Wanamaker served as the first paid secretary of a North American YMCA and then as president of the Philadelphia branch, where he oversaw the construction of its first building. He believed that architecture creates a powerful moral ambience capable of changing people, leading him to embrace the City Beautiful and Gothic Revival movements.[13] He subscribed to the principles of the temperance movement and Sabbatarianism, and he invested heavily in the development of religious education. He supported the Moody revival and later Billy Sunday's evangelistic efforts. He bankrolled large sums for the Salvation Army, made record donations to the organization, gave the Philadelphia branch a building, and kept a portrait of its founder, William Booth, in his home.[14] In other words, he believed in moral influence and its potential for shaping people and places.

Dwight L. Moody was not the only critic of Wanamaker's decision to remain in his business. Moody's concerns for his friend echoed the popular negative view of business in the second half of the nineteenth century, a view that continued into the twentieth century. Merchants, in particular, suffered from an image problem and invited criticism for a host of unseemly business practices. They were also regularly lampooned in the press as modern greedy tricksters known for their "duplicity" and "hardened hearts."[15] The press claimed that businessmen "too much loved the world" and thus devoted themselves to business to such a degree that family and religion fell into eclipse.[16] These perceptions conflicted with an emerging model of the working man whose tenacity and hard work moved him from poverty to success.

Popular opinion also laid the blame for the four major economic collapses of the nineteenth century squarely at the feet of businessmen, depicting the financial catastrophes as a result of an "emotional excess" of lust and greed.[17] A series of books detailed the charges, most famously one by William T. Stead, a journalist and moral advocate who later would get himself into trouble over his righteous zealousness. Stead published his provocatively titled book, *If Christ Came to Chicago!*, in 1894 after his visit to the city during the World's Fair. In it, Stead took readers on an imagined visit to Chicago through the eyes of Jesus. He directed the blame for the ills of society at Chicago's business leaders, particularly its merchants, including department store tycoon Marshall Field. He accused Field of mercenary business practices, claiming that Field had built his store on a "pyramid largely composed of human bones" and accusing the department store founder of destroying small businesses by undercutting prices.[18] The luxury rail car maker George Pullman and mass meat producer Philip Armour shared the scathing spotlight with Field for what Stead called their "quest of the almighty dollar."[19] As evidence of their immorality, he chronicled their lavish lifestyles in comparison to those of their workers. The book became a runaway bestseller.

The growth of companies into huge, abstract corporations invited the charge that large businesses and their proprietors were unethical, "amoral," and "soulless."[20] The problem was more than just the increasing size of businesses: Americans had trouble identifying where large corporations fit in the familiar relational frameworks of home, church, and local business. Exposés that uncovered disturbing business practices and the growing power of corporations led to perceptions of businesses as uncaring, distant, and morally questionable in their drive to make more money.[21]

Cultural historians and journalists in the late twentieth century took up the critique of businessmen, equating the birth of modern consumerism with a decline in Protestant Christianity.[22] Their studies of the intersections of religion and business suggested that the business leaders of the late nineteenth century helped to create "a commercial environment steeped in pecuniary values."[23] For these scholars, Wanamaker and others like him represented a cultural turn in which uncritical "accommodations of religion" to consumerism" led to a marginalization of religion.[24] Merchants, in this view, used religion merely as a convenient gimmick to sell more goods. The behavior of those prominently involved in religious activities was seen as a naive attempt to bring together religious sentiments and the developing world of consumerism or as a malicious intent to use religion for business profit.[25] Religious commitments were assumed to have little to no effect on their business practices, which frequently appeared to operate in opposition to professed religious belief.[26]

Yet, while some historians suggested that business leaders used religion either to insincerely increase profits or to assuage guilt—a thesis that equates the rise of business with the decline of religion—a new generation of scholars has demonstrated the intermingling of Protestantism and business stretching back as far as the Puritans.[27] As historian Mark Noll has noted, religion and business have always been intertwined in "extraordinarily complex ways."[28] Their histories have shown how revivalists and Protestant Christian organizations employed business techniques to further religious aims long before the nineteenth century.[29] And they have demonstrated how American evangelical business leaders geared their businesses to promote and support their religious agendas.

Were Wanamaker's religious activities and his store's holiday promotions merely a ploy to increase sales? Was his incorporation of Christian themes into the material world of his store self-serving and a corruption of his spiritual message? Or were his efforts part of a larger endeavor to breathe new life into an evangelical Protestant message to meet the challenges of the time?

This book examines how and why a well-known and leading American businessman, John Wanamaker, blended commerce and religion in his massive Philadelphia department store. It offers a historical exploration of how the relationships among evangelicalism, commerce, and urban life in the late nineteenth and early twentieth centuries merged in unexpected and public ways, and how these relationships contributed to the creation of an American Protestant Christian ethos that was expressed, shaped, and supported by commerce. Wanamaker aimed not only to shape the budding American retail experience, but also to evangelize his consumers and employees, creating model middle-class Protestants. Wanamaker saw his retail empire not as separate from religion but as an instrument of it, as a means for achieving moral reform in business, in the city, and in individuals' lives. Wanamaker, like many others during this period, developed a new way to deliver "old-time religion." He harnessed the material world and aesthetics for his ministry, seeking to influence and define the moral order of the urban milieu through architecture, material goods, and public religious and civic events.

For many years, Wanamaker and his retail business made appearances in histories of American retail, department stores, holidays, and the rise of the middle class. The store and its art displays have also been a staple source for art historians and scholars of material and visual culture exploring the public display of religion. Yet, a fuller treatment of Wanamaker's store and his religious commitments has not been undertaken, until now. This book traces earlier developments in the blending of religion and business and their roots in the emerging moral reform movements of the nineteenth century. Attending to Wanamaker and his approach to business and religion reveals much about the role Protestantism played in the formation of a middle-class aesthetics, the way that Protestantism was tied to the emergence of consumerism, and how Protestantism changed through its moral-religious response to shifts in population and religion in the urban landscape.

Urban Crisis

The nineteenth century was a period of moral anxiety for Protestants, centering on cities.[30] American cities changed dramatically in layout, density, architecture, size, and social strata in a relatively short period of time. While new technology offered more affordable goods and greater personal comfort, it also upended traditional business methods and work life.[31] "Progress" was touted as a positive moral value, but it came at a high cost. The familiar structures of communal life and business became nearly unrecognizable.[32]

Developments in transportation and jobs lured people to cities from small towns at the same moment that Protestant churches faced diminishing authority. A flood of newcomers with little experience of urban living arrived looking for jobs, housing, and a sense of identity in an unfamiliar environment.[33] Business shifted away from small establishments operated by "self-employed proprietors to large corporations run by salaried managers" and their army of workers. Historian Alan Trachtenberg has noted the sharp contrasts that erupted during this period between the wretched effects of industrialization and the hopeful, upward mobility of some members of the population.[34] New technologies introduced improvements to life while at the same time creating new detriments.

Adding to the ferment, urban populations swelled with an influx of millions of immigrants who came in successive waves starting in the 1820s and lasting until the 1920s. Between 1840 and 1890, 7.5 million Irish and German people poured into American cities, forever changing the cultural and religious demographics.[35] Most of these immigrants were Catholic or Jewish, upsetting the Protestant majority at a moment when Protestants already felt vulnerable because of changes stemming from the industrialization of cities.[36] The surfeit of newcomers broadened the increasing culture gaps between city residents and country dwellers, rich and poor, educated and uneducated.[37]

Cities were not prepared for the swift expansion that took place in the nineteenth century. Insufficient water supplies and waste systems, poor street conditions, and a lack of suitable housing plagued cities and yet did little to stymie growth.[38] New transportation lines extended the boundaries of cities to meet outlying communities, eventually absorbing them. Wealthy residents moved out of cities to escape declining conditions, forcing their religious institutions to decamp from their urban homes. The old pattern of cities composed of small neighborhood enclaves that created tight-knit communities broke down with a surge in unregulated development.[39] As cohesive neighborhoods disappeared, traditional institutions of support destabilized and became overwhelmed by the needs of a larger area and a more diffuse complex of problems. Customary lines of authority and power weakened as established families found themselves competing with new wealth in a jostle for power and prestige.

Women's roles also began to change as a large number entered the workforce outside the home. At first, women's occupations opened largely in the arena of domestic service. By the 1890s, women found jobs in factories, business offices, and early department stores.[40] Upper-class women discovered new opportunities outside the home through women's groups, volunteer activities, and businesses, like department stores, that catered to them. The social needs of the urban context also drew women into reform work and offered new opportunities for leadership.

An increase of violence and unrest also marked the period, with inadequate police forces and many city governments hampered by corruption.[41] Bloody gang wars, street brawls, anti-Catholic riots, and protests broke out regularly.[42] Unemployment and pockets of deep poverty contributed to the disquiet, while workers toiled long hours doing backbreaking work for low wages. The second half of the century saw several eruptions of labor unrest, including the Great Railroad Strike of 1877, Chicago's Haymarket Affair in 1886, and the Pullman Strike of 1894, in addition to smaller, localized outbreaks.[43]

Starting at the same time that the first wave of young men from rural areas and immigrants settled into American cities, a surge of popular literature warned of the moral dangers of urban spaces. A new popular genre, what historian R. Laurence Moore has called "moral sensationalism," soared in popularity, feeding the masses a never-ending stream of salacious tales of crime and vice in the city.[44] Cities were cast in the popular imagination as sinister places that eroded more than the physical health of their occupants; they were a danger to their moral health too. Slums and tenements in particular were painted as places of sexual licentiousness, lawlessness, and drunkenness. This genre contrasted cities with a romanticized depiction of domestic life in agrarian small towns.[45]

Congregationalist minister Josiah Strong, starting in 1885, authored several works identifying the need to focus Christian mission work in American cities and the West. Alarmed by the changes in population, the perceived moral danger of the city, and what felt like diminishing

Protestant religious authority and cultural dominance in the face of a soaring Catholic presence, Protestants responded with a proliferation of reform strategies in what historian Paul Boyer has called a "moral awakening."[46] These programs—which included new forms of church and an array of agencies, movements, and morality campaigns—aimed to take back the city, domesticating it, and transforming it morally. What had been seen as a dire situation turned into an opportunity. Unable to combat the problems alone, Protestants set aside major doctrinal differences and banded together, pooling resources and ideas to address the problems of the city in creative ways that led to what was ostensibly a rebirth of American Protestantism.[47] At the heart of these moral reform movements stood both a real community and what scholar Benedict Anderson has called an "imagined community."[48] The imagined community links people together who may never meet and yet share a similar set of values and ideals that make them recognizable to one another.

The real community consisted of a network of Protestant churches and leaders who, throughout the nineteenth century, worked together toward common goals across denominational lines. In many ways, these leading Protestants were the economic beneficiaries of the changes in American commerce. In this period, Protestantism began to embrace the concept of moral influence or persuasion and moved away from a sudden conversion model to one of religious formation over time.[49] Popularizing these ideas, Horace Bushnell, in his book *Christian Nurture*, advanced an organic approach to religion in which home developed into a religious and spiritual center.[50] A child became Christian through the influence of properly maintained family, home, and church. Good taste and refinement came from God.[51] These ideas transformed the way people looked at housekeeping, the arrangement of furniture, and home design—elevating them to new importance in religious life. Home, as historian Colleen McDannell has observed, became an intentional "vehicle for the promotion of values."[52] Reformers embracing this viewpoint and expanded the vision beyond the home with the belief that beautiful and orderly cities and green spaces had the power to transform their inhabitants morally.[53] Bushnell and other reformers had combined piety with taste.

Art critics such as John Ruskin, Charles Eliot Norton, and others broadened this thinking to include civic and religious architecture, landscape design, and artwork as sources of moral refinement. Ministers picked up these themes in their preaching and led their congregations to construct new buildings that paid attention to the aesthetic expression of Protestantism.[54] They wanted to reestablish moral authority and the prominence of Protestantism; in that process they redefined American Christian churches, institutions, architecture, and white identity. The YMCA, Sunday school mission movement, development of religious education, Moody-Sankey revivals, settlement house movement, social gospel movement, City Beautiful movement, Gothic Revival, and Arts and Crafts movement, among many others, shared this perspective.

Tying these moral reform movements together was an "imagined" pan-Protestant community rooted in a nostalgic, idealized vision of rural small-town life remembered as moral, virtuous, orderly, and supported by neighbors' supervision.[55] Reform movements contrasted this vision with the seemingly chaotic urban landscape where everyone appeared to be a stranger. The romanticized agrarian past informed a shared vision of what it meant to be Protestant, white, and middle- or upper-class. Print media, such as religious publications, books, religious education materials, magazines, advertisements, and sermons, helped white urban Protestants to "imagine themselves and their identities in relationship to others," identified what they aspired for themselves to be, and articulated a longing for a mythical, utopian past.[56] The Protestant imagined community allowed the exchange of ideas and approaches to move between Europe and the United States, making it a trans-Atlantic phenomenon. Attempts to bring unity among Protestants found their way into the design of church architecture, liturgy, and Sunday school classes.[57] They redefined and reinforced what it meant to be Protestant. It was a Protestantism suited for the urban world and new wealth.

Protestant reformers translated desired values into practices of decorum and material expressions. Historian Richard Bushman has noted, "The refinement of America began around 1690" and by the "end of the eighteenth century and beginning of the nineteenth . . . the middle class . . . [began] to believe they should live a genteel life." In part, material markers of a genteel life became accessible to a wider range of people when they became more affordable with the changes in mass production and transportation. By the Civil War, "vernacular gentility," a gathering of elements of refinement and taste, had become the possession of the American "middling classes."[58] Values perceived to be derived from rural life included purity, cleanliness, discipline, honesty, order, neatness in dress, and refinement in manners, and these values were also articulated into house furnishings and domestic architecture. Those who wished for "simple respectability had to embody the marks of the genteel style in their persons and their houses."[59] Social theorist Pierre Bourdieu calls the adoption of genteel style "cultural capital," the idea that values could be translated into "culturally authorized tastes, consumption patterns, attributes, skills and awards."[60] Increasingly, for many Protestants "good taste became virtually a principle of Christian morality."[61] The combining of good taste with morality gave permission to purchase material goods and imbued material goods with moral power.

Good taste, then, had the power to change people. Material acquisitions and deportment determined "good taste." With morality thus connected to taste, good taste signaled to bystanders an individual's moral disposition.[62] It became a shorthand way for urban Protestants to recognize moral individuals and those with whom they wished to associate. Protestants intentionally mobilized architecture, fashion, art, and music to promote morality and conversion in what I term an "aesthetic evangelism."[63] In the urban context, these small-town values that were meant to shape the immigrant population became associated with, attracted, and simultaneously helped to create the developing middle class.[64]

This book examines how John Wanamaker not only participated in these urban moral reform movements but creatively adapted these approaches for his department store, making it an instrument for moral reform. He also attempted to convert retail business into a moral-ethical, Christian endeavor by changing and promoting new business practices. From the Philadelphia store's architecture to the ritual use of space, from the art and educational exhibits to employee education programs and their physical presentation, Wanamaker understood his department store and his employees as an extension of his religious work. Contrasting himself with his Chicago competitor Marshall Field, who had said, "Give the Ladies what they want," Wanamaker told the public, "To give people the things they want is not enough." Instead, he sought to be "an educator in taste."[65] For him, taste was not simply fashion, although it was that too. "Good taste" was an outward expression of an interior state—a reflection of one's moral character. He believed, as did other

Protestants, that disciplined dress, bearing, behavior, and lifestyle had the power to shape one's morality—to improve one's interior. Wanamaker hoped that through his store's aesthetic education his customers and employees would experience moral uplift. His approach to business was an exercise of his Christian piety and practice. While pursuing traditional avenues of Protestant Christianity through his continued work in revivals, his Sunday school, and the YMCA, Wanamaker helped to transform Protestant Christianity by infusing the developing commercial culture with new meaning. Wanamaker's blending of religion and business altered our understanding of Protestant Christianity in the late nineteenth and early twentieth centuries. By following the trajectories of the braiding together of business and religion, we gain insight into the intertwining strands of aesthetics, material goods, and architecture with the developing middle class.

1

Retail Reform

On a May evening in Philadelphia in 1914, the carriage carrying Russell Conwell and John Wanamaker crawled along a three-mile parade route linking Conwell's Broad Street home to the Academy of Music, the home of the city's symphony orchestra. A large crowd had gathered along the street to celebrate the lawyer turned Baptist minister, founder of Temple University, and first president of the Samaritan Hospital.[1] On this night, Conwell would present his wildly popular lecture "Acres of Diamonds" for the five thousandth time to an eager audience of three thousand.[2] Providing the introductory remarks for this grand occasion was Conwell's fellow philanthropist and friend of more than thirty years, John Wanamaker.

Before moving to Philadelphia in 1882, Conwell had gained fame as an orator on the Chautauqua circuit and speaking at churches. He had delivered "Acres of Diamonds" across the country to eager audiences who wanted to reconcile their Protestant theology with their changing economic circumstances. The growth of commerce and industry opened the way not only to financial security but to affluence. A growing middle class needed a new way to think about money unencumbered by Protestantism's negative interpretation of wealth.

In "Acres of Diamonds," Conwell advanced the surprising message that seeking wealth was neither a sign of greed nor the root of evil. Instead, it was a godly pursuit. He passionately told his listeners, "I say that you ought to get rich, it is your duty to get rich. . . . Because to make money is to honestly preach the Gospel."[3] He spoke plainly of the advantages of money, linking it to the prosperity of churches and reminding audiences, "Money is power, and you ought to be reasonably ambitious to have it. You ought because you can do more good with it than you could without it." Indeed, money supported evangelism, he pointed out: "Money printed your Bible, money builds your churches, money sends your missionaries, and money pays your preachers, and you would not have many of them, either, if you did not pay them." Money underwrote the church and its outreach.

Conwell's lecture marked a startling transformation in tone among Protestants. He promoted the accrual of riches as a reform tool, which he claimed Jesus would wholeheartedly approve. Speaking of assumptions that piety and affluence were mutually exclusive, he pointedly told his audiences that to say "'I do not want money,' is to say, 'I do not wish to do any good to my fellowmen.'" He instructed his followers to pursue prosperity in an honest, morally upright way. And he warned them, "It is an awful mistake" to believe that you have to be "awfully poor in order to be pious."[4] You could be pious and rich. A strong work ethic combined with moral living would be rewarded by God. Becoming wealthy demonstrated God's approval and allowed one to do more of God's work. This idea, which would later become known as the "prosperity gospel," was part of a larger movement that emphasized individualism and the "self-made man," and altered the relationship between business and Christianity in the late nineteenth and early twentieth centuries. Material goods played a key role in Conwell's message—prosperity was expressed by accumulation and quality of goods. It was natural for Wanamaker and other prosperity gospel adherents to turn to aesthetics as an expression of God's blessing and as an educational tool.

John Wanamaker epitomized Conwell's gospel.[5] Although Conwell was a Baptist and Wanamaker was a Presbyterian, they shared a theological perspective that spanned denominational divides. Conwell's concept of money and wealth provided Wanamaker and other Protestant entrepreneurs a much-needed positive interpretation of their dizzying success and helped him make sense of how to be deeply religious and prosperous at business. It also explained why he spent his money both to purchase luxury goods and to build institutions that served the poor.

Wanamaker never grew tired of Conwell's "Acres of Diamonds." He published dozens of editions of the speech at his printing press. The lecture helped him make sense of his world and he wanted others to learn it. It bridged the worlds of religion and commerce. For the six thousandth delivery of the lecture, Conwell gave the speech at the store's radio station. Wanamaker's treasured religious philosophy of material wealth radiated from the store for hundreds of miles.

"A Country Boy"

It is hard to say how much Wanamaker and his biographers embellished the details of his early life. His version of the story emphasized how hard work, moral fortitude, and Christian devotion resulted in social mobility and impressive economic success. He cast himself as a "self-made man" straight from a Horatio Alger novel.[6] His early biographers, many of them friends and admirers, perpetuated this image with their laudatory accounts produced shortly after his death in 1922.

During his life, Wanamaker presented his biography—long used as part of the advertising for the store—to help establish the moral character of his department store.[7] His personal stories emphasized his hardworking, religiously devout brickmaking family and the simplicity of living among the riverside marshes and farms of Philadelphia in an unexpected juxtaposition of country and city life.[8] The virtues of hard work, mutual support, loyalty, and sacrifice, mixed in with familial devotion, served as signposts of Wanamaker's character.

Born to Nelson and Elizabeth Wanamaker in the summer of 1838, the first year of a crushing economic depression that gripped the nation, John Wanamaker was the oldest boy of six children and was named after his grandfather.[9] His father and grandfather before him were brickmakers, sharing a small brickyard in the South Philadelphia neighborhood of Grays Ferry.[10] His mother, Elizabeth, the daughter of a local farmer and described as a descendent of French Huguenots, was a deeply religious woman who "communed with God, and to this end, she was regular and diligent in her readings and devotions."[11] Her uncle ran the local inn, the Kochersperger Hotel.[12] Grays Ferry sat between South Street and the Schuylkill River on one side and the Delaware River on the other. In the early and mid-nineteenth century, it was home to various light industries, including leather tanning, lime burning, lumber, and fertilizer and chemical companies. Of the nine Philadelphia brickmakers listed in the *McElroy Business Directory* of 1859, six of them made their home in Grays Ferry, in part because of the high clay content in the soil—an essential element for making bricks.[13] The area also was home to a number of small farms and the impressive Naval Home, a hospital for disabled veterans modeled after a Greek temple in Athens.[14]

A marshy rural area, Grays Ferry was sparsely populated compared to bustling downtown Philadelphia. It formed one of the many "island" neighborhoods that made up American cities in the early nineteenth century.[15] Perhaps not surprisingly, Wanamaker liked to call himself "a country boy" and liked to recount childhood memories of fishing, catching frogs, and frolicking with friends among the fields and marshes.[16] However, the extent of his modest upbringing remains uncertain. Wanamaker mentions that his birth took place in a house on a small farm initially belonging to his mother's family. His adult descriptions of his childhood home were thoroughly Victorian—the home was a bright and cheery oasis ruled by his devoted mother. In a store advertisement, he sweetly described it as "a little white house with its green shutters and a small garden of marigolds and hollyhocks." It is most likely that the Wanamakers were decidedly working middle-class, although unstable in their social ranking.[17]

One of the challenges of living in Grays Ferry was its lack of schools. At best, a child's formal schooling was occasional in the mid-nineteenth century. Families frequently relied on their children to provide labor on farms and in family businesses, making regular school attendance challenging. A lack of accessible schools compounded the problem. At the age of ten, John received his first taste of organized education when a small schoolhouse was set up at the edge of his family's brickyard for the neighborhood children.[18] However, the schoolmaster meted out blows with his spelling lessons, making John's schoolhouse experiences stressful.

Over two winters starting in 1847, Trinity Lutheran Church surveyed the Grays Ferry neighborhood for the establishment of a mission Sunday school. During this period, churches started mission Sunday schools to serve poor urban areas and provided moral education and lessons in reading and writing rooted in the Bible.[19] A local farming family, the Landreths, offered an empty house for the school, and one of the workers from the church, John A. Neff, became its superintendent. John Wanamaker's father, Nelson Wanamaker, and his grandfather, John Sr., a longtime Methodist lay preacher, volunteered to teach Sunday school classes. Later in life, he claimed "the Sunday School as the principal educator of my life" and the Bible as the source for "knowledge not to be obtained elsewhere, which established and developed fixed principles."[20]

Wanamaker also kept busy at the family business, where he turned bricks to dry in the yard with his brothers.

Grays Ferry did not remain bucolic. The fields and marshes Wanamaker fondly recalled gave way to increasing industrialization, pushing out longtime residents. The routing of new rail lines through other parts of the city isolated Grays Ferry from the wave of new economic development springing up in Philadelphia.[21] Competition increased as larger brickyards swallowed up small, family-run businesses. Racial tensions grew between workers as opportunities for work became competitive. Long an abolitionist, John Sr. employed free and formerly enslaved African Americans in his brickyards despite protests and sporadic attacks by white workers.[22] Unemployed men started gangs, and young local ruffians began roaming the streets to stir up mischief.[23] By 1850, John Sr. looked for an escape for his extended family from the deteriorating area and struck upon the idea of moving to Indiana to be near his father's family. Nelson and Elizabeth followed with their five children, moving into a homesteader log cabin on an isolated farm of about 250 acres located seven miles from Leesburg, Indiana.[24] But homesteading through Indiana's harsh winters offered a harder life than Grays Ferry. John Sr.'s sudden death sealed the fate of the pioneer adventure. The Wanamaker family returned to Philadelphia, buying back the old business to take up brickmaking once more, first living in Grays Ferry and later moving to a home on Lombard Street, closer to the center of town.[25]

Upwardly Mobile

John Wanamaker grew up in a swiftly changing country. At the point his family headed to Indiana to improve their fortunes, other Americans left their homes searching for new opportunities. Some moved west to try their luck at homesteading, farming, or getting rich in one of the gold rushes. Others made their way to cities lured by steady jobs and paychecks, leaving the fickleness of agriculture and small-town life behind.

Philadelphia bustled with growth and activity throughout the nineteenth century. By the late nineteenth century, it served as a publishing, finance, and manufacturing hub.[26] The city had experienced rapid development earlier than other cities.[27] Its growth spurt began in the antebellum period and continued through the early part of the twentieth century, making it one of the wealthiest and largest cities in the country by 1920.[28]

It was a religious center for the nation as well. Not only did Philadelphia remain an anchor for the Quakers, but it was also the home of the mother diocese of the Episcopal Church, the birthplace of the African Methodist Episcopal Church, and one of the first places Catholics openly worshipped in the American colonies.[29] The first presbytery in the United States started in the city, making it a center for Presbyterianism. Two major synagogues were established in the eighteenth century, giving Judaism an early foothold that allowed it to prosper in the city. Later, Philadelphia became the headquarters for a number of national religious organizations, agencies, and boards.[30] And like other major American cities, Philadelphia experienced the complex problems and conflicts of rapid urban growth.

An embrace of innovative technology and transportation spurred Philadelphia's expansion.[31] Situated on two rivers with ocean access, the city augmented its transportation system with the construction of a series of canals. The arrival of railroads connected Philadelphia and New York with a growing network of cities on the Eastern Seaboard. Philadelphia was especially adept at constructing an urban transportation infrastructure.[32] The establishment of a streetcar system allowed urban workers to live farther afield and increased the city's footprint. Telegraph wires went up in 1845 and quickly expanded. The emergence of Philadelphia's industrial center in the 1850s led to a remarkably diverse set of industries and businesses, including heavy manufacturing, steel, textile production, pharmaceuticals, and chemicals. Cheaper transportation meant cheaper consumer goods, so items such as household furnishings became affordable to a growing middle class.[33] At the same time, wealth became more widespread with an increase in industrial and especially white-collar jobs, allowing individuals and families to buy more goods than what was essential. The time was ripe for new developments in retail to meet the changing needs.

For the Wanamakers, the move to Indiana and back did not improve their financial situation. While his parents wanted to educate their children, a lack of schools and the family's financial distress made it necessary for thirteen-year-old John to find a job to help support the family. Nelson and Elizabeth hoped for a position for their son outside the brickyards. Using their religious ties, they consulted with John Neff, who had been the superintendent of the Landreth Mission Sunday School. Wanamaker's mother implored Neff, "I want you to find my John a good place in a good store; somewhere near where you are so that you can keep an eye on him."[34] Neff suggested that Wanamaker accept the opportunity to be an errand boy first at a bookseller and later at a law firm.[35] By the next year, John had moved from being an errand boy to sweeping floors and dusting mannequins at a dry goods store—a shop that carried a variety of nonliquid (that is, dry) goods, including textiles, and that became an early model for emerging department stores.[36] His parents' vision of upward mobility for their oldest son was a propelling force in John Wanamaker's life, and he would later interpret his stint at the dry goods store as a source of his interest in retail.[37]

Despite what he described later in life as a limited education, Wanamaker proved to be a fast learner with an entrepreneurial streak. He grew restless as a store janitor and began to develop ideas for improving the store's business. He already knew he wanted to be a successful merchant and decided to find a job at one of the city's larger retail establishments. Wanamaker set his sights on a job at Tower Hall, a leading men's clothier in downtown Philadelphia specializing in men's ready-to-wear clothing. An up-and-coming trend, "ready-made" or "ready-to-wear" clothing was still a novelty at a time when customers typically made their clothes at home or had them made by dressmakers or tailors.[38] Tower Hall was one of many businesses changing the way people dressed and shopped. It was a shift away from businesses that sold the materials to produce goods at home to purchasing items created in a factory. Tower Hall's proprietor, Colonel Joseph N. Bennett, a man often described as eccentric, hired the young Wanamaker because he had known John's grandfather well.[39]

Wanamaker wanted to learn how to sell. However, Bennett assigned him menial tasks as his first jobs around Tower Hall. Perhaps sensing that it was a test, Wanamaker enthusiastically performed small jobs. In an effort to prove himself, he polished the brass doorknobs of the store until they gleamed. Bennett took a liking to the young man, recalling years later, "He was the most ambitious boy I had ever met." Wanamaker repeatedly told Bennett that "he was going to be a great merchant someday."[40] In particular, Bennett admired John for his "natural born" organizational abilities, saying, "He was always organizing something."[41]

For the next three years, Bennett tutored Wanamaker on the ins and outs of the retail business, from managing stock to sales to buying the store's inventory. His apprenticeship at Tower Hall put him into a relatively small pool of white-collar workers that in a few short decades would grow exponentially into the thousands. In those early years, a white-collar salesman possessed a set of skills that placed him in an elite group of workers. Many of these young men would take their leap into business, founding what would become thriving dry goods and wholesale businesses in America's booming cities.

"A Religion to Live By"

Elizabeth Wanamaker had wanted her oldest son to be a minister.[42] Wanamaker recalled, "My first love was my mother. . . . Leaning little arms upon her knees, I learned my first prayers."[43] Church and Sunday school were constants throughout his boyhood. But it was not until Wanamaker's late teens that the religious devotion of his family became fully his own. He started attending worship services at First Independent Church at the corner of Broad and Sansom Streets on the edge of town, where the well-liked Irish preacher, the Reverend John Chambers, was known for his creative and sometimes rebellious approach to ministry.

Chambers started First Independent when local Presbyterians refused to ordain him for his "unorthodox" views.[44] He opened a new church, and in another maverick move, Chambers advertised worship times and his sermon titles in the newspaper. Like many Protestant leaders in the mid-nineteenth century, he preached a message that increasingly placed an emphasis on moral and ethical reform as the heart of the gospel. A big champion of the temperance movement, Chambers insisted on total abstinence from alcohol, despite the fact that some of his parishioners made their money from distilling liquor. A Sabbatarian, he urged parishioners to keep a strict sanctity of Sunday as the "Lord's Day."[45] Chambers rejected creedal statements like the Westminster Confession because they lacked a practical emphasis. He felt that creeds interfered with "holy living" and outreach to those in need.[46] And as the Baptist Russell Conwell would later preach to great effect, he taught his followers that "time and talents no longer belonged to himself but to the Lord and should be used in his service." Chambers stressed the humanitarian impulse of Christianity, an idea that would crop up in the teachings of Josiah Strong and Washington Gladden, leaders of what became known as the social gospel movement later in the century. He argued that people needed to be "like the good Samaritan, to go out of his way to help people in trouble, lend a helping hand in life to those who had fallen, and help to start them on their way again."[47]

Wanamaker discovered Chambers's First Independent Presbyterian Church by accident. One evening as he was walking by the church, the sound of singing drew him inside.[48] He had walked into a prayer meeting where men were talking about how religion gave meaning to their lives. The first speaker—an older gentleman with wispy white hair who stepped forward and began to speak of the importance of religion for him and of the way that he now "had a religion to die by"—failed to impress young Wanamaker.[49] He recalled that as a young man he was seeking "something not to die by, but to live by."[50] His attitude changed with the next speaker, a hatter named R. S. Walton who walked to the front of the room and spoke of the "practical" side of religion—how as a Christian, he felt that his religion was part of his trade as a hat maker.[51] The hatter told the small gathering that business and religion were not mutually exclusive; they were part of one another. Religion informed his trade, and trade informed his religion. In a letter written later in life, Wanamaker remembered that evening and how after the meeting he searched the building for the Reverend Chambers to tell him that "I had given my heart to God that night." The minister replied with a firm handshake and said, "You will never regret it." Wanamaker described those words in his later years as "the truest thing that I know."[52]

After Wanamaker's experience at the prayer meeting, he threw himself into a frenzy of religious activities at church, Tower Hall, and then the streets of Philadelphia. He taught Sunday school at First Independent, gathering neighborhood boys for lessons, led prayer meetings during his lunch break, and, like many young men in cities, joined the city's newly established YMCA. He invited coworkers to church, circulated a temperance pledge to promote abstinence from alcohol, and started prayer meetings.[53] The more he devoted himself to religious work, the more zealous he became.

Tireless at first, Wanamaker eventually found that his religious fervor combined with his long hours at Tower Hall took a toll on his health.

He suffered from skin infections, and his lungs filled with congestion. He had never possessed a robust constitution.[54] Growing up among the chemical-laden industries of Grays Ferry likely exposed him to harsh chemicals. His profession as a store clerk consisted of long hours toiling in improperly ventilated rooms full of textile dust. Poor respiratory health was a constant struggle for retail clerks of the time. Wanamaker consulted a doctor, who prescribed he leave Tower Hall and his religious work to rest and recover. Wanamaker interpreted the doctor's orders as an opportunity to travel. Taking his savings, he set off to see what was beyond Indiana. He traveled to Chicago and then on to Minnesota, spending time in the woods and fresh air.

The time away afforded Wanamaker a chance to reflect, especially on matters of religion and business. He wrote to a friend of his desire for Christians "to be faithful and true to their profession that they led abroad by their example a power that will grow and expand in the hearts of those around and induce them to join with us."[55] He told his friend that he would come home with recovered health and "renewed energy to engage in the service of the Lord."[56] He returned to Philadelphia at the end of 1857, just as a financial panic took hold of the nation and a religious response to the panic began to stir in American Eastern Seaboard cities.

Urban Prayer

Throughout the second half of the nineteenth century, the United States experienced a series of economic downturns and panics rattling the stability of businesses and financial institutions. In late 1857, credit disappeared, banks closed, and unemployment surged in Northern cities. In the face of economic instability, religious revival movements sprang up in business districts and on Wall Street itself. The grassroots Protestant phenomenon that became known as the Businessmen's Revival cropped up first in Boston and then, through a series of religious meetings, near Wall Street in New York City. In New York, Jeremiah Calvin Lanphier, a former businessman turned church worker, started a weekly prayer meeting for businessmen at noon on Wednesdays.[57] Within a few weeks, over a hundred men attended, and new meetings quickly sprang up.[58]

The Businessmen's Revival was at once "a mass stirring of affections" and a disciplined movement. Prayer meetings followed a controlled agenda in a strict one-hour format that ran like a business meeting.[59] Revival leaders encouraged attendees to "make an appointment with God."[60] The prayer meetings found immediate success, especially because of their location; the New York City prayer meetings took place at the North Dutch Street Church, a quick five-minute walk from Wall Street.[61] New meetings appeared in unusual places, including stores, firehouses, and movable tents, to make them more convenient.[62] Though Lanphier spearheaded the nascent days of the revival, the religious movement gained momentum as the country sank deeper into economic crisis by the end of 1857. The revival spread without the orchestration of a high-profile leader and soon found new fertile ground in other major urban centers, including Philadelphia.[63] An embryonic Young Men's Christian Association branch begun three years before by dry goods salesman and banker George Stuart, assisted in catapulting Philadelphia's Businessmen's Revival into high gear.[64]

The YMCA was one of the new and creative evangelistic approaches developed to address the rising tensions in urban areas around the influx of young men looking for work. In London in 1844, a twenty-two-year-old department store sales clerk, George Williams, and a group of eleven friends generated one of the most fruitful and creative institutions to address Protestant concerns. The young men decided to combat what they saw as the unwholesome temptations of urban life that seduced naive young men seeking a new life in the city. Taking inspiration from Charles Finney's revival preaching, which emphasized moral living and character, Williams and his friends began holding prayer meetings for their coworkers in 1842. Over a two-year period, the prayer group reportedly raised "the morals and morale" of attendees and even converted the owner of the store.[65] Soon Williams's colleagues took their program to other dry goods firms in the neighborhood. They declared that their goal was "the improvement of the spiritual condition of young men engaged in the drapery and other trades."[66] By the summer of 1844, they had founded the Young Men's Christian Association. While the propagation of Christianity was the initial purpose of the YMCA, it quickly expanded its scope to the mental, physical, and spiritual welfare of young men from a variety of trades.[67]

The concept spread to other urban areas. Chapters of the YMCA sprang up in Boston and New York City, quickly taking root in the fertile North American evangelical soil among those who sought creative ways to mitigate the threats of the city.[68] American YMCAs espoused a "concern for the young man away from his home in the great city" with a particular focus on the "spiritual, mental, and social condition of young men."[69] The Y also built bridges between Protestantism and business—training men for a productive work life and shaping businesses.[70] While the YMCA was not the first foray into benevolent societies for the welfare of young men, earlier efforts struggled to gain firm footing.[71] Spreading from successful chapters in Eastern Seaboard cities, new YMCA chapters emphasized evangelism in combination with relief services, libraries, and social facilities.[72] Hoping to start a branch of the Y in Philadelphia, George Stuart sought out Williams for advice while on a visit to London for business.[73] In 1854, three years after Stuart's visit, Philadelphia's YMCA branch opened with fifty-seven members, five of whom were clergy. Stuart served as the branch's first president. The group rented a building at 833 Arch Street that included two of the earliest features of the typical Y: a small library and a reading room.[74]

The new organization struggled at first. Many Philadelphia churches condemned the local Y, some going so far as to threaten to withhold church membership from any person connected to the organization.[75] Ministers feared that the Y would steal away their young men, making congregations unnecessary. Some congregations protested against the YMCA's habit of welcoming, at least as associate members, Catholics, Jews, and other non-Protestants who wanted to partake in what the Y had to offer.[76] Despite initial resistance, the Philadelphia YMCA began to deliver a wide variety of services that emphasized building moral character and encouraged honesty, frugality, and hard work.

During the early months of the Businessmen's Revival, Stuart redoubled his efforts for the Y, leading revival prayer meetings and generating excitement through publicity.[77] His application of business techniques to fundraising put the Y on stronger financial footing. It was Stuart's grueling schedule that led him to create a paid secretary position to lead the Philadelphia Y, the first such position in a North American YMCA. He approached Wanamaker about filling the position and offered him a generous salary; it was an offer he could not refuse.

Stuart felt that hiring the young, evangelically spirited Wanamaker as secretary could harness the excitement of the revival for his struggling YMCA chapter. Business and religion proved a potent mix—a recipe Stuart communicated to Wanamaker during his service as secretary.

Wanamaker had accepted the position as secretary in part because of the large salary; Stuart personally guaranteed a hefty $1,000 annually. However, Wanamaker soon discovered that, in reality, he needed to raise nearly the entire amount of his salary each year.[78] Stuart charged him to "seek out young men taking up residence in Philadelphia and its vicinity, and endeavor to bring them under moral and religious influences by aiding them in the selection of suitable boarding places and employment, by introducing them to the members and privileges of this Association, and, by every means in their power, surrounding them with Christian associates."[79]

Under Wanamaker's leadership, the Philadelphia YMCA experienced a swift expansion in membership and in its physical plant. He focused part of his energy on raising the profile of the Y.[80] Advertising played a key role: Wanamaker placed daily advertisements broadcasting YMCA-sponsored prayer meetings—a technique he had learned from Chambers.[81] By 1857, the YMCA had garnered favor among some congregations, largely through Wanamaker's efforts.[82] It was an uphill battle, with Wanamaker recalling later, "I never worked harder in my life to stem the tide of prejudice."[83] During his tenure, Wanamaker added an estimated two thousand new members in the three years he served as secretary.[84] He recalled, "I went out into the byways and hedges, and compelled them to come in."[85] Wanamaker focused his outreach to the "rougher edges" of Philadelphia society. After all, although he was transforming himself into a white-collar worker, he had grown up in Grays Ferry.

Wanamaker enthusiastically supported Philadelphia's Businessmen's Revival in his role as Y secretary. In collaboration with Stuart, he guided the local Y's efforts to fan the flames of the revival by offering space for evening meetings, and when the embers of the movement appeared to cool, the Y "reactivated it with the Union Tabernacle, a movable tent set up in various parts of the city." The mobile worship service aimed to spread "the Gospel to masses who would not enter a church."[86] He also organized and led noontime prayer meetings at a local hall. The meetings quickly mushroomed, making it necessary to rent out the largest auditorium in the city for the meetings.

Wanamaker also focused his energy on religious outreach to the city's infamous firemen; he wanted to "reform their character."[87] Firefighters in mid-nineteenth-century Philadelphia had a reputation for rowdiness and the use of profanity. Because they were paid based on who arrived first at a fire, an intense rivalry developed between competing fire companies, leading to gang-like behavior that resulted in outrageous pranks and sometimes violence.[88] Wanamaker brought the prayer meetings to the firehouses, making attendance for firefighters almost impossible to avoid. His efforts appeared to pay off, with hundreds of firefighters attending revival meetings and joining religious organizations.[89] Wanamaker learned about the power of persuasion.

Near the end of his tenure with the Y, he helped the Philadelphia branch save enough money to purchase a dedicated building to house its wide-ranging services and offer a consistent moral atmosphere. Stepping down as secretary, he moved into Stuart's role as president of the branch—steering the group to raise funds and complete its first two buildings. Wanamaker felt that dedicated buildings and spaces aided the work of the YMCA. Wanamaker's faith in the potential of a "built environment" to stir change began to grow.

As Wanamaker moved into his new role as secretary of the Philadelphia Y, he also returned to the Sunday school work he had begun. He attended an American Sunday School Union meeting and volunteered to start a mission Sunday school.[90] In 1790 a consortium of Philadelphia Protestant groups had founded the Sunday School Union, which was part of a wider religious and education movement in the United States and Great Britain.[91] Its successor, the American Sunday School Union, began in 1824 and focused on planting Sunday schools in impoverished areas. Working as a Sunday school missionary was a path to the ministry for many young men. By the 1840s, eager Sunday school workers poured into poverty-stricken areas, urban and rural, to establish Sunday schools. Wanamaker's success with the noontime prayer meetings during the Businessmen's Revival fed his confidence for church work. By starting a Sunday school, he would have a chance to shape the character and beliefs of young men and women in his community.

Wanamaker decided to start his mission Sunday school near his childhood home in a working-class immigrant neighborhood ruled by gangs of boys and young men called the Schuylkill Rangers, or sometimes simply the "killers," or the "bouncers."[92] It was a predominantly Catholic enclave. On a snowy day in early February 1858, Wanamaker held a preliminary meeting in a vacant house loaned to the cause with the help of the Reverend Edward H. Toland, an American Sunday School Union official. They encouraged those who attended to give their names and addresses and to invite their friends when the next meeting gathered. Outside, the loud jeering and shouts of the neighborhood gang marred the session, and, fearing for their safety, his potential students fled out the back door.[93] Wanamaker attempted to confront the gang and was physically threatened.[94] Undaunted, he held the first official meeting of the Sunday school a week later in the second-floor room of a cobbler's shop. Wanamaker had spent the week canvassing the neighborhood to ensure that a large group of children would attend. He asked his sister Mary and her friend Mary Brown to assist.[95] During the meeting, the neighborhood gang returned, interrupting the meeting. They "broke in the lower door" of the cobbler's shop, "raced up the stairs, chased out the children and warned" Wanamaker and his two teachers "to leave and never to return."[96]

Wanamaker remained undeterred. He planned another gathering of the budding Sunday school for the next week despite the threats. His sister and her friend agreed to return. Wanamaker needed to secure a new location after the cobbler complained of damage caused by the gang; however, word had spread about the Sunday school. Fifty children and adults appeared for the third meeting. The Rangers not only attacked again but escalated their assault, this time pelting Wanamaker and the Sunday school children "with rotten eggs, bricks and snowballs until a policeman drove off the gang."[97] Despite this setback, and likely shaken, Wanamaker promised the children and their parents to return the next week. He made a plan to thwart the gang by calling on the local firefighters he had befriended during the revival for help.[98] The firemen spread the word that they would not tolerate attacks on Wanamaker and his Sunday school.[99] The fourth meeting of the Sunday school was not interrupted, and even more children came, though sporadic harassment by the gang continued throughout the first months.[100]

Wanamaker's Sunday school flourished even as he divided his time between the school and the YMCA. Now established, the group returned to the cobbler's shop, only to outgrow the space by spring. They needed a new place to meet. A member of Chambers's congregation, an elderly German man named John Oberteuffer, surveyed the neighborhood for a meeting spot to no avail. He then suggested collecting discarded sails from the wharves off the Delaware and Schuylkill Rivers and using them to build a tent for the Sunday school. Oberteuffer personally collected the sails, Wanamaker and boys from the Sunday school cleared an old ash lot loaned for the purpose, and the mothers of the Sunday school children sewed the old sails together to create the tent. Not everyone was pleased with the new tent Sunday school. A Catholic neighbor threatened to burn it down if it was erected. Ignoring the threat, the Sunday school raised the tent and set up a schedule of overnight guards to protect it.[101] By July 1858, the school held its first meeting inside what Wanamaker called "a beautiful little white church" situated on a borrowed lot.[102] To accommodate large crowds, especially when popular ministers preached, the tent flaps were raised. Wanamaker reported that three hundred children attended the first tent meeting. Although it was initially called the Chambers Mission School after his beloved minister, Wanamaker and his followers decided to name the Sunday school Bethany, after Luke 24:50, a text that focuses on the risen Jesus blessing his disciples.[103] Wanamaker said that the new name mirrored his hope for the school, that it would be "a place of blessing, a home where spiritual food, comfort and love can be found!"[104] The school focused on service and on creating a moral environment rather than emphasizing doctrine or creed. It continued to grow, and by January 1859 a simple building had been constructed. Barely a year had passed from the beginning of the Sunday school mission.[105]

In 1862 an attempt was made to add a church to the Sunday school. Continuing what would be a lifelong flexibility in denominational labels, the first minister called to Bethany was the Reverend Augustus Blauvelt of the Dutch Reformed Church to serve as the first "Missionary" of the congregation. He served the church for a year before departing due to ill health, leaving the church side of Bethany in disarray.

Bethany drew over half its members from what one historian describes as "a mix of lower white collar and blue collar laborers."[106] Despite the outbreak of the Civil War, the Sunday school grew, and by the end of the war there were over nine hundred on the Sunday school rolls. In the summer of 1865, Bethany welcomed the Reverend Samuel Lowrie to try once more to launch a church alongside the Sunday school. This time the effort met with success, and the congregation broke ground on another building, at the corner of Twenty-Second and Bainbridge, to accommodate the congregation's rising membership.

By end of the Civil War, the Sunday school had become too large for Wanamaker to handle alone, especially as his retail business took off. He signed on new staff to run the congregation and Sunday school.[107] One of the first individuals he hired was John Neff, the man who found him his first job, who was employed to assist with the school. A series of ministers followed Lowrie, attracted by the opportunity for urban missionary work. They served for a few years and then departed, often to purse foreign missionary work or revival preaching. This became a pattern at Bethany. Wanamaker's constant presence as a leader may have been another reason for the high turnover. Initially, he was the only ordained elder in the congregation and was a permanent member of the church's governing board. Bethany's ministers answered to him.

Bethany's building, at the corner of Twenty-Second and Bainbridge, was as much a part of the mission as its location and services. Members of the Sunday school raised the money, many sending notes with their weekly donations explaining what they had originally budgeted the money for and how they instead were donating it to Bethany. The first building was a lofty square brick Greek Revival structure with poor acoustics; Wanamaker recalled that "no one could speak in the building so as to be heard."[108] Despite the money and time invested in the building and potential embarrassment, they tore it down, saving only a large stained-glass memorial window from the building. The congregation again started construction.

Bethany's new building bore little resemblance to its first iteration. Designed by the up-and-coming Philadelphia architect Addison Hutton, the much larger building wrapped the corner of Twenty-Second and Bainbridge, reaching down the block in two directions. The architect used a Gothic Revival style that had surprisingly become "*the* generic Christian style" of church architecture in the United States starting in the 1840s and continuing into the first two decades of the twentieth cen-

Figure 1.1. An undated postcard (ca. 1870s) of Bethany Presbyterian Church's second building at Twenty-Second and Bainbridge in a Gothic style. Over time, Wanamaker purchased nearby buildings to house the expanding services the church offered to members and the surrounding neighborhood. The postcard's inset shows a young John Wanamaker, and advertised the connection between the merchant and the church.

tury.[109] Proponents of the design believed that Gothic structures possessed an aesthetic power that had the ability to uplift the city through beauty. And it was more than aesthetics. It was a reassertion of clerical and Protestant authority through spatial politics.[110] Gothic structures made imposing additions to neighborhoods and city skylines and challenged the Catholic cathedrals sprouting up at the same time. Wanamaker's fascination with Gothic architecture and Catholic forms would increase in the coming years.

Hutton's conception of Bethany produced a tall brick-and-stone multigabled structure with large Gothic arch windows. A slim bell tower protruded from the middle. Signaling its public nature, the bell tower contained an immense clock. At the corner intersection of the building, wide steps led to the main entrance. It made a statement in the neighborhood with its size and dignified style without taking on the more ostentatious decorations of Gothic Revival architecture.

Inside, the sanctuary incorporated the fashionable theater style used by many evangelical Protestant congregations. Bethany's chancel had a broad stage with a centrally located pulpit. A large organ anchored the chancel, and its pipes offered a dramatic backdrop to the pulpit and choir.[111] The auditorium seated fifteen hundred and had a sloped floor to improve visibility and acoustics. The wooden pews faced the central pulpit and were curved on the sides so congregants could maintain eye contact with the preacher. Tiffany stained-glass windows filtered outside light from a clerestory above and large windows opposite the chancel stage.[112] The round room allowed parishioners to see and be seen by one another. The seating arrangement promoted not only attendance but concern over proper decorum.[113] It also engendered an intimacy that older box pew churches lacked. A balcony wrapped the upper story of the mahogany-trimmed auditorium, adding more seating with a good view of the chancel below. Delicate ironwork decorated the balcony railings. Support pillars in the front of the sanctuary framed the chancel much like a theater's proscenium.[114]

Wanamaker and his handpicked teachers instructed his Sunday school using the latest methods in religious education in a smaller auditorium that seated five hundred. The portion of the building devoted to the Sunday school also had an extensive series of rooms for meetings and education. The large room employed the "Akron model" of folding partitions to make classrooms "entirely isolated from one another, thus grouping the pupils into classes according to their ages and needs."[115] The model offered maximum flexibility for the large Sunday school. After the age-group classes finished, the group convened "for the general lesson," which Wanamaker frequently led. The large Sunday school room decorated by a fountain in the middle was equipped with curved desks and benches for the young scholars pointed toward the front of the room.[116]

Wanamaker saw Bethany as a moral force in the neighborhood. Thirty years later, at the International Sunday School Convention, Wanamaker reflected on the effectiveness of Sunday schools. He told the audience, "It is the only School organized to teach the Bible at the most teachable age; to inform the mind, influence the heart and mould the life in the highest principles of unselfishness and uprightness in the fear of God and love for our fellow men."[117] He felt that Sunday schools leveled social strata and opened opportunities for all: "The Sunday-school door, wide open to all alike, lets in a ray of hope that there are no levels marked 'Reserved,' and places of equal footing and equal opportunity for all men." As historian Jeanne Kilde has noted, "In Protestant churches of the late nineteenth century, then, location, architecture, and mission intertwined, influencing and altering one another, merging in the process of meaning creation."[118] A part of this meaning placed these churches at the intersection of public and private, a "spiritual armory" against the onslaught of urban changes and a hub of outreach to the working class and those who struggled on the margins.[119]

At its height, Bethany boasted 6,097 enrolled in the school, making it one of the largest in the country.[120] Its Sunday school rolls and membership numbers were points of pride for the congregation and were regularly quoted. And although Bethany began under a Presbyterian flag, the congregation had an independent streak running through it, much as Chambers's First Independent did; it had more in common with the popular revivals of the day led by Moody and others. After the Civil War, Bethany broadened its focus beyond religious education and salvation to community service under the leadership of Wanamaker and its ministers. Wanamaker took the lead in opening a series of institutions and programs to support the working poor. In particular, calling the Reverend Arthur Tappan Pierson solidified Bethany's standing as what would become known as a social gospel church.[121]

Making a Social Gospel Church

Wanamaker and Pierson had struck up a friendship sometime in the 1860s, most likely through their Presbyterian and YMCA connections. They also shared a passion for urban mission outreach and the temperance movement, and both were friends with Dwight L. Moody.[122] Pierson turned out to be a prolific writer, penning dozens of articles, sermons, and lectures that led to a rapid rise in prominence. Interested in foreign and domestic missionary work early in his career, he read extensively and traveled to Europe to learn about British urban missions.

On a visit to England in 1867, Pierson wrote a letter to Wanamaker that shows the extent of their friendship. Visiting a number of urban mission tabernacles and leading British preachers, Pierson explained to

Wanamaker, "I am seeking to find, that I may carry back the information for use among our own members," "how the most successful churches here are carried on especially among the same class as we are seeking to reach." He attended services at the famous Metropolitan Tabernacle, the largest Baptist church in the world, to hear the eminent Charles Spurgeon preach. The church was designed architecturally with an opera house in mind to help make city dwellers feel more comfortable coming to worship.[123] The experience made an impression upon Pierson, and he had carried the ideas of the Metropolitan to his work in Detroit and Philadelphia. Pierson held Wanamaker in great esteem and harbored the same worries Moody had for the merchant and his growing business. Pierson confided in his friend, "I want you to be like a star in god's right hand. May he keep you in the hollow of that hand." Unlike Conwell, who saw Wanamaker's success as a sign of God's blessing, Pierson had warned his friend, "You need [God's] keeping, you are in a high place—a fall would be correspondingly deep," and urged him to "hide yourself in his [God's] deep shadow."[124]

The year before Pierson's European trip, he joined the Evangelical Alliance. Founded in 1847 in London, the American branch of the Alliance took twenty years to gain momentum. Following the Civil War, the organization gathered a group of elite, educated Protestant evangelicals: urban ministers, seminary professors, businessmen, and college presidents. They wanted a "social Christianity" that addressed the practical and religious needs of the working poor and foreign-born without losing the importance of individual conversion, moral living, and the centrality of the Bible.[125] The group emphasized Christian unity and partnership among the denominations while pointedly opposing Catholicism.

The Alliance's social gospel approach promoted a "moral equivalent of war" on a variety of social ills fought by Protestants from numerous denominations holding a variety of theological perspectives.[126] Institutional churches served as a major "weapon" in the social gospel war.[127] As one scholar notes, "With its emphasis on ministering in the community and making the church a vital part of its neighborhood, institutional churches brought many middle-class Protestants in the pews face to face with the problems of an industrializing urban society."[128] It provided a way for white Protestants to cope by actively responding to the social ills they saw around them.

Pierson was one of the younger members of the Alliance, but it was a comfortable space for him—his theology professor, Henry B. Smith, and several other members of the Union Seminary community were leaders in the renewed organization.[129] The secretary of the Evangelical Alliance was Josiah Strong, one of the leaders of what became called the "social gospel movement" and author of the bestseller *Our Country: Its Possible Future and Its Current Crisis*, published in 1884.[130] In the book Strong made a case for mission work in the United States to reach the immigrant working-class masses. Pierson completed his own acclaimed book, *The Crisis of Missions*, shortly after Strong's. His book had a foreign mission focus and set the stage for Pierson's later leadership in foreign missions.

Pierson had left the congregation he served in Massachusetts in 1869 to settle at Fort Street Church, a prominent and wealthy Detroit church with railroad barons among the parishioners. Espousing a strong social conscience, Pierson fretted over the growing "materialism" of his congregation, especially among the emerging middle class. The congregation had disappointed him with its lackluster response to Reconstruction and to the newly freed people of the South. Observing the changes in society around him, he felt conflicted by the ways Native Americans and immigrants were treated and believed that without Protestant Christianity, the social fabric of democracy was threatened.[131]

For seven years, Pierson had urged his parishioners to be more attentive to the urban poor and to the need for missionaries abroad. Expressing a strong missionary impulse, he recognized the need to evangelize the city as much as the foreign mission fields. Successful at encouraging his church members to fund foreign missions, he struggled to make the church, with many wealthy members, into one that served the neighborhood's working poor and immigrants. The congregation refused to get rid of "pew rentals," which would have enabled Pierson to open the doors of the church to those who could not afford them, what he called the "unevangelized masses."[132] He dreamed of his own Tabernacle church like Spurgeon's and Finney's as a way to reach the masses who did not feel comfortable in ornate churches. Pierson grew more agitated over his congregation's lack of response to the urgent need around them. On March 24, 1876, a sudden fire answered his prayers. The blaze gutted the elegant Gothic building of Fort Street Church, toppling its mighty spire, one of the tallest in the country, and creating an opportunity for the change Pierson craved.[133]

After the fire, the congregation rented Detroit's Whitney Opera House to conduct worship services while they decided how to rebuild. Pierson convinced the congregation's leadership not to reserve seats for members as they had done before and instead allow the poor to mingle with the rich and sit where they wished. He adopted a more casual "gospel style" of worship that was the hallmark of revivalists and the worship service of the Broadway Tabernacle and other earlier experimental churches.[134] He made the service less formal, took up extemporaneous preaching, and held an altar call at the end of every service for those who sought prayer or conversion. Local newspapers called Pierson's worship services a revival, and for sixteen months the Opera House services were packed, with thousands turned away at each service.[135] Pierson begged the church leadership not to rebuild a church for the wealthy but instead to construct one that continued to welcome and serve the poor. The Great Railroad Strike of 1877, during which West Virginia railroad workers went on strike over repeated wage cuts and other workers joined them across the country, only to be broken by state militias and federal troops, deepened Pierson's resolve to create a missionary church in the city. He wanted the congregation to serve the real needs of the neighborhood by offering services. The congregation's answer to his pleas was clear. They rebuilt the church within the walls of its original Gothic structure, complete with an opulent interior, and reinstated pew rentals.[136]

Pierson began looking for another congregation that would welcome his ministry. He landed briefly in Indianapolis at the centrally located Second Presbyterian Church in 1882. There he found the same obstacles he had encountered in Detroit. From the outset, Pierson's strong moralizing sermons against drinking, playing cards, and other amusements prevented him from forming a warm relationship with the congregation members. Although he rented the local opera house for evening services and again drew large crowds, Pierson resigned after six months. He felt that the church was not a good match for his vision. Wanamaker began courting Pierson to be the minister of Bethany after a YMCA meeting in Milwaukee. The congregation was between ministers once again, and the merchant knew that he and Pierson held a similar vision for the church. At the meeting Wanamaker implored Pierson to visit his church in Philadelphia. He wanted to share the work of Bethany but the invitation also had another purpose: Wanamaker had possibly heard rumors—or had heard from Pierson himself—that he was not happy in his new parish.

Pierson was very direct with Wanamaker, laying out his vision of the church to convert and serve the urban poor.[137] He would not accept another post that failed to align with his ideas about the purpose of the church. He also suggested a shift to full-immersion baptism, a surprising move for a Presbyterian. Wanamaker agreed to the minister's vision. He had already made adjustments to Bethany's worship by adding a printed program with popular gospel hymns, a choir, and a church orchestra. Wanamaker reported to Pierson that when they built the church they had installed an immersion baptism pool that was yet unused. Pierson was impressed that Wanamaker had planted the church in a poor Philadelphia neighborhood as a Sunday school mission, deciding perhaps he had more in common with the department store magnate's church than he had realized. Pierson accepted the offer to come to Bethany, but he insisted on being paid less than the original offer and stipulated that his entire salary would be raised through free will offerings rather than through pew rentals.[138] In this church, he would live the social Christian experiment he had been dreaming about.

Pierson discovered a like-minded Presbyterian in Wanamaker. Professing similar beliefs about morality, temperance, and the evangelical purpose of Christianity, they set about creating an "institutional church," one of the expressions of the social gospel movement. Historians have long disagreed on the definition of the social gospel movement and whether social gospel churches are identifiable by actions or beliefs.[139] It was a more multivalent movement than often presented, with fluid boundaries and no single theological center; many different people and institutions identified, promoted, and endorsed social Christianity.[140] Even without a definitive theological statement from the movement, scholars tend to place social gospelers in the liberal progressive camp. Contrary to common interpretations that often place the social gospel and revivalism on opposite poles, many leaders of social Christianity thought, wrote, and spoke as evangelicals who valued campaigns for conversion. Their social awakening, social salvation, and social evangelism were expressed in revivalist terms; they did not deny the prevailing emphasis on individual salvation but instead added a social dimension to it.[141]

Wanamaker and Pierson moved Bethany into a full-blown social gospel church, founded on the mission Sunday school, that attempted to address the problems of urbanization and of the burgeoning working and middle class.[142] Under their leadership, Bethany created dozens of social outreach programs offering a wide variety of "services" to the neighborhood through a network of institutions that expanded the church's geographic presence far beyond the corner of Twenty-Second and Bainbridge.[143] While the church housed some of the services, over time Wanamaker bought buildings for the dedicated use of the congregation's service branches. Bethany's services included the Friendly Inn, a home for unemployed men; an infirmary offering medical services to those in need; and a Deaconess Home for older single women who dedicated themselves to the church and gave back to the community by running a small kindergarten. Wanamaker acquired a building for the Bethany Mission on Bainbridge and Carpenter Streets to serve the neediest in the community. Mary Wanamaker continued to work at Bethany and particularly enjoyed leading classes on sewing, proper hygiene, and cleanliness for working-class women.[144]

On what had been the original site of the Bethany's tent church, Wanamaker constructed a men's clubhouse for the local branch of the Andrew and Phillip Brotherhood, an organization that promoted Bible study, community service, and physical fitness and was a part of a national, cross-denominational movement that had started in 1883 in Chicago.[145] Wanamaker founded the chapter at Bethany and regularly attended Brotherhood meetings before teaching Sunday school. The Brotherhood House offered books, wholesome entertainment, and an art gallery.

In 1888 Wanamaker opened the Penny Savings Bank in the basement of Bethany, a concept similar to Philadelphia's Cardinal John Neuman's Beneficial Bank, which helped immigrants keep their money safe and helped them learn to save. As the bank's name advertised, it accepted very small deposits, even as little as a penny, with the hope that it would encourage children and their families to save. When the bank outgrew its church quarters, Wanamaker found a building a few blocks away to house the institution as he was to do many times over the years, for service organizations he supported in the United States and abroad.[146] The year before Pierson arrived, Wanamaker opened a night school he called Bethany College, to equip unskilled laborers with a vocational education in an effort to help them secure better employment.[147] Pierson took up teaching at the college on a range of theological topics.

In many ways, Bethany emulated the YMCA, which had shaped and inspired the services the church offered. Most of Bethany's outreach programs sought to instill "middle-class values" such as frugality, cleanliness, and temperance steeped in moral living and religious devotion.[148] A booklet describing the Sunday school's methods listed—in addition to Bible classes, prayer services, and mission and temperance work— wholesome entertainment and life skills coaching that covered how to make a household budget, dietary instruction, sewing, and more. Pierson and Wanamaker remained a team until 1889, when the minister felt a pull to return to missionary work.

By 1904, long after Pierson had left and other ministers had served at Bethany's helm, Wanamaker remained the ever-present thread in the life of the congregation. A visitor that same year described Wanamaker's bustling church and Sunday school: "There were thousands of children, with their fresh faces and in their Sunday dress, from little girls and boys of six or seven years to young men and women of eighteen and twenty."[149] Sunday mornings began at eight o'clock with the gathering of men and women who studied scripture texts as a source for "practical religion." Impressed by the gathering, the visitor remarked, "When I looked out over the Sunday-school of Bethany Church, I seemed to see before me a garden of God."[150] Bethany continued to draw visitors and impress them with the Sunday school.

* * *

Wanamaker's life had taken a big turn at the beginning of 1858. He participated in the Businessmen's Revival, led noontime prayer meetings, started work at the YMCA, and planted a mission Sunday school that would grow to be one of the largest institutional congregations in the country. In 1860 he married Mary Brown, the young woman his sister brought along to help teach his first Sunday school class at the cobbler's house in South Philadelphia. His father died around this time, leaving the care of his beloved mother on his shoulders.

Choosing between ministry and business proved challenging. Wanamaker's passion for ministry only grew with his Sunday school and YMCA work. However, some friends advised him against ministry, noting his fragile health. Others suggested he become a minister of a small congregation in the country to protect his health. Wanamaker, in turn, began to think about business in a new way: "I thought that if I became a man of means through my business, I might be able to accomplish as much or even more for Christ than I would have as a minister."[151] Perhaps his business could help his religious endeavors.

Now with a wife to support, Wanamaker left the YMCA, and with the money he had saved he decided to open a men's store with his new brother-in-law, Nathan Brown. The young men tried to buy the store of Wanamaker's old employer, but Bennett refused their offer. So, with their combined savings of $3,500, the men leased two floors of the six-story McNellie Building on the corner of Sixth Street and Market Street (at that time called High Street), near the Pennsylvania State House (Independence Hall), and bought a small supply of men's suits, collars, shirts, cuffs, neckties, and other accessories.[152] The new store was situated on the same block as Colonel Bennett's establishment in the retail district of town.

War was brewing and the economy was still recovering from the economic crisis of 1857–1858, but the two entrepreneurs appeared to pay little attention to problems of timing.[153] They called the store Wanamaker & Brown, Oak Hall, perhaps in a competitive nod to Colonel Bennett after he had refused to sell Tower Hall to the young men. Oak Hall held its grand opening on April 8, 1861, two weeks after Wannamaker's first child, Thomas was born. Only one customer entered the store on the first day.[154] Within a week, the Civil War began.[155]

The war began slowly; it was July before the first major battle broke out at Bull Run. As news of the battle spread to Philadelphia, Wanamaker attempted to enlist in the Union Army despite his obligations at home and in the store, but the army physicians refused him for his poor lung health. His rejection was a wound he carried throughout his life, calling the army's refusal "his greatest humiliation."[156] But Wanamaker found another way to support the war effort. At a fledgling national YMCA meeting in New York City in November 1861, delegates voted to create a Christian service commission to attend to the "spiritual welfare" of soldiers and sailors by providing chaplains in hospitals and on the battlefields. George Stuart was tasked with leading the newly developed organization and once again enlisted Wanamaker to help recruit volunteers, raise money, and organize the massive undertaking.

Many of Wanamaker's friends predicted that Oak Hall was doomed to fail.[157] They thought that Wanamaker and Brown were too inexperienced and that the war and economic landscape were not favorable for a new enterprise.[158] The early days of the store were challenging. Wanamaker's connections through the YMCA and other evangelical organizations gave the young shopkeepers a reputation of integrity and trustworthiness, leading banks to extend credit, a resource that made the difference between success and failure.[159] The war also contributed to the new store's survival. An order for uniforms for local Union regiments provided income that kept the store afloat during the lean years.[160]

To draw customers to their shop, Wanamaker and Brown created innovative advertisements before their doors were even open. For the first half of the nineteenth century, retailers considered store advertisements gauche. Store location, word of mouth, and quality of goods were the primary attractors for businesses.[161] Yet Wanamaker had watched Chambers bring visitors to the church through advertising. Colonel Bennett had attracted customers with attention-grabbing poems in the newspaper without ever mentioning his merchandise. To draw attention to their new establishment, Wanamaker and his partner took a similar approach and covered Philadelphia with mysterious advertisements displaying their initials "W & B" with no explanation.[162] Thirteen painted billboards, some a hundred feet tall, went up all over the city, and balloons carrying prize certificates were released. Anyone who returned with a certificate received a free suit of clothes. These campaigns succeeded in drawing attention and excitement to Oak Hall's opening.[163] The favorable outcome of the initial advertising onslaught fueled their efforts. Soon, the name "Oak Hall" plastered fans, postcards, posters, and other small goods, leading one observer to jest about "the universal Wanamaker & Brown chiseled on the street crossings, painted on rocks, and mounted on house-tops. That they have not been wafted to the clouds, and tied to the tail of a fiery comet, is only because Yankee ingenuity has not yet devised the ways and means."[164] Wanamaker & Brown, and later Wanamaker's stores—he never liked or adopted the label "department store"—maintained the tradition of creative and unconventional advertising.[165]

Surviving the lean war years, Wanamaker and Brown's Oak Hall reaped the benefits of the postwar boom economy.[166] The two men had expanded their clothing store from two floors to the entire McNellie Building. The men established a wholesale and mail-order enterprise on the top floors of the building and made a name for themselves selling reasonably priced and high-quality men's wear. When Brown died three years later in 1868, Wanamaker bought Brown's shares from the estate and continued to enlarge the business under its original name. A year later, he was again ready to expand his store and the merchandise it carried but found the adjacent properties too expensive to acquire.

Abandoning the idea of one large store, Wanamaker purchased property next to one of Philadelphia's upscale hotels, the Continental, on Chestnut Street between Eighth and Ninth. The new store featured an open floor plan lit from above by a large skylight. Galleries open to the main space formed the upper floors of the store. Wanamaker outfitted the new establishment with high-end finishes, thick carpets, and large, gilt-framed mirrors and experimented with hanging artwork.[167] A man decked out in livery stood at the front door, a practice Wanamaker had abandoned at Oak Hall when customers deemed it too pretentious.[168] On the street, large show windows topped with "mediaeval stained glass" provided space for displaying merchandise—an approach that scandalized other merchants.[169] He called his new luxury store John Wanamaker & Co. and opened its doors under the management of his brothers.

By the end of 1871, Oak Hall and John Wanamaker & Co. had surpassed Colonel Bennett's Tower Hall as the largest men's store in Philadelphia with the purchase of adjoining buildings.[170] That same year, inspired by previous fairs and a Wabash College professor's vision of a great fair to celebrate the centennial of the Declaration of Independence, Wanamaker, along with a group of businessmen and state political leaders and with the blessings of the city and state, petitioned Congress to hold a world's fair in Philadelphia. That year he also traveled to Europe for the first time.[171]

"A School for the Nation"

Over the span of fifteen years, Wanamaker had withstood a series of painful economic panics, financial downturns, and the personal tragedies of losing two children, his son Horace as an infant and his little girl Hattie at the age of five. He had transformed a small men's store started on the eve of the Civil War into a thriving retail establishment with a luxury branch. But neither Wanamaker & Brown's Oak Hall nor John Wanamaker & Co. constituted a department store. During a visit to Europe to inspect a wool manufacturer, Wanamaker arranged a visit to London's International Exhibition. The visit gave him his first inkling of an idea for what he called "a new kind of store."

London's Annual International Exhibition in 1871 was not the first international display of the latest technology, goods, and art gathered in one place. Previous exhibitions in Paris, London, and New York City had evolved out of a century of fairs and trade gatherings that were initially aimed at the working class. In 1851, under the guiding hand of Queen Victoria's husband, Prince Albert, London hosted a spectacular exhibition in a dazzling glass structure built for that purpose. Inside what became known as the Crystal Palace, a series of grand displays presented the latest in technology and luxury goods. The exhibition demonstrated the power and riches of the British Empire and served as a rationalization of colonialism. Technological advancements and artistry were positioned as the pinnacle of Western white civilization. Organizers had developed new "ways of showing" goods and created organizational concepts to categorize the massive collections of objects, people, and machines brought together for the exhibits.[172] Luxury items were displayed in great abundance and with dramatic flair, inviting the onlookers to see high-end goods and then to make the leap that luxury was not just for the aristocracy anymore. From the architecture to the exhibits, visitors were invited to look, with no other purpose, at the wonders of the modern industrial age.[173] In the open and protected spaces of the Crystal Palace, fairgoers also were able to watch one another.

London's successful exhibition spawned a proliferation of world's fairs from Dublin to Calcutta throughout the nineteenth century.[174] In particular, Paris fell in love with the expositions and held them in 1855, 1867, 1889, and 1900. The fairs coincided with the French capital's rise in prominence for American tourists. The century before, it had been a way station en route to Italy, but now Paris served as a primary destination for Americans to obtain culture and taste.[175]

Publicity for the Exposition Universelle Internationale de 1900 in Paris boasted of the democratizing power of the exposition: what was "once the exclusive possession of a few noble spirits of the last century today gains ground more and more."[176] The event, and others like it, offered an opportunity for a shared experience for a large number of people. The promoters asserted that the displays were "the common religion of modern times," imparting a "powerful impetus . . . to the human spirit."

The great exhibitions' displays did bring people together, making them a temporary and seductive "pilgrimage" site for all classes.[177] Education and the demonstration of technology served as themes for the majority of the exhibitions.[178] Each exposition offered innovations of industry, science, art, music, and luxury goods presented in an ever-increasing spectacle of power, fantasy, and beauty. Cultural critic Walter Benjamin called it "the enthronement of the commodity."[179] Machines, commodities, and objects from the host city and country, and from around the world, were gathered together and meticulously organized and categorized.[180] Drawing millions of visitors, the great exhibitions proved to be some of the most significant events in the nineteenth and twentieth centuries.[181] In turn, the exhibitions inspired and shaped the emergence of art museums and department stores.[182] All three institutions—exhibitions, art museums, and department stores— concentrated on the display and organization of a wide range of objects. Each sought to educate the masses and guide public taste.[183]

London's International Exhibition of 1871 acted as a catalyst for Wanamaker. At the exhibition, his traveling companion, Dr. Samuel Lowrie, Pierson's predecessor at Bethany, recalled that Wanamaker was "like a child" at the fair, reveling in the majestic pipe organ at the center of the building that led a large crowd in singing.[184] He loved seeing the latest technology mixed with paintings and unusual objects. He returned home full of ideas for the upcoming Centennial Exhibition and new possibilities for the expansion of his two stores.

Wanamaker pondered the possibility of enlarging his store again by merging the two stores under one roof. He launched a search for a larger

space with the idea that more space would allow him to try new merchandising techniques. On the hunt for affordable options, he looked
west of the retail district where, in 1865, the Union League Club had
built an imposing French Renaissance building. Nearby, city hall had
broken ground in 1871 for a massive "New Public Building" at the intersection of Market and Broad Streets, and the Masonic Temple started
construction on a new edifice in 1873. The plan for the new city hall had
blocked the Pennsylvania Railroad's right of way and necessitated moving its freight depot to another location. The move had left behind the
empty train shed and a four-story building.

Wanamaker did not at first see the old train depot as a possible location for his new store. In the fall of 1874, the now-empty depot hosted an
exhibition by the Franklin Institute. For the fair, the institute adapted the
old depot by enclosing the glass train shed. Underneath the glass can-
opy, with natural sunlight from above, fair organizers laid out a series of
display booths that featured new inventions in engineering and mechanics. As Wanamaker walked through the building, he began to visualize
the freight depot as an unlikely but nevertheless creative location for a
new store where a larger selection of merchandise could be categorized,
systematized, and grandly displayed.[185] The train shed's glass-and-iron
ceiling mimicked the Crystal Palace and had much in common with the
plans for the Centennial Exhibition's Main Building.

The depot site also offered an enormously flexible space and, at the
time, the largest open floor in Philadelphia. Wanamaker recalled, "The
idea came to me that it was the greatest situation for a large store, but
I was perplexed and frightened at the idea of making the purchase."[186]
Relocating his stores away from the established retail district would be a
daring move full of uncertainties. All indicators—particularly the construction of several new buildings—pointed to Thirteenth and Market
Streets becoming the new center of Philadelphia. But it was still quite a
distance from the retailing district. His original store was on the same
block as the Pennsylvania State House (Independence Hall) on a street
filled with stores. The depot was just over a half mile across town. Filling the depot space proved to be another problem. Initially, Wanamaker
planned to entice other businesses to partner with him and to open specialty "departments" in his depot. When this scheme broke down, he
decided to move forward with the new store alone.

The location posed a danger; he could lose regular customers if he overestimated how far they were willing to travel. To balance the risk, Wanamaker decided to maintain his original stores, Oak Hall and John Wanamaker & Co., under the management of his brothers and to use the depot as a place to advertise the stores to the Centennial Exhibition visitors by offering similar goods and the same level of service.

Wanamaker purchased the cavernous freight depot as a retail experiment. He negotiated an option on the train shed and left for Europe with his family to take notes on the methods for storekeeping, displays, and selling different kinds of merchandise employed by the multidepartment stores of Paris.[187] They were also taking part in a rite that wealthy and middle-class American families had begun before the Civil War—a tour of Europe.

While the Wanamaker family traveled in Europe, a group of Philadelphia Protestant businessmen received the good news for which they had been waiting anxiously. Moody and Sankey, now among the most famous revivalists in the country after their triumphant tour of England, Ireland, and Scotland, sent word that they would be coming to Philadelphia. Although the Philadelphia Academy of Music was available for the revival, the businessmen wanted a larger space to host what they hoped would be the most successful Moody revival in the United States. They contacted the Pennsylvania Railroad about their old train depot, only to discover that Wanamaker was in the process of purchasing the building. The men, all friends of Wanamaker, sent word to Europe asking whether the train depot was available for the revival. Hosting the revival would delay construction on his new store, but Wanamaker agreed to rent the freight depot to the committee for one dollar, declaring, "The new store can wait a few months for its opening; the Lord's business first."[188]

Later, critics of Wanamaker contested the story, accusing him of timing the revival at his train shed to serve as a store advertisement. It is highly likely he had foreknowledge of the revival. Wanamaker first met Moody through their shared work for the YMCA's U.S. Christian Commission during the Civil War. He had hosted Moody and his family on their trip to Philadelphia in 1871, and Wanamaker was friends with many of the leaders on the committee. When Moody lost his church and home to the Great Chicago Fire, Wanamaker led a national fundraising campaign to help the evangelist rebuild.[189] He also would have under-

Interior of the Old Pennsylvania Railroad Freight Depot, Thirteenth
and Market Streets, Philadelphia, used for the First Moody and
Sankey Revival Meetings, November 4, 1875. Small pictures
show Dwight L. Moody on the left and Ira D. Sankey on the
right.

Figure 1.2. Inside view of the Moody and Sankey revival in the train shed that John
Wanamaker later turned into his new store. Note the sparse décor and the chairs lined
up for the event in orderly rows. Wanamaker had the number of chairs mentioned in
revival advertisements to emphasize the size and scale of the religious gathering. It was
a technique he honed in his store advertising.

stood the publicity advantage in hosting the revival at the location of his future store and the potential that Protestants would associate his store with the evangelist, casting a moral glow on his business. After months of daily revival meetings, all of Philadelphia would know the location of Thirteenth and Market Streets, John Wanamaker & Co.'s Grand Depot.

One of Philadelphia's leading architects, Addison Hutton, drew up plans to redesign the train shed into a space for the revival.[190] Construction began immediately. A sloped floor was installed to improve Moody's visibility for the audience, walls went up on the peripheries to create several inquiry rooms for those who converted and needed prayer, and evenly spaced "long rows of chandeliers" were added over a space that covered an entire city block and held almost nine thousand chairs.[191] In the front, workers fabricated a substantial stage to hold a large choir, a cabinet organ, and a small pulpit on an elevated platform with just enough space to lay an open Bible. A barrel roof over the stage created dynamic acoustics, allowing Moody to be heard in the back of the enormous room and Sankey's baritone voice to climb the rafters. Printed banners declaring God's love and sharing scripture quotes solemnly garnished the sparsely decorated space. Behind the pulpit, over a thousand chairs provided ample room for Philadelphia's leading business leaders and visiting dignitaries to be seated and to be seen. Their regular presence legitimized the religious proceedings and modeled the desired decorum. Within hours of the last night of the revival, a team of workers mustered at the depot to turn part of Moody's tabernacle into a temporary store—Wanamaker's "fair annex"—in time for the opening day of the Centennial Exhibition on May 10.

The Grand Depot

Philadelphia hosted the Centennial Exhibition in its vast green space, Fairmount Park. Positioned as a "school for the nation," it was the first of a series of American fairs where, as historian Robert W. Rydell has pointed out, business leaders, politicians, and intellectuals attempted to cultivate a "consensus about their priorities and their vision of progress" that supported American imperial desires, promoted economic growth, and portrayed white Protestants as the pinnacle of civilization.[192]

Philadelphia constructed five massive temporary buildings that originally were intended "to carry the spectator through the successive stages of human progress."[193] The colossal Main Building echoed London's earlier exhibition building, the Crystal Palace, with displays of science, industry, and engineering. The grand Machinery Building hummed day and night with machines, especially the remarkable Corliss steam boiler engine. Described as an "athlete of steel and iron," the Corliss engine not only showcased American ingenuity but also served as a workhorse for the fair by powering all the exhibited machines in the Machinery Building.[194] The Agricultural Hall showcased agricultural machinery, and Horticultural Hall housed a lush display of exotic plants. The only permanent building constructed for the fair was Memorial Hall. It accommodated numerous paintings and sculptures from around the world.[195] After the exhibition closed, Memorial Hall turned into Philadelphia's first art museum. A large cluster of smaller edifices sheltered the state and foreign exhibits and the fair's amenities.

Drawing over ten million visitors, the fair brought together unprecedented numbers of people and proved to be one of the most significant American events in the nineteenth century.[196] A visitor to the fair told the *Atlantic* magazine, "No account, however close, however graphic, can give a just conception of the variety and interest of the things to be seen." Open to fairgoers twelve hours a day, the Centennial Exhibition offered more than could be consumed in a single day. Inside exhibition buildings, miles of objects, machines, plants, art, and commodities from around the world were organized and categorized hierarchically.[197]

Wanamaker's Centennial annex shop and exhibit took up only part of the cavernous depot, but Wanamaker created a more uniform appearance for the building and mounted a sign, "John Wanamaker & Co.," running its entire length, prompting one visitor to exclaim that it was "the most colossal sign I ever saw."[198] Unapologetically, Wanamaker's store emulated the architecture of the exhibition. He festooned his store with flags and towers in a jumble of architectural elements mimicking the Main Building.[199] On the inside, Wanamaker took pains to copy the fair's display and organizational techniques. One newspaper noticed the correlation between the Centennial Exhibition and the new store immediately, noting, "A view of the main floor from the antique gallery west . . . strikingly recalls the Centennial Exhibition." Although it was not yet a department store, the annex catered to the city's thousands of visitors and cemented Wanamaker and his new store in the minds of Philadelphians.

Six months later, at the close of the fair, construction workers once again congregated at the freight depot—this time to transform the annex store into John Wanamaker & Co. at the Grand Depot, "A New Kind of Store." The onetime tabernacle and world's fair annex was converted into one of the nation's first department stores. Local papers predicted the store's failure, giving it three months. To combat these dire predictions, Wanamaker went out of his way to create an exciting spectacle of merchandise in the expansive space of the depot. Since his invitation to other retailers to open specialty departments at the Grand Depot had failed, Wanamaker undertook the task himself of expanding his stock, although he had limited experience with merchandise outside men's fashion. He began with five departments. Every few months, he added more shops with their own lines of stock and personnel. Over time, "Grand Depot" and "a new kind of store" dropped from the name, and it became simply Wanamaker's.[200]

A reporter from the *Public Ledger* told readers that the depot was now "remodeled to accommodate the new trade, and is very attractive." Natural light came from the train shed's old vaulted glass ceiling. Wanamaker installed a large pipe organ with an ornate case, like the ones that had thrilled him at the London and Centennial Exhibitions. The organ served as a focal point for the huge space while providing music to entertain shoppers. The morning before the store opened, he invited employees to join him for a morning sing-along with organ accompaniment.

To fill the vast floor, Wanamaker crafted an ingenious layout for his display counters that featured a visually commanding "circular counter . . . radiating from the central counter" with long aisles of "196 feet in length" and an additional "thirty-three blocks of counters, numbering 129 in all."[201] The floor plan signaled orderliness, in stark contrast to the chaos of the city and to the merchandise arrangements of many older stores, where sample goods lay in large heaps and on cluttered shelves. Much like the world's fairs, merchandise was categorized hierarchically.[202] Clothing for boys and men, the original clientele of Wanamaker & Brown, landed outside the circle in a large section of neat rows and aisles. The counters that created the radiating circle featured women's and girls' merchandise and small household goods. To coax women into the heart of the store, Wanamaker positioned the most luxurious goods near the center. Inside the innermost circle, where the finest silks were sold, a special carpeted "dark room" lit by gas fixtures allowed women to see how different silks looked in conditions mimicking a ballroom.

The geometrical nature of the circular counter system provided a focus for the open floor space and conveyed a sense of reason and elegance for those viewing the floor from the store's mezzanine. Although the building had no more floor space than Oak Hall, it was laid out so that an individual could take in the entire floor in one view.[203] The four street entrances divided the store into four quadrants making it appear, from some perspectives, like a giant compass.[204] Wanamaker would use an image of a compass on store receipts reminding customers of his four store promises—one price, cash returned, full guarantee, cash payment.

The *Ledger* gushed over the features of the new store, from the variety of its stock to its parlors and comfortable retiring rooms for shoppers. The newspaper recognized that the depot imitated the great exhibitions with its extensive display of goods "extending about as far as the eye can reach."[205] Another journalist would note that the store had gathered together "the riches of the world brought together from all lands" in ways that were "tastefully arranged to be shown with advantage."[206] The reporter felt that the store communicated "veracity, courtesy, and accommodation" through its "organization, order, and discipline."[207] The store did not fold in three months, as critics had predicted; instead, the store's location and approach to retail proved a raving success.

Within the first year of business, Wanamaker started buying abutting property to provide room for future expansion. These efforts culminated in 1885 with the purchase of a small street between his properties, giving him an entire city block.[208] To link the spaces, he constructed a stained-glass enclosed walkway—which, in a nod to European shopping streets enclosed by glass, he called an arcade—to channel customers into the store.[209] Newspaperman George Childs described the entrance to the new arcade as "handsomely ornamented" and noted that marble tiles paved the enclosed walkway.[210] To make the arcade attractive at night, Wanamaker installed large gas chandeliers with reflectors to maximize light and invited shoppers to experience a "grand illumination" of the

BIRD'S-EYE VIEW OF THE INTERIOR OF THE WANAMAKER GRAND DEPOT SOON AFTER ITS OPENING, 1877.

Figure 1.3. The floor plan of the Grand Depot in the train shed. From the beginning, Wanamaker made his store displays eye-catching and changed displays frequently to entice repeat visits by customers. Note that the overhead light fixtures are the same ones used for the Moody revival and the exposed trusses remain, making it easy to identify the store as the same space as the revival.

store from seven thirty to ten o'clock on November 11, 1878. The event allowed participants to do nothing more than view the merchandise that he had readied for the Christmas season—creating a holiday exhibition. He was training shoppers to understand the store as a place to stroll and browse and not necessarily as a place to always buy.

Dissatisfied by the dimness of the gas lamps, one month later, Wanamaker installed the newly invented electric arc lamps he had seen at the Centennial Exhibition and powered them with his own electric generator.[211] However, his enthusiasm for cutting-edge inventions was not always shared by his customers. For a short time after the installation of electricity, some customers stayed away because they feared the store might explode from the electrical current pulsating through it. The fear passed and customers returned to the store in droves.

The whirlwind pace of installing new technology continued with additions of steam heat and elevators. Soon, Wanamaker added an elaborate and visually stunning pneumatic tube system to move money from the sales counters to the central cash desk. He wanted to change the sensory aspect of the shopping experience by making it beautiful as well as comfortable through convenience, services, and climate control. By the next Christmas, he had increased the size of the store from two acres of sales floor space to three. In 1879 he began buying full-page ads in the local papers as well as in newspapers all over Pennsylvania and up and down the East Coast.[212] He promoted his store as a permanent exhibition—a place worth visiting even if you lived hours away. The store soon boasted forty-six departments with the pace for additions hardly slackening. Nearly constant updating and change characterized Wanamaker's store as he tried new ways to improve his store and keep the customer experience fresh.

Huckster or Holy Man?

By 1885, Wanamaker knew his gamble on the depot had paid off, and he had finished a large construction project consolidating the buildings he had acquired into one connected edifice. He had invited his friend Robert Ogden and his oldest son, Thomas, to help manage his other stores, but he now decided to sell his first two retail locations to a partnership composed of his brothers and trusted friends. He was now a wealthy man and busy grooming his sons Thomas and Lewis Rodman (who went by his middle name, Rodman) to take over his stores someday. Both sons joined the business when they graduated from Princeton University, starting at the bottom and working up through the ranks to learn the business. Wanamaker had expanded his philanthropy beyond the YMCA and Bethany by serving on a variety of boards to improve the city, especially through education and art. Growing more confident in his ability to lead, he decided to become more involved in politics.

Wanamaker had initially avoided politics. His admiration for Abraham Lincoln had led him to the Republican Party, but he refused a series of invitations to run for office and to accept nominations, preferring to donate money to campaigns. With the hotly contested presidential election of 1889, Wanamaker entered the political fray of a nationally and locally divided Republican Party. He continued his fundraising and, in addition to personally contributing tens of thousands of dollars, secured large sums of money for the struggling Republican candidate, Benjamin Harrison.

Harrison won the election and promptly awarded Wanamaker a cabinet position as postmaster general. The appointment initiated a period of public woes for the department store merchant. Political pundits did not like the Pennsylvanian upstart with no government experience who, by all appearances, had purchased his placement in the cabinet. Democrats implied that he bought his way into a cabinet seat by spreading rumors that Wanamaker donated far more money than he had.[213]

Used to running his own business, he lacked the diplomatic skills to make changes to the postal department in a politically savvy way. Further stoking criticism, Wanamaker fired all the Democratic postmasters—some thirty thousand people—as his first move in office, throwing the postal service into disarray.[214] Despite his efforts to modernize the system and to introduce innovative ideas such as the Rural Free Delivery (RFD) service and commemorative stamps, his time as postmaster general garnered mostly condemnation.

The cabinet post also placed Wanamaker in the national spotlight. Suddenly, the lives of the entire Wanamaker family attracted scrutiny—from questions about who attended the parties given at their home in Washington to which dresses his wife, Mary, and his daughters wore. Back home, visitors to Bethany skyrocketed, with people wanting to visit the postmaster's congregation and perhaps to catch a glimpse of him at his Sunday school desk. But this heightened interest also had a downside. Wanamaker's prominence as a fundraiser and a businessman with no political experience made him a popular target for the press.

The reputations of Wanamaker and President Harrison took an additional hit when midway through the president's term a group of wealthy businessmen, led by Wanamaker, presented the president's wife, Caroline, with a luxurious home on Cape May Point. Political opponents vehemently attacked the extravagant gift of a summer house as an attempt by Wanamaker to influence the president. The summer house episode led to bad publicity for both men, moving Harrison to return the house to Wanamaker, and instead vacationing at a local Cape May hotel.

Fueling the mounting vehemence against the merchant, Wanamaker's insistence on traveling to Philadelphia nearly every weekend to lead

Sunday school at Bethany smacked of duplicity to some. His proficient fundraising skills made him a target for those who felt that money corrupted government.[215] Political cartoonists took notice. They exaggerated Wanamaker's rotund figure and his conservative black suit to symbolize his wealth and to criticize his religious devotion. Critics nicknamed him "Holy John."

Critiques of Wanamaker came to the fore when cartoonists at *Judge*, an illustrated dime humor weekly out of New York City, picked up Wanamaker as a subject in the first month of his cabinet post.[216] A rival dime weekly, *Puck*, soon began running color cartoons of Wanamaker as well. He became a familiar face in the papers as both a solo target of the cartoonists and as part of Harrison's cabinet.[217] The cartoonists attacked Wanamaker from a variety of angles; some of their accusations were based on truth, while others were unsubstantiated. Surely one of the most upsetting cartoons for Wanamaker showed him in cahoots with his sworn enemy, Matthew Quay. Quay was a Pennsylvania Republican, a shrewd party boss known for his cronyism, who chaired the Republican National Committee and attempted to thwart Wanamaker's political ambitions.[218]

Increasingly, the cartoonists ridiculed Wanamaker's unflagging devotion to the church. In the summer of 1891, *Puck's* front cover featured a cartoon titled "The Two Wanamakers." One Wanamaker was depicted as "Pious John," praying while dressed in his Sunday best—a somber black suit—and clutching a Sunday school lesson book and an umbrella. The other figure, "Smart John," a huckster character dressed in a loud plaid suit and top hat, with a book of "Political and Business Schemes" jutting out of his pocket, was whispering in Pious John's ear.[219] Wanamaker was depicted as a schemer and backroom deal maker—the very attributes he strongly condemned in other Republicans, especially Mathew Quay.

Although many of the Philadelphia newspapers, run by friends of Wanamaker, attempted to counter the accusations, some of the papers joined the attack. When Wanamaker complained about the misrepresentations in the news, J. Keppler drew a cartoon entitled "The Righteous Man Has No Fear," with Wanamaker in a conservative black suit, sour-faced at what the newspapers were saying, with President Harrison in one pocket and a clutch of newspapers in the other. In a parody of Wanamaker's perceived self-righteousness, the text read, "Behold,

THE TWO WANAMAKERS.

Smart John *to* Pious John.—I guess you'll have to look a little extra holy, John, till this Philadelphia trouble blows over!

Figure 1.4. "The Two Wanamakers." Magazine cover for *Puck* magazine, 1891, showing two versions of Wanamaker: "Smart John," a savvy trickster figure, in the process of trying to corrupt "Pious John," a clueless and religiously zealous figure.

brethren, the reward of True Goodness. I collected $400,000 from the Truly Good to elect a Truly Good President." Wanamaker's certitude was criticized for its cost: "[It doesn't matter how many] Good banks are wrecked, or how many Truly Good bank officials go to jail, so long as I have the protection of the Truly Good press made solid by my Truly Good advertisements, and a Truly Good President to back me up."[220]

When Harrison lost the next election, political cartoonists nearly forgot about Wanamaker when he stepped away from the political limelight.[221] Before fully retiring from politics, however, he made unsuccessful bids for a Pennsylvania Senate seat and governorship. These efforts caught the attention of *Judge* cartoonist Grant E. Hamilton in 1897. Featured on the cover of the June 12 issue was the most scathing

Figure 1.5. "Another 'Stuffed Prophet.'" Cartoon by Grant E. Hamilton for the cover of *Judge* magazine in June 1897, which provides a clever and detailed critique of Wanamaker and his blending of business, religion, and politics.

of the cartoons attacking Wanamaker. Titled "Another 'Stuffed Prophet,'" the caricature showed an overly plump Wanamaker dressed as a Moses-like prophet nearly bursting out of his tunic and crowned with a fake halo. Standing on a pedestal marked "Bargain Counter," he held a stone tablet with a list of "The Profit Sighs of Wanamaker," a play on the word "prophecy." The "Profit Sighs" listed a mix of store sale announcements and Wanamaker's investment in political skirmishes. In a nod to the Old Testament Ten Commandments, the first "Profit Sigh" declared, "You shall have no other boss before me," followed by a warning to those who supported fellow Republican and sworn enemy Matthew Quay. In a coy reference to Wanamaker's advertising prowess, the tablet also predicted a sale on collar buttons, so cheap "they will almost be given away." In a final blow, the last "Profit Sigh" summarized the cartoonist's take on Wanamaker as insincere and only looking out for himself: "I Profit sighs any old thing for the sake of profit."[222] The cartoon publicly called into question Wanamaker's honesty and sincerity as a Christian businessman. Rodman Wanamaker closely followed the reporting on his father and family during the political years. He kept a large scrapbook of clippings from national and local papers that both heralded and lampooned his father.[223]

Despite these harsh public parodies, Wanamaker continued to believe that blending religion and business was beneficial to both—in particular, that religion would be more successful with the help of business. Over the years, he frequently received letters from strangers and friends questioning how business worked with his religious beliefs. He also reflected on this question in public arenas. In a speech he gave near the end of his life, Wanamaker shared with a large gathering the importance church played for him: "I became a member of a country Sunday school when a boy ten-years old and have been a member continuously for seventy-three years."[224] Aware that there were those who criticized him for his religious zeal, he reflected, "Why people think my Bethany work is either virtue or pose, I cannot imagine. I have just always liked it. And there isn't anything else, not business certainly, that I have just always liked and have gotten always satisfaction and blessing, not worry out of it."[225]

* * *

Concerned Protestants formulated a number of approaches to the problems of immigration, industrialization, poverty, and the loss of religious authority in the second half of the nineteenth century. Working across denominational lines and international borders, leaders launched dozens of programs targeting immigrant men as well as native-born men arriving from the countryside for work. Leaders freely borrowed techniques from one another, eager to find the right formula to address the problems. Ultimately, these tactics transformed American Protestantism. Like many urban leaders, Wanamaker joined multiple efforts to combat the scourges of modern city life with the balm of a new form of Protestant Christianity.

John Wanamaker's engagement with evangelical Protestant Christian moral reform programs began early and continued throughout his life. His participation in these groups was not separate from his business interests. As he developed his business, he began to apply the ideas he learned from the YMCA and his Sunday school work to his retail business. Protestant nonsectarian movements, his involvement with the YMCA, and his efforts at Bethany demonstrated to him the power of practical, nonreligious means used for religious purposes to inspire change in people's lives. While the spiritual was more important than the material, the two became intertwined for Wanamaker. The material was a powerful tool that could be harnessed to do ministry.

John Wanamaker felt that his store had "a broader, higher purpose," something more than only selling goods. It was public space created and orchestrated with a dual purpose—to make money but also to proffer a mix of religion, genteel manners, and curated goods intended to battle the corrupting moral influences of the city. The store's so-called higher purpose "was the general uplift of sentiment and the refining of all influences and ethics," which would shape not only the store customers but business practices as well by the "harmonizing of discordant elements in a business whose moral tone should be commensurate with its artistic supremacy."[226] He urged shoppers to see the luxuriously appointed spaces in his store as not an exercise in "ostentatious display but [as] DEDICATED TO THE PATRONS OF THE WANAMAKER STORE for their use and for the higher education of their children."[227]

Wanamaker understood himself as a moral reformer fueled by the desire to combat moral corruption. As he saw it, to reform the character of business necessitated changing its rules.

With the success of the Grand Depot, Wanamaker had started to accumulate a massive fortune. He funneled his money into dozens of Protestant reform movements and to his beloved church Bethany. But he wanted to do more. After the failure of his political ambitions, he began to think of designing a store building that would advertise his Christian business values and bring a moral ambiance to the heart of the city. By 1901, he had begun plans for a new store building in Philadelphia whose moral aesthetic would influence the city.

2

Moral Architecture

A building is an argument in stone.
—Peter Brown, historian[1]

French writer Émile Zola expressed amazement that modern department stores mimicked churches. In his 1883 ethnographic novel *Au bonheur des dames* (*Ladies' Paradise*), he compared the architectural wonders of his semifictional Parisian department store to a cathedral, observing, "Space had been gained everywhere, light and air entered freely." The open spaces of the stores were "as vast as a church," and the store entrances were "as high and as deep as a church porch."[2] Zola noted the ease of movement of the shoppers "beneath the bold curves of the wide-spaced trusses," proclaiming the department store "the cathedral of modern business" and "the cathedral of commerce."[3] He associated these new stores with the Catholic cathedrals of Paris, especially Notre Dame. His scrutiny contained admiration and critique. He wondered whether these cathedral-like stores were "producing a new religion," and whether or not it was a dangerous one.

Zola noted that churches "were being replaced" by department stores, as the stores attracted more worshippers than the churches. Women who used to spend hours in churches now spent "thrilling disturbing hours" in department stores in pursuit of "the ceaselessly renewed cult of the body, with the divine future life of beauty."[4] Both the church and the department store catered to women and their relationships. Luxury goods and high fashion, once the obsession of the wealthy, were now accessible to the growing bourgeoisie for purchase or, at the very least, close inspection. Zola felt that department stores had mesmerized their devotees to the extent that if the stores were to close, "there would have been a rising in the street, a desperate outcry from the worshippers" as no less than their "confessional and altar" was abolished.[5]

To some, Zola's assessment of department stores as churches seemed cynical, an exaggeration. Yet his keen observations described one of the major developments in Western urban architecture and consumerism. Department stores changed the landscape of the urban milieu, helping to create and structure modern consumerism and to shape middle-class, upper middle-class, and gender identities.

While Zola saw the department store as a threat to religion in the city, American department store impresario John Wanamaker saw it as a tool to extend his religious aims. With the success of his "new kind of store" at the Grand Depot, he began to dream of constructing a modern building for his Philadelphia department store. The edifice would do more than house an impressive array of merchandise and services. Wanamaker envisioned his new store building as a way to telegraph the nature and character of his business to the public and transform the urban context through architecture.

Glass and Iron

Arguably, Paris gave birth to the modern department store.[6] In the West, the development of retail shop design and methods progressed slowly, with little change from the early second century to the 1830s.[7] The creation of department stores symbolized the great social and economic developments of mid- to late nineteenth-century Europe and of the late nineteenth- and early twentieth-century United States. New production methods, labor practices, and merchandising approaches revolutionized retail, both supporting and creating the conditions for an emerging consumer culture.[8] Ready-to-wear clothing was one result of these transformations and was one of the innovations that opened up the potential of new stores.

Expanding prosperity broadened the consumption of luxury goods beyond aristocratic circles, lifting the criticism of moral ineptitude. Social classes developed, although the lines remained blurry for quite some time. Luxury consumption by the middle class became not only possible, but acceptable.[9] As the middle classes grew, leisure time increased. Children moved to the foreground of family life and were viewed as a reflection of their parents' social standing. New products emerged to meet these shifting needs.[10] In turn, new merchandise "raised consumers' standards and broadened their material wants" as stores took "careful note of consumer preferences."[11] Stores addressed these new desires by altering their retail approaches. In the 1830s and 1840s, stores in France called *magasins de nouveautés* (fancy or luxury goods stores) expanded the variety of materials they carried beyond dry goods and drapery.[12] Some *magasins de nouveautés* strung together a series of shops and buildings to create multidepartments of goods.

The forerunners of *magasins de nouveautés* were arcades. Moving out of the medieval tradition where "one trade kept to one street," arcades were "glass-roofed, marble-paneled corridors" and narrow streets "extending through whole blocks of buildings" where an assortment of shops clustered together protected from the elements, dust, and dangers of carriage traffic on the cramped Parisian streets.[13] Decorative elements, such as ornate mosaic tile floors and artful clocks, and elaborate storefronts began to multiply, attracting shoppers to experience not only the shops but the luxurious atmosphere. The glass roof invited in natural sunlight during the day, and the spaces were illuminated by dancing gaslights at night. It was an urban world enclosed.[14] But these first stores were labyrinths, like the streets of old Paris.

Inside most arcades, the shops featured sumptuous luxury goods that shopkeepers found ways to enticingly display. One arcade in Paris, Le Passage des Panoramas, offered shoppers a restaurant, "reading room, music shop, Marquis, wine merchants, hosier, haberdashers, tailors, bootmakers," and a variety of other shops and entertainments.[15] This combination of goods and recreation would find its way into department stores. The arcades demonstrated how to link multiple types of spaces and goods.

Arcades invited looking. The smorgasbord of goods created a sensory shopping experience, leading an observer to compare the shops to a church: a "nave with side chapels."[16] Unhurried by the press of a crowd on narrow sidewalks, shoppers could stroll and look at the shop displays without entering a store or buying anything. Cultural observers coined the term *lèche-vitrine* to describe this way of looking. While the phrase is often translated as "window shopping," its literal translation, "window licking," captures the embodied nature and hypnotizing effect of this new form of shopping.[17] It was possible to spend a day in the arcades and their shops, as they were often located near one another. Cultural critic Walter Benjamin reflected that the arcades became "dwelling places."[18] Arcades experienced their greatest popularity in France, where they were called *passages*; Germany, where shops clustered in *passagen*; and Italy, where shoppers strolled through *gallerie*.[19] Many of the shopping customs of the arcades extended to the emerging department stores.

The roofs of the arcades featured an early application of two great advancements in nineteenth-century architecture: glass and iron. Glass had been used with stone and lead in churches and palaces. Greenhouses had employed wood frames covered in glass. With the production of stronger iron and larger sheets of clear glass, they became key ingredients in a proliferation of new architectural forms. Soon, glass roofs sheltered food markets, such as Covent Gardens in England and Les Halles in Paris, and train depots, such as the one in Liverpool and the Strasbourg Platform's first building (now Gare de l'Est) in Paris. However, not until London's Great Exhibition did architecture, the display and organization of goods, and the emerging consumer culture come together in a spectacular way, making the department store possible.

London's 1851 Great Exhibition expanded the idea of the arcades by producing a grander rendition with its magnificent Crystal Palace. The palace's designer, Joseph Paxton, was a celebrated horticulturist who had long experimented with building glass conservatories. Paxton employed sheets of plate glass to create an unprecedented structure of soaring glass-clad iron that amazed visitors. The building design enabled natural light to pour over the exhibition's diverse exhibits and proved flexible enough for Paxton to save several mature elm trees that stood in the path of the building by enclosing them inside the structure.

An enormous structure, the palace enclosed twenty-three acres of London's Hyde Park, giving ample room for more than eight miles of display tables. The palace's design embodied the wonders of the Industrial Revolution. Many of its displays celebrated the superiority of British culture as the pinnacle of a great civilization and empire.[20] For architects, the palace demonstrated new practical possibilities for erecting structures with large open spaces filled with light, and it became the standard for exhibition building design. Shopkeepers took note.

London's palace inspired New York City's first attempt at a world's fair in 1853. Copying the design of a glass-clad iron structure, New

York's much smaller Crystal Palace also featured an adjacent observatory, where Elisha Otis demonstrated his new safety elevator to the public—an invention that would later make the multistory department store possible. Like London's fair, the New York exhibition promoted itself as a place where innovation was on display and ideological expression at the forefront. Although Franklin Pierce, the sitting U.S. president, opened the fair and over a million visitors passed through its displays, it was not as successful as subsequent American fairs, in part because of its remote location away from the center of the city.[21]

An ongoing series of fairs in Europe, especially in England and France, further inspired shopkeepers. Retailers imitated the new architectural designs and technology from the exhibitions to create dramatic spaces and exhibit their wares to a greater advantage.[22] In France, the *magasins de nouveautés* copied elements of the exhibitions and the arcades, transforming dark labyrinth-like spaces into glittering houses of sumptuous goods that cultural critics would later call "intoxicating." The *magasins* became "a vertical arcade, a stack of streets lined" with a wide selection of goods.[23]

The great exhibitions helped transform retail practices as well. Prevailing practices actively discouraged browsing in stores. Customers entered knowing what they were looking for and were expected to make a purchase. The exhibitions introduced a different approach to display and recognized that casual looking stirred interest. Shopkeepers began to alter traditional retail practices in response: now they invited browsing.

French merchants Aristide and Marguerite Boucicaut became leaders of this new approach when they creatively blended the display techniques of the *magasins de nouveautés*, the exhibitions, and new architectural forms. When they laid the cornerstone for Le Bon Marché (a French play on words meaning both "the good deal" and "the fair market") in 1869, they set out to construct a building explicitly designed to be a department store instead of adapting existing space.[24] Other *magasins de nouveautés* shopkeepers quickly followed suit. The Boucicauts' new store turned into a twenty-year building project as it repeatedly outgrew its space.[25] These new stores were called *les grands magasins* (literally, the large stores). Le Bon Marché also had benefited from the remaking of Paris.

Changing conditions in transportation, manufacturing, and consumption were essential ingredients in the development of department stores. Elected in 1848 as president of the French Republic,

Louis-Napoleon Bonaparte dreamed of remaking Paris as a modern city. Cramped serpentine streets made it difficult to traverse the city and created unhealthy living conditions for the poor. The Seine River served as the city's sewer. Crime flourished in dark alleys and narrow streets. By 1852, Louis-Napoleon Bonaparte had made himself emperor and moved forward with his vision to modernize the capital. He hired civil servant Georges-Eugène Haussmann, a man who had impressed Napoleon with his ability to lead large projects but had no urban planning or engineering experience. With the power of the emperor and the state behind him, Haussmann razed parts of "old Paris" and reassembled it. Aesthetics and politics led the redesign, guiding architectural design and layout. New wider boulevards made it possible for people to move freely through the city and protected against civil unrest by making the city more easily accessible to police. A remade Paris with wide boulevards, parks, and beautiful buildings drew visitors and spurred population growth—potential customers for *les grands magasins*. A similar phenomenon unfolded in other European cities and in the United States as large cities rapidly developed.

Changes that Haussmann made provided the Boucicauts an opportunity to construct a new, larger retail building. The first building constructed specifically for Le Bon Marché sported large windows and a magnificent staircase but did not employ an iron framework. They embraced the use of iron in the 1873 and 1876 store additions. For a second building expansion, they worked with the engineer Gustave Eiffel—before he had designed the famous Eiffel Tower for the 1889 Paris Exposition—to build an impressive iron-and-glass dome reminiscent of another cultural institution, an opera house.[26]

Ironwork skeletons, and then steel frames, enabled department store buildings to grow taller and stronger with thinner supports. The metal frames permitted the installation of massive and elaborate glass-covered roof sections. Glass roofs admitted sunlight into the center of the store and invited store designers to express a decorative flair with stunning stained-glass patterns. Iron and steel structures also permitted the installation of larger windows in buildings. The plate-glass Paxton employed in the Crystal Palace and in subsequent exhibition buildings became mainstream in retail establishments. Shopkeepers started skirting their buildings with enormous windows to bring more natural light into dark interiors and to tantalize customers with carefully orchestrated displays of the merchandise inside.[27]

Exhibition structures were not the exclusive source of architectural inspiration for department store buildings. European stores looked to historic palaces and cathedrals and the newer monumental designs of opera houses and train stations as examples of magisterial and permanent public buildings. The magnificent structures created for Parisian stores, such as Le Bon Marché, Les Grands Magasins du Louvre (usually called Le Louvre), Bazar de l'Hôtel de Ville, Samaritaine, and Printemps, sparked creativity in the design of other massive stores. Architecture began to be a defining principle of department stores.[28]

Department stores caught on quickly and by the turn of the twentieth century had spread across Europe. Germany had one hundred department stores by 1907 and two hundred by World War I. While England's department store growth was slower, it launched three particularly famous stores: Harrods, Whiteleys, and Selfridge's—although Selfridge's was started by an American and former associate of Marshall Field, Harry Selfridge.[29] The department store soon became a symbol of a new bourgeois culture in Europe and the developing middle class in the United States.[30]

American Department Stores

American department stores developed later than their Parisian counterparts. It was not until the 1870s when the dynamics of population growth, increased wealth, the advent of reliable transportation, and improved production made it a fertile time for the establishment of multidepartment stores in the United States. Now, there were more people with money to spend on merchandise and leisure. Trains and streetcars made movement through the urban landscape easier and more appealing.[31] In turn, department stores gathered a wide variety of goods under one roof and offered lower prices.

From 1870 to 1920, American department stores sprang up in cities across the United States. Nearly every American city boasted one department store—or more—with grand displays and ample floor space for a plethora of goods, and by 1900 there were over 8,900 such stores.[32] But long before them all, there was what many name as the first American department store, A. T. Stewart's Emporium in New York City.

Alexander Turney Stewart, a transplant from Ireland working as a grade school teacher, accepted a small dry goods store in New York City as payment for a loan in 1823. To add to the store's stock, he invested a small inheritance in a shipment of Irish linens and laces he handpicked on a trip back to Belfast in hopes that these additions to the stock would quicken sales.[33] Similar retail establishments popped up around the same time, like Lord and Taylor.[34]

Stewart's little shop did well, and over the next twenty-three years he moved his store to larger and larger quarters until, in 1848, he gathered enough money to build his own store at Broadway and Chambers Street. Stewart built a marble edifice with extensive street frontage. People called it the Marble Palace and found the size of the establishment exciting—the building itself was as much a draw as the merchandise. It boasted one of the most extravagant exteriors of the time, with Piedmont windows on the lower levels and other Federalist-inspired decorations.[35] Shopping at the Marble Palace constituted an entirely new experience and drew retailers from England and Chicago to visit.[36] At the time, it was the largest American building devoted solely to retail. However, Stewart's Marble Palace was not a full-fledged department store—it catered only to women.

By 1859, Stewart decided to build an even larger store on lower Broadway between Eighth Avenue and Twenty-Third Street. Called the Iron Palace for its intricate iron frame, its completion made Stewart's establishment the biggest retail store in the country, with acres of floor space to sell a wider variety of goods. This five-story building included a glass rotunda that delivered sunlight into the depths of the building, an architectural flourish reminiscent of the European department stores and great exhibitions. Two winding grand staircases accented the dome, affording access to the floors above.[37] The stairs also allowed customers to see and be seen as they shopped for goods or spent the afternoon taking advantage of the growing number of services the store offered. The open space offered visual access to multiple floors of merchandise. The building symbolized the new mode of retail. It housed nineteen departments offering merchandise far beyond women's clothing. Stewart's impresssive new store offered a wide variety of goods for men, women, children, and the home, organized into departments.[38]

Yet Stewart's Iron Palace boasted few comforts. It lacked carpet and additional elegant appointments at a time when other storekeepers started layering their interiors with luxurious touches to attract customers. The only convenience was a women's restroom.[39] Stewart's new location drew other large-scale shops to the area, creating a shopping district along Broadway that became known as the Ladies' Mile.[40] Competitors sought to emulate and surpass Stewart's success. New stores sprouted up, emphasizing sheer size as a marker of the variety of merchandise they had for sale.[41]

But Stewart did not have the first American department store. Having more in common with European forerunners, *magasins de nouveautés*, it lacked the variety of merchandise, services, and luxury appointments that came to define a department store. Stewart's placement as the mythical source of the first store was in part encouraged by John Wanamaker. After Stewart's death, the store struggled. In 1896 Wanamaker purchased the store and claimed he was the heir of the famous retailer's legacy in store guides and signage. By 1878, only three stores in the United States had advanced from their dry goods and wholesale roots into full-fledged American department stores: Wanamaker's in Philadelphia, Macy's in New York City, and Jordan Marsh in Boston.[42]

By the turn of the century, there were numerous large-scale retail establishments across the United States, in buildings adapted and enlarged for that purpose, hawking a bewildering assortment of merchandise. Some even assumed the name "bazaar" or "emporium" to signal the new type of business that gathered many different types of goods together in one place. Many were highly profitable and looked to magnify their success by commissioning buildings to house their retail businesses. Large cities were the first to experience a surge in store construction, sparked by a growth in population and better transportation systems.

Building Morality

For twenty-five years, Wanamaker had made do with the complex of buildings that had been the old freight train depot as the home of his expanding store. He had added onto the Grand Depot numerous times, surging upward and outward, buying neighboring property and a small alley to protect himself from the growing incursion of other Philadelphia retail establishments and to house his swelling hoard of merchandise.

After a burst of construction that joined the various parts of the Grand Depot together into a cohesive whole in 1885, Wanamaker gathered a large contingent of his employees in the central space of the store to give a speech on the store's progress. His staff now numbered in the thousands, and the space could no longer hold all of the employees. Wanamaker likened the moment to the biblical story of Jacob and his seven-year search for his wife Rachel. He told his staff, "I have been serving more than seven years for this night to come. It was a kind of wedding night. The old building and the smaller buildings—the Market St. building and the Chestnut St. buildings are married tonight."[43] To mask the cobbled-together spaces of the store, Wanamaker and his team of workers decorated the space lavishly inside and out. His first iteration of the Grand Depot as a Moorish sibling to the Centennial Exhibition slowly gave way to a straightforward series of storefront edifices anchored by a tall clock tower at one corner of the property. Despite these ongoing construction efforts and the ones that followed, the store maintained a thrown-together look, as if "a village of temporary shops" had popped up without walls between them.[44]

By the late 1890s, Wanamaker had survived a few tumultuous years in political office and another series of national financial downturns. He had purchased Stewart's New York store, which, despite its age, remained more dignified architecturally than his Philadelphia store with its two grand staircases and glass-capped rotunda. The neighboring New Public Building (Philadelphia city hall) was finally finished after twenty years of constant construction, putting Wanamaker's store in the shadow of the imposing and ornate building. At the corner of Market and Eighth, a cluster of department stores—Gimbels, Strawbridge and Clothier, and Lit Brothers—were either building or expanding.[45]

A visit to Chicago's Columbian Exposition in 1893 gave Wanamaker, along with millions of American and international visitors, an experience of monumental architecture and city planning. Visitors experienced a study in contrasts between the city where they stayed for the exhibition and the idealized city inside the exhibition gates. The exposition gave life to a utopian vision of the urban world. Dubbed the "White City" for the gleaming white stucco exteriors of the buildings, the fair's stunning Beaux Arts classical architecture and visual uniformity reportedly stirred the "higher consciousness" of fairgoers and created a "morally

Figure 2.1. The exterior of the Grand Depot around the time of the Centennial Exhibition, sporting a Moorish motif to visually link Wanamaker's store annex with the exhibition's Main Building.

uplifting environment" even for the "commonplace crowd."[46] Beautiful, elegant, and harmonious surroundings were believed to have contributed to the courteous behavior of the mammoth crowds.[47] For many, the fair buildings exemplified the best civil architecture of the period.[48]

Wanamaker had grown aware that the store's jumbled architecture did little to communicate the character of his business. On his visit to Chicago, the difference between his Grand Depot and the latest trends in architecture and design was stark. It became impossible to ignore that his building lacked the aesthetic power of the Chicago's Exhibition architecture.

Chicago also, however, offered answers to the problem. In the city's nascent high-rise architecture, and the design of the new Marshall Fields store then under construction, Wanamaker found new ways to think about exploiting multistoried space.[49] For a while, the purchase of the Stewart store in New York delayed any building plans. By 1901, other major department stores broke ground on new buildings. In New York, Macy's and Adams Dry Goods Company hired the same architecture firm, De Lemos and Cordes, to design palatial buildings with huge footprints.[50]

On the twenty-fifth anniversary of Wanamaker's business, the pride he professed in 1885 to his employees had disappeared, and he now referred to the Grand Depot as "no more than a glorified shed" and an "old one-story shack."[51] Wanamaker wrote to his son Rodman that it was time to replace "this queer patchwork building."[52] Constructing a new building would modernize the store and, he believed, contribute to the moral reform of Philadelphia. The construction of a new flagship Philadelphia store offered Wanamaker the opportunity to create an edifice to serve as an instrument of moral reform in business, in the lives of his customers and employees, and in the city of Philadelphia. As his interest and support for moral reform movements grew, so too did his vision of how his store could contribute to this endeavor.

It was no coincidence that Wanamaker felt a strong impulse to use architecture for moral reform. Since the early nineteenth century, Protestant clergy, reformers, religious educators, and architects in the urban milieu sought new ways to infuse "civic uplift" into the urban environment.[53] These reformers and activists saw the aesthetic design of public spaces, architecture, churches, gardens, and parks as a way to combat the city's damaging environmental ills resulting from urbanization and the mechanization of society.[54] Architecture had the power to shape and influence behavior, and the experience of "good" architecture could be a form of worship.[55] Ministers such as the Reverend Frederick W. Sawyer linked together beautiful "parks and gardens" and "churches and public edifices" with the power "to mould the taste."[56] Urban aesthetics mattered.

Tenement reform, the settlement house movement, the development of city parks and playgrounds, and city planning grew out of these efforts to improve the lives of city inhabitants.[57] As reformers saw these programs progress, some brought these elements together in a more comprehensive approach to urban planning and design known as the City Beautiful movement. Proponents reasoned that if parks and recreational spaces made a difference in crime, a well-planned city would have an even more powerful effect. Properly designed buildings and public spaces could morally uplift urban inhabitants. The City Beautiful movement also emphasized the role of public spaces and buildings in creating a civic spirit.

Wanamaker saw a connection between "a city's physical appearance and its moral state."[58] He concluded that a new building for his Philadelphia store could do more than house his successful business; it would also foster a physical environment that would gently cultivate morally responsible citizens. It was a wider application of Horace Bushnell's concept of "Christian nurture." If a Christian home life cultivated Christian children, then a Christian building had a similar power. If the proper construction of space helped with Christian formation, why not a department store building?

After all, Wanamaker had direct experience with the effectiveness of a built environment through the Sunday school movement and especially the YMCA. Sunday school missionaries planted their schools in impoverished areas to provide basic reading and writing along with religious education steeped in emerging middle-class values. Sunday school teachers served as role models to their students, week after week exhibiting proper behavior, dress, and physical presentation.[59] Some of these schools turned into churches and further influenced the neighborhoods they served, providing the benefits of settlement houses and social service centers.

Indeed, this was a point of pride for Wanamaker and his Bethany Sunday school. Surveying what he had built, he measured Bethany not by how many souls had been saved but by how the church and its services had revitalized the neighborhood. He proudly claimed that "the [Sunday] school is generally and fully credited with having made this entire section of the city what it is today." For Wanamaker, not only did the church define the people it attracted, but it also improved the city itself and "made this parish a desirable place for residence."[60] He saw evidence that Bethany and its many programs had enhanced the neighborhood, transitioning it from a collection of run-down homes to a working- and middle-class neighborhood.[61]

Wanamaker's involvement with the YMCA proved to be the greatest source of inspiration for the new building. The Y had helped Wanamaker reconcile business and religion in his youth, and now it helped him envision an attractive place of shopping leisure where customers experienced moral uplift. From its earliest days, the YMCA promoted the purposeful articulation of space as a tool for religion. Leaders of the Y in London discovered that "well-furnished" rented rooms attracted young men from less savory recreational options in the city.[62] Once the young men were inside, the Y socialized them.

In the United States, the desire for YMCA buildings before the Civil War emerged as a concern for financial stability and greater permanency.[63] By the time the first building plans were being drawn in New York, Boston, and Philadelphia, a larger vision for the role of the YMCA had surfaced. Now, a Y building represented the organization's values through its exterior design and the services offered inside. It would be a wholesome clubhouse that offered respectable leisure and a chance to socialize young men in middle-class, Protestant values.[64] Y buildings were instilled with the potential to heal the nation after the war and to create a visible connection to the "Great Master Builder," God.[65]

New York City's building led the way for Y branches across the country. Although Wanamaker left the position of secretary to start Oak Hall with his brother-in-law, his relationship with the organization never ceased. From the position of secretary, he moved into the role of president in 1869 and shepherded the Philadelphia branch in fundraising and the construction of its first building at Fifteenth and Chestnut. Philadelphia's Y imitated the New York City building design and offered similar amenities, including a reading room, classrooms, a parlor, and a gymnasium, as well as storefronts on the street level to produce income.[66] Wanamaker was intimately involved in the Y building project. Addison Hutton, the architect who had drafted the design for Bethany's second building and who, that same year, transformed Wanamaker's Grand Depot into a tabernacle for the Moody revival, served as the architect for the undertaking. Wanamaker's faith in the power of the building program grew so strong that he personally sponsored the construction of YMCA buildings for branches in Madras and Calcutta, India; Peking, China; Kyoto, Japan; and Seoul, Korea.[67] As historian Paula Lupkin has traced, "From the beginning, the YMCA was invested in defining class, race, and ethnicity as well as gender through its buildings."[68] It was a principle that Wanamaker applied to his stores. As he saw it, the material world was a powerful tool and, if employed correctly, could be mobilized to do ministry.

The Golden Rule of Business

In 1896 Wanamaker wrote a letter to an R. M. Luther on his mixing of business and religion. He explained that he had done more than run a successful store; he had also "tried to be in one sense a preacher of at least good business habits" and to train his employees to be better people. The merger of business and religion was a complete one: "I would like to use my store as a pulpit on week days, just as much as my desk at Bethany on Sundays, to lift people up that they may better lift themselves up."[69] There was a lot at stake in constructing a new building. In the Grand Depot, Wanamaker had slowly assembled a store and a business model that he believed exuded a moral and, at least for him, religious ethos. Wanamaker felt that the new building could advertise the character of his retail business, and that those same values could influence the city. The structure needed functionality and moral merit.

In a speech to his employees in 1885, Wanamaker explained the connections he saw between his business and religion. He urged them to not "fail to recognize God's Providence over us." Although Wanamaker desired success, he wanted the store to be known by its "character" and "integrity" as well as by its new methods. Though acknowledging that some people saw the store's extensive advertisement campaigns as "offensive," he saw his advertising as one of the tools he used to change business. In full-page newspaper ads, day after day—except Sundays—Wanamaker penned his own "folksy" editorial columns educating his customers in understanding the quality of his merchandise, the character of his business, and his generous treatment of employees. He used advertising as a way to educate customers and competitors about a new, moral way of doing business. He wanted to expose "the old methods that have helped many to go wrong: the false tickets, the short measures." He wanted to let shoppers know that his store was "about honesty."[70] It was more than image making, although it was that as well. Wanamaker saw it as a part of his business mission—to make business a Christian enterprise and profitable. If he was successful God would reward him.

The reputation of retail had not been good in the previous decades. Wanamaker reminded his workers of the uphill battle they were facing: "It was said, once, that a man or a woman to be a salesperson had to tell falsehoods—had to throw their conscience overboard." His guiding principle was "anything to be done either in the counting room or the Private Office, or on the Floor or in the Basement that we cannot think of with comfort when we go to church, and when we say our prayers" was a disservice both to the firm and to those who had engaged in the action. Cheating customers did not help the store; rather, it detracted from the reputation Wanamaker had built with his employees' help.[71]

Wanamaker's impulse to align his business with his Christian principles was not an isolated one. As historians Mark Valeri and Leigh Eric Schmidt have shown, the mix of business and religion has a long history in the United States.[72] From 1880 to 1925, there was an uptick in experimentation with applying Christian principles to business across the United States.[73] An early leader in this movement, Wanamaker used this trend—and his acceptance of the prosperity gospel—to reconcile his decision to become a merchant instead of a minister. He sought to align retail business and his Christian values with a "Golden Rule of business." He had learned that nonreligious means used for religious purposes inspired change in people's lives.

Wanamaker's efforts to infuse business with Christian values commenced at Oak Hall. Wanamaker and his brother-in-law Nathan Brown had decided to treat their customers in a manner that was different from standard trade practices. At the time, most stores did not allow customers to browse freely. To enter a store meant that the customer was expected to make a purchase, and customers were harassed until they did so. Prices depended on a customer's ability to haggle with the sales clerk, and exchanges were not accepted. In disreputable retail establishments, "sample" goods laid out for a customer's inspection—in a bait-and-switch move—were of a higher quality than the items sold to the consumer. To differentiate themselves, Wanamaker & Brown implemented a one-price system for all; there was no haggling—all customers paid the same price for the same item. Moreover, their store was an early adopter of price tags (some claim it was the first) and a limited money-back guarantee (for a full refund). "One Price and Return of Goods!" became their first motto, and they routinely promoted a schema with four cardinal points: "one price; cash payment (no credit); full guarantee; money refunded." To illustrate the need for changes, Wanamaker repeatedly told two boyhood stories. When, as a child, he visited a store to look at merchandise, he had been kicked out because he did not make a purchase fast enough to satisfy the store clerk. On another shopping excursion, Wanamaker recalled purchasing a gift for his mother only to discover a better gift in another display a few minutes later. Returning to the salesperson to make the exchange, he was sternly told, "No refunds," and left the store disappointed.[74] As the shop grew, Wanamaker & Brown launched additional business reforms in 1862 and 1864, adopting the motto "A Square Deal Upon Solid Principles," which they described as being reached "by three connecting roads—Standards of Merchandise, Standards of Value, Standards of Service."[75]

Other American retailers experimented with similar practices. James Cash Penney, for example, started his career at a dry goods store run by Thomas Callahan and Guy Johnson in the 1890s. Located in Colorado and Wyoming, they called their stores the Golden Rule Stores to advertise the New Testament principles of their business. Penney eventually bought Callahan and Johnson out and made the Golden Rule Stores the basis for his franchise, J. C. Penney. Wanamaker & Brown drew on the idea of the "golden rule" and made these changes prominent as a marker of the integrity of their business.[76]

A pamphlet produced in 1899 made the argument that Wanamaker's store was "more than a store—more than a money-getting business— more than a material result of individual enterprise." Instead, the store represented a comprehensive and intelligent system, "a system capable of the widest application in the business world; and yet a unique system" capable of changing the world for the better.[77] The store married "scientific business practices with ethics," which meant "treating all people alike—of preserving their self-respect in buying, and of respecting the confidence which they have been asked to bestow."[78] The subtext was that the store's business practices were moral and Christian. In his later years, Wanamaker explained that, through his efforts at reform, "the Golden Rule of the New Testament has become the Golden Rule of business." This new "Golden Rule" was a way "to raise the standards" of retail that would be "tolerably free from practices that had gradually lowered mercantile character."[79] What began as four cardinal principles quickly expanded into a series of rules and regulations Wanamaker imposed on his business.

Now, he wanted his store building to message the moral character of the business through its intentional design and beauty.[80] Other department stores had mobilized building design as a form of advertisement, emphasizing "no-nonsense message of thrift and bargains," "an orgy of exuberant consumption," or "progress, modernity, youthful stylishness."[81] During a trip to Chicago, Wanamaker ruminated on what he wanted his building to stand for and wrote down in a small diary the words "simplicity" and "straightforwardness" to signal his honesty and loyalty as a businessman. He recorded "granite" as a contender for the exterior of the building, noting that it would "stand for integrity and strength."[82] Beautiful architecture also had the capacity to increase profits—an aspect that was not lost on Wanamaker.[83] Research for potential building designs took him back to Europe, where he again studied department stores, especially the new building for Printemps in Paris and the new and architecturally daring buildings in Berlin.[84]

The Wanamaker Building

When it came to selecting an architect for his project, Wanamaker passed over Addison Hutton, the architect he relied upon for several of his biggest construction jobs. In a surprising move, he turned to Chicago architect Daniel Burnham and his firm, whose vision he had admired at the 1893 Columbian Exposition and with whom he had a working relationship.[85] Wanamaker had retained Burnham for a large addition at his New York store along with an elevated connector between the old and new buildings. The two shared an appreciation for French architecture, with Burnham relying on many designs from French architects for the 1893 exposition buildings. But Wanamaker's selection of Burnham was not without controversy. Despite Burnham's firm's previous work designing the Land Title Building in Philadelphia in 1897, Philadelphia architects angrily complained that Wanamaker chose an "outsider" for his new building.[86]

But the tide of Burnham's architectural influence on the American department store was too strong to turn back. Within a ten-year period, Burnham and his firm designed Marshall Field's State Street store and related buildings in Chicago, Gimbel Brothers in New York, and Filene's in Boston.[87] In each case, Burnham adapted his famous office building high-rise design.[88] Like his office buildings, the department stores featured large atriums to admit natural light into the depths of the store, and, by providing multistory open space, he carved out interior public spaces as well. The store exteriors carried various articulations of his developing classicism. Although Burnham's store designs shared similarities in basic form, size, and stature, each building had a unique layout and differing exterior decorations, windows, and cornice style.[89] Wanamaker's building displayed the cleanest lines of Burnham's buildings and was the largest.

From his earliest years working with John Wellborn Root, Burnham pushed American cities to new heights by designing their arts and commercial interests. Burnham's platform, solidified by the fair, gave him a national reputation that attracted other department store merchant princes contemplating change at the turn of the nineteenth century. His massive office buildings, the Rookery in Chicago and the Ellicott Square Building in Buffalo, established him as an authority in creating large, beautiful, yet practical public buildings.

The success of the Columbian Exhibition convinced Burnham that his legacy rested on creating buildings whose beauty enhanced cities and that the classical style his team executed there should be the style for his future work.[90] Burnham advocated for urban planning and was a leader in the City Beautiful movement. He felt drawn to create public spaces that conditioned the public's morality and fostered moral order.[91] However, Burnham initially saw public and commercial spaces as distinct from one another. Wanamaker challenged this perspective, understanding his building as both a commercial and public building. Burnham soon agreed.

Like Marshall Field, Wanamaker wanted his new building to be built in a series of phases so that business could continue uninterrupted. This construction process also served as a working advertisement for the new building—shoppers could buy their goods and see the new building's progress in one stop.[92] It was a challenging endeavor, with pressure placed on store employees charged with freighting merchandise from one section of the building to another as parts were destroyed, rebuilt, and opened.[93]

Wanamaker was intimately involved in the design of the building and traveled to Chicago to meet with Burnham and go over his specifications.[94] Initial plans for the building were drawn in 1902 and worked over by Wanamaker for several months. Extensive excavations of the massive basement slowed progress at first. Construction spanned a seven-year period, with the last section finished in 1911. The length of time was not entirely due to the size or scale of the project; labor disputes and financing problems took their toll.[95]

Ultimately, the design Burnham and Wanamaker agreed upon echoed an Italian Renaissance palazzo with clean lines on the exterior and large windows.[96] They called it "Roman Doric." The design itself was neither inherently Christian nor moral. It was the idiom of American business and modernity: the mid-rise skyscraper dressed in granite. It was a symbol of modernity standing out in Philadelphia's developing Center City. Through its clean lines, the design aligned Wanamaker's edifice with other public buildings going up in this period, especially banks, museums, and courthouses with their attendant associations of discipline, balance, honesty, integrity, and respectability—the same values Wanamaker saw as Protestant and moral. By adopting this style, he not only wanted to communicate these same values but also hoped to signal "good taste."[97]

Squat in comparison to modern skyscrapers, Wanamaker's building made a memorable statement in Philadelphia's city center in 1911. Although not as tall as the New Public Building crowned with a statue of William Penn, Wanamaker's building was much taller and much wider than its neighbors. The building's cornice, which differentiated Wanamaker's store from surrounding buildings, was less ornate than some of Burnham's other buildings, yet its detail gave the store a neat and crisp ornamentation. The uniform use of elements on the entire building made it distinctly different from neighboring buildings that were executed in more flamboyant designs. The building facade consisted of three distinct layers. Just below the cornice, small square windows punctuated the building at even intervals, giving way to a row of arched windows that spanned two stories. The middle section maintained six rows of evenly spaced windows topped by large arch windows as broad as two arched windows just above. Pilasters decorated the lower part of the building, changing into temple-like columns at the entrances.[98]

The fluted columned entrances, like those of a Greek temple and the new courthouses and museums popping up in American cities, lent gravitas to the store's four entries, one on each side of the building. Emphasizing the temple connection, two fierce Japanese bronze statues flanked the main entrance. The statues were Ni-o, the traditional guardians against evil spirits at the entrances of Japanese Buddhist temples. The temple correlation continued in the gleaming brass doors, which were framed by embedded columns and panels decorated with intricate knot designs and marble panels. Here, Burnham maintained stronger historical references than in his other work because the building was situated in an older city.[99] Plate-glass windows encircled much of the sidewalk level of the building, inviting shoppers into the store through imaginative displays. The spacing of the granite blocks over the whole facade brought visual interest to a building that covered an entire city block.

Burnham described the Wanamaker Building in a letter to a friend, noting that it was "in the center of the city." Detailing the scale of the design and its beauty, he wrote, "There are three stories below the sidewalk and twelve stories above. . . . The exterior is of very beautiful granite, the Italian Renaissance style being employed in the design." These attributes made the Wanamaker Building awe-inspiring and confident in the city landscape. Burnham declared, "The building as a whole, both inside and outside, is the most monumental commercial structure ever erected anywhere in the world. Its total cost has exceeded Ten Million Dollars."[100] Burnham was right. Once finished, it was for a time the largest retail space in the world.

Wanamaker advocated for modern technology, insisting on installing the latest in electric wiring, lighting, elevators, dumbwaiters, and fire safety. Prominently placed on the store's new rooftop were two Marconi wireless telegraph towers. The telegraph was promoted as a service to customers, although its primary purpose was to allow the Philadelphia store to communicate affordably and quickly with the New York store. Later, the store boasted its own radio station, which Wanamaker used to promote both store and religious programming and music from the store organ. The first radio broadcast, on August 7, 1922, opened with Bethany Presbyterian's minister, the Rev. Dr. Macauley, reading the Twenty-Third Psalm and Wanamaker giving a formal speech. Bethany's Sunday services were also broadcasted from the station, making the store a promoter of Wanamaker's church.[101]

Good ventilation persisted as an abiding concern in stores. One of the chief complaints of shoppers and store employees at the turn of the century remained the lack of fresh air in retail establishments. At the

Figure 2.2. Undated postcard of the Wanamaker Building in Philadelphia. Building postcards typically showed the edifice absent surrounding buildings.

Grand Depot Wanamaker had experimented with ways to cool and re-fresh the air, adding ductwork and a series of fans in a bid to control the air flow and temperature in the building. In the new store, he installed a sophisticated ventilation system to keep fresh air moving through the store, continually exchanging fresh air for stale air.[102]

The construction of a large building brought fire safety concerns to the fore. Wanamaker worried about fire; he had nearly lost his store to a blaze that swept down Market Street in 1896. In 1906 a fire erupted under one of the store's display windows at the height of the Christmas season when the store was packed with shoppers. A cigarette or cigar had been tossed down in a grate below the window and smoldered into a blaze. A policeman noticed smoke and helped put out the fire just as flames began to burst inside the display window.[103] Fires in other cities, such as the 1903 Iroquois Theatre fire in Chicago, raised concerns about fire safety and the importance of multiple building exits when more than 550 people died trying to escape the flames in what had been touted as a "fireproof" building. Making the threat of fire even more real, Wana-maker lost his summer home to a fire just as the new Philadelphia store neared completion.

Customers worried about fire too. In the spring of 1900 one shopper took the time to write, at length, about the lack of fire safety he had observed at the Grand Depot—listing the lack of exits and the time it would take to evacuate thousands of customers and employees.[104] The concerned citizen told Wanamaker, "You May thank God you have escaped thus far, but have you the moral right to continue this public menace?" The stranger called the store a "complete death-trap," citing only eight exits from the massive building.

Wanamaker took fire concerns seriously and resolved to solve the problem in his new building. However, the attention to fire safety did not succeed in squashing the new store's central atrium. Rotundas and grand staircases were common features in late nineteenth-century department stores but were largely abandoned because large open spaces between floors helped fires spread quickly.[105] It was the one area Wanamaker compromised on fire safety by keeping a multifloor atrium in the plan. Wanamaker was particularly proud of these achievements and consistently mentioned store technology in advertisements. In keeping with the great exhibitions' incorporation of the latest technology, he showcased the building's mechanics in store publications.

A year after the groundbreaking, as workers finished the first section of the building and a power plant to run the building, Wanamaker wrote a newspaper editorial expressing excitement and enthusiasm for his new building. He invited readers to "compare, if you can, the old freight station's miserable lamps with to-night's mighty blaze of electricity shining from the three hundred and sixty-three windows of the little section of our new building." Light, both natural and artificial, was a major feature of the new store. With the power plant in place, the store would light up in new ways with the first Christmas light show launched that year.

With only one-third of the building complete, Wanamaker encouraged his readers to imagine the "whole place . . . when the other sections are completed." Then, in an explosion of enthusiasm, he shared the genealogy of what stood before them: "Back of the light—electricity; back of electricity—dynamos and engines; back of dynamos and engines—MIND!"[106] The store was more than just the sum of its various elements, more than just a building for that matter, "It was the idea behind it that counted."[107] It had spirit; it had mind; it had soul.

Promotional materials for the store's anniversary and in celebration of the new building expounded on the meaning of the design, declaring, "It is the spirit that counts. . . . The great granite building that houses the Wanamaker merchandise in Philadelphia says this on the face of it." The text asks a rhetorical question, "Suppose [the design] had been a gingerbread, fantastical sort of building, with turrets and fretwork, minarets and Renaissance carvings, and stucco gorgeousness, would it have been art?" Wanamaker answered the question clearly: "No—because it would not have been SINCERE. It would not have been SUITABLE. It would not have been SIMPLE. It would not have been expressive of the SOUL within it."[108] The soul of his store and how it got there, Wanamaker never explicitly explained. But his treatment of the store, his passion for its potential to change people's lives, and his fondness for his employees, whom he called his "store family," leave little doubt that Wanamaker believed that the store had a Christian "soul within it."

With simplicity, elegance, and sturdy beauty, the new Wanamaker store did in fact stand in sharp contrast to the New Public Building, built over a thirty-year period (1871–1901) across the street from Wanamaker's. The New Public Building boasted a French Second Empire style that was heavily ornate, with 255 sculptures and a thirty-seven-foot-tall statue of William Penn standing atop a tower.[109] Where the New Public Building stood as an elaborate profusion of Victorian enthusiasm, Wanamaker's building looked steady, reliable, modern, and inviting, and he argued that these characteristics depicted it as morally sound. In many ways, the Wanamaker Building appeared more suitable as the center of city business in its Renaissance palazzo style. From the main entrance framed grandly by columns to the granite facade, the Wanamaker Building echoed the design of museums, libraries, and courthouses popping up across the country.

A Building for the People

Six years later, when workers finished the store, Wanamaker and his son Rodman prepared for the building's dedication by planning a spectacle of seemingly endless celebrations and visiting dignitaries honoring the achievement of the new building and Wanamaker's fifty years in business. Thomas, the oldest son, had died unexpectedly while the store was still under construction. Rodman had returned from living abroad to support his father in running the business.

The vision for the dedication ceremonies was to inaugurate the store as Philadelphia's newest public building. While Wanamaker had always thought of his store as a public entity, his new store better played the role of public building with its monumental architecture and size. Geographically, it was already at an advantage. The location next to the city hall marked its role as a civic building by association. Wanamaker invited Republican colleague President William Howard Taft to speak at the dedication. To Wanamaker's surprise and delight, Taft accepted the invitation. The dedication ceremony would be an inauguration of Wanamaker's as a public building with the blessing of the president of the United States. It was the first time a sitting U.S. president took part in the dedication of a commercial enterprise.

Other American department stores also identified themselves as public buildings, often through architecture, size, or location.[110] Some stores, including Marshall Field's and Halle's in Cleveland, placed large clocks on their exteriors to emphasize their service role in the public square. European department stores took on the architecture of public buildings and offered a host of services, and American stores followed their example. One historian notes that department stores typically "encouraged a perception of the building as a public place, where consumption itself was almost incidental to the delights of a sheltered promenade in a densely crowded, middle-class urban space."[111]

Burnham also came to understand the Wanamaker Building as a public building: "Commerce is the heart and lungs of a community." He said at the dedication, "[Wanamaker's] monument is his store—a thing of beauty and dignity enhancing the appearance of the city, a building that the entire community is from this time on to take the greatest pride in, for in a high sense it is theirs, and they are to use it."[112] The structure was available for the citizens to use, and its beautiful aesthetic enhanced the city.

Wanamaker imbued his new building with meaning—publicly and personally—at nearly every opportunity. At the laying of the last cornerstone in 1910, after those who had gathered sang the hymn "My Faith Looks Up to Thee," he confidently told the gathered crowd, "After many rejected plans of the exterior of the building, the one accepted faces the world on all sides with a bold and classic front. It will be unhesitatingly interpreted from the outside as meaning something good and strong."[113] When contemplating what was considered by many architects to be one of the two most beautiful and distinguished department stores Burnham designed (the other being Marshall Field's State Street store), Wanamaker saw more than beauty. His new department store building symbolized something more permanent than the structure itself. In a vein he regularly revisited, he described the force behind the store as the human spirit: "The oak rises, flourishes and dies; the hardest granite, as time wears on, shows the sign of age; but the mind of man, renewed and cultured at each generation, grows on forever preparing for wider and nobler service."[114]

It was a poignant speech, especially given that he had nearly lost everything in the economic downturn of 1907 and that he was grieving the sudden death of his heir apparent, his son Thomas, at age forty-six. Even in this moment, Wanamaker thought of education—how the building itself housed the possibility for the store customers as well as the employees to grow. Ever paternalistic and yet ever sincere, he was confident in his authority to serve as moral guide and teacher. In his speech Wanamaker solemnly claimed, "I am so glad to add to that, whatever be the attainments of the mind of man, God, the Father of us all, is saying to us, Come up higher. Come up higher. That is the everyday speech of the Maker."[115] This growth would occur in Wanamaker's department store itself. "From today our lives must start from this new center. The blessing of all this is the permanence about us."[116]

* * *

Protestants responded to a changing society with new architecture. Churches moved to remodel old buildings and design new ones with imposing facades, towering spires, and eye-catching designs that went up in cities across the country.[117] Reform organizations like the YMCA and Sunday schools joined the building boom by constructing impressive, centrally located structures. Protestant leaders invested in these buildings by serving on the planning committees, raising funds, and seeing the projects through to completion. America's urban landscape was changing.

Wanamaker's new building took up more prominently his religious work of moral reform. He reimagined the space, a new building dedicated to bringing his Christian principles to bear—to morally influence the city—not only in his business practices but also in the building's architecture. It would, he hoped, shape the city into its image, inspiring responsible, disciplined, and moral behavior by its mere presence.[118] This "aesthetic evangelism" promoted Christian evangelical values through the built environment in the center of the city.[119]

Inside the store, Wanamaker peddled the latest fashion and home goods, and through his advertisements and displays he hoped to educate his customers in Christian taste. But the exterior of the building was as important as the goods hawked inside. Just as he hoped that the tasteful clothes, home goods, and decorations moved people toward a more genteel and moral middle-class life, he believed that his store building had the power to do the same for Philadelphia as a city. Wanamaker worked toward a cohesive approach, much as city beautification programs did in the late nineteenth and early twentieth centuries. The new building would house his entire store in one unified facade. He later reflected: "What profound change it has made in the city, this neighborhood, and the methods of commercial life everywhere."[120]

Department stores had become a symbol and co-creator of the new bourgeois culture in Europe and the middle class in the United States. In the end, Zola's description of department stores and Wanamaker's were not too far from one another. At a gathering of employees, Wanamaker told a story of two bishops—one compared himself to a "little sparrow" feeling insignificant in the space of a cathedral, while the other bishop experienced the cathedral as a place of "vastness and beauty" and consequently was "filled with exaltation." Wanamaker confided to his employees that he shared the feeling of exaltation and saw beauty all around. The store, he explained, was "a great cathedral of magnificent opportunity."[121] He believed that "men are changed by changing their environments" and that "cities are changed by changing their architecture."[122]

3

Christian Cadets

With all my STRENGTH
With all my MIND
With all my HEART
With all my WILL
I SERVE THE PUBLIC at THE WANAMAKER STORES.
—*Wanamaker Rule of Four Pledge*

Pomp marked the dedication of Wanamaker's "new house of business" on December 30, 1911. The elaborate ceremony began shortly after 1:00 p.m. at the Broad Street train station with the arrival of the president of the United States, William Howard Taft. On the station platform, Wanamaker stood with the governor of Pennsylvania and the mayor of Philadelphia to greet the president. The First City Troop, a prestigious unit of Pennsylvania's National Guard consisting of male members of Philadelphia's oldest families, escorted the president's motorcade down the street, dazzling the crowd with their "bright uniforms" accented by "dashing sabers" and colorful helmets against the gray buildings and low-hanging clouds.[1] Arriving at the store's Juniper Street entrance, the City Troop lined up to the right of the store's entrance along a large carpet stretching from the street to the building's threshold.

On the left side of the entrance, another troop and a bugle corps stood at attention in their dress uniforms awaiting the president's arrival. Described by one newspaper as "dapper little fellows," the troop was made up of boys and young men employed at Wanamaker's store, with the exception of his African American workers. They represented the hundreds of youth employed at the business who took part in a military-style store education program; they were the Wanamaker Cadets.

As the president disembarked from his car, the City Troop gave him a saber salute. The Wanamaker Cadets sounded out a bugle greeting and then marched the president and his entourage inside the store, delivering them to the store's regal atrium for the dedication ceremony. The crowd roared when they saw the president enter with the smartly dressed cadets. Later, the full regiment of Philadelphia-based cadets, numbering in the hundreds, joined the bugle corps to present specially designed store flags to commemorate the day.

On display to the crowd of an estimated thirty thousand that afternoon was more than the new store building, leaders of the state of Pennsylvania and Philadelphia, and the president of the United States. To a rapt audience, Wanamaker demonstrated the success of his employee education programs. The store was a place to buy goods and a laboratory for the socialization of his working-class employees—an effort other businessmen like George Pullman and Henry Ford embraced with mixed results. The cadets' lean and physically fit bodies decked out in crisp, impeccably kept uniforms and their sharply choreographed movements were a physical performance of Wanamaker's religious values. The store's education programs were part of a larger Protestant movement that focused on character formation and strong bodies, helping to shape the middle-class, gender, and white identity in a time of uncertainty and change.[2]

"Raw Recruits"

Wanamaker had faced three pressing challenges with the opening of the Grand Depot.[3] His hiring had focused on recruiting white male Protestants with a mercantile background for his men's and boy's store, Oak Hall. His staff needs continued to multiply as he broadened the types of merchandise he offered. By 1880, he employed more than three thousand workers. Wanamaker turned away potential candidates who, he claimed, "would not feel at home in" what he had come to call the ranks of his employees, "the store family."[4] The "essential" qualities he sought in employees were "honesty, loyalty, good taste, enthusiasm, and native intelligence."[5] While he did not state it directly, maintaining race, class, and ethnic homogeneity was a core value for Wanamaker, as it was for many white Protestants in their businesses.[6] He preferred to hire employees with a "long residence in America."[7] In other words, he sought white nonimmigrant Protestants with some retail experience. They were becoming increasingly scarce in a competitive employment marketplace. Initially, Wanamaker took referrals for new hires from employees, contacts at the YMCA, and church members—people he described as "personal friends and faithful people"—but the store's growth swiftly outpaced his social and religious networks.[8]

By the turn of the century, Wanamaker's employee base mushroomed to ten thousand between his two stores, and during the Christmas and Easter seasons it temporarily ballooned by an additional five thousand.[9] The store's meteoric expansion necessitated new methods to find suitable employees. Men and women readily applied for open positions; however, more and more they lacked the basic skills needed for retail. Bemoaning the lack of skilled retail workers, Wanamaker lamented, "The world seems to be filled with men who can do 'most anything.' It often happens that the man who says he can do 'most anything' turns out to be the man who cannot do anything specific."[10] In developing "rationalization of retailing," Wanamaker and other retailers had changed their minds about the nature of sales. It was not an innate talent; instead, it was a skill that could be taught.[11] Nevertheless, it became "increasingly difficult" to find appropriate new recruits who expressed what Wanamaker felt was the right disposition for his stores.[12] He said he wanted employees who valued "the fear of God" and "order."[13] He agonized over the deportment of his clerks and salespeople.

For Wanamaker and many of the Protestant leaders of this period, behavior and appearance expressed moral character. An individual's exterior presentation reflected the state of the individual's moral interior. Increasingly, moral character took on a strong association with emergent middling class manners, dress, and housekeeping. How store employees walked, talked, and interacted with customers attained greater importance. Employees presented the day-to-day face of Wanamaker's store, and their work immersed them in a world solidly planted in white middle- and upper-middle-class aspirations, goods, and customers.[14]

Children played a central support role in large-scale stores like Wanamaker's until after the turn of the century. In the late nineteenth century, child labor laws allowed retail establishments to hire children as young as thirteen years old—and certainly some children and parents lied about age to secure employment at younger ages. Before the advent of pneumatic tube systems and cash registers, young boys called "cash boys" acted as conduits for money, receipts, and goods between the sales floor clerks, a central cash station, and a floor inspector who reviewed sales transactions for accuracy.[15] It was no small task as stores added more and more floor space, making the journey from cash station to sales clerk a long one. While some stores employed cash girls, Wanamaker felt that positions that offered "less freedom" were "safer" for his girls and he placed them in other roles.[16] Children also ferried stock from the back rooms to the sales floor, dusted displays, and ran errands. Children working in retail had little hope for advancement, as they lacked the education and manners to move into skilled sales and management positions. These youths came from working-class or struggling middle-class households, and their wages went to support their families.

Stores expanded their pool of workers when they began to hire women for clerical jobs. With the addition of merchandise for women, children, and the home, stores hired women as sales clerks to put female customers at ease in their shopping experience. A shortage of potential male employees quickened the trend. The majority of women available for these positions hailed from working-class backgrounds, which posed a whole set of problems on the sales floor when working-class norms clashed with emerging middle-class decorum. Everything from speech and grammar to dress and manners merited attention by department stores and correction. Yet managers also discovered that women interacting with women delivered sales.[17]

Rarely did women find working in a department as a path to management in this period, although Wanamaker made a few exceptions when he promoted a handful of women over the years to the position of buyer—an employee who selected merchandise to sell at the store.[18] By the late nineteenth century, Wanamaker had opened a women's hotel to house the growing number of single, working-class women that he had hired.[19] The hotel placed the women in a nearby, supervised location that acted as a de facto training ground on proper behavior, housecleaning, dress, manners, and hygiene.

While many department stores refused to hire African American employees at all, Wanamaker enlisted African Americans for positions as elevator operators, janitors, maids, porters, servers in his restaurants, and other low-skill work at the store. With the exception of the store post office, African Americans were not hired as store clerks.[20] Most American department stores did not employ African Americans as sales clerks for fear of driving white customers away. Store managers rationalized their exclusionary practices by asserting the need to hire clerks who mirrored the clientele they hoped to attract and serve. However, some African Americans did work as sales clerks when the lightness of their skin tone allowed them to "pass" as white.[21] The racial composition of employees and shoppers also signaled the class and stature of the store's customers, even for African Americans. The whiter the employee and customer base of a store, the more elite it was.[22]

When writer, sociologist, and activist W. E. B. Du Bois surveyed black Philadelphians in 1898, he discovered that African Americans who were employed as sales clerks or held other white-collar positions worked for African American businesses.[23] Problematically, black businesses never grew very large, typically employing five to ten people, and the failure rate of the businesses was high.[24] Black-owned businesses struggled to survive without the same resources available to white-owned businesses. This combination of factors diminished blacks' opportunities to learn management and sales skills and to find advanced employment. African Americans who attended business school programs found that education credentials had no effect in bringing down hiring barriers. Wanamaker's and the other Philadelphia Market Street department stores contributed to the situation by banding together in their refusal to hire black employees.[25] In white-run businesses that did hire African Americans, black workers received substantially less pay than white workers in the same positions. Working in a white-run establishment had additional drawbacks. African American workers in department stores were often routinely demeaned and treated harshly by white customers and other employees. Another survey taken in 1912 reaffirmed what Du Bois discovered the decade before: despite the activism of the local NAACP, black newspapers such as the *Philadelphia Tribune*, and the Armstrong Association's employment bureau, Philadelphia department stores still did not hire African Americans for clerk positions.[26]

Wanamaker liked to brag that his black workers came from the "best kind of backgrounds." What constituted the "best kind of background" was never spelled out, although it was likely class-related, since this was an abiding concern for his white workers. When it came to hiring children, women, and black employees, Wanamaker attempted to rely on referrals from current employees or his religious connections, favoring his employees' relatives over strangers.

School Days at Wanamaker's

The search for "appropriate" workers grew more arduous every year. Wanamaker decided to address the problem head-on two years after opening his Grand Depot location by offering classes to the youth who worked in his stores.[27] He would shape the next generation of employees under his store roof and have more control over the outcome. If they left the business for other work, they would spread the gospel of business he instilled in them. Initially the curriculum consisted of mathematics, reading, and writing—courses that benefited retail work. The classes also likely assuaged his discomfort in employing a considerable number of children, a practice that attracted growing criticism. Yet to refuse children employment came with a downside Wanamaker knew intimately. He connected their situation to his own, when at the age of thirteen he was sent out to earn money for his family as an errand boy. Wanamaker said that he understood that a child "who comes into a store" was "forced by the driving necessity to begin the task of earning a livelihood."[28]

Child labor did come at a cost—it was likely that working children would not finish school. His own lack of education was one of Wanamaker's regrets in life. He believed that each youth he employed "must not . . . be permitted to stand dead to development, content to live on the small stock of educational provisions" acquired "before his working days commenced."[29] Educating the store children furnished additional benefits. Providing an education for the children had the potential to shape the employees' families too. He applied techniques similar to those used at the YMCA and the Bethany Sunday school, and in a reverse model of Bushnell's "Christian nurture," he believed children educated by the store would morally influence their mothers, fathers, and siblings.

Wanamaker's fledgling school garnered enough benefit that by 1890 he moved to invest in creating a comprehensive education system for employees. He named the school the John Wanamaker Commercial Institute (JWCI). At first, the school served the store's boys, ages thirteen to sixteen. He created it "as a way to directly shape his employees," especially his "younger employees."[30] Soon, older boys clamored for their opportunity for the store's "free" education, and a "senior branch" of the school, for ages sixteen to eighteen, opened. Next, the store's young women asked to attend classes and take part in cadet exercises, so he created a separate "girl's branch." The girl's branch had easier requirements that Wanamaker felt suited their gender. Older employees had access to a well-stocked library, a regular offering of lectures, self-organized classes, and pamphlets and rules to instruct them on proper behavior.[31]

Education was on the mind of other Philadelphians during this period. Wanamaker's friend Russell Conwell had gone in a similar direction across town at Grace Baptist Church. As a key component of his prosperity gospel message, Conwell told his listeners that education, godly hard work, and community service led to God's blessing of success.[32] When a young printer approached Conwell for assistance in preparing for the ministry in 1884, the minister started teaching lessons in his office. The young man rarely came to his lessons alone, often bringing working-class friends hungry for education. The classes moved to the church's basement, and the numbers swelled to over forty, quickly inundating the resources of the church. To meet the needs, Conwell founded and chartered Temple College in 1888 to educate working men; three years later, he broadened the charter to include working women.

Public and employer education gathered momentum in the late nineteenth century. Certainly, for some companies the development of education programs constituted part of a larger response to labor concerns in the wake of strikes, riots, and violence that peppered the late nineteenth and early twentieth centuries.[33] A series of investigative reports exposed to the public horrific working conditions in factories and department stores that entailed long hours, low pay, and job instability.[34] Novels like Upton Sinclair's *The Jungle* painted a graphic picture of the human toll of factory work and abuse by employers. Fear of a tarnished public image led some businesses to organize "corporate welfare programs."[35] These programs ranged from profit sharing and pension plans to death benefits and corporate housing.

Department stores pioneered many of these approaches to stave off criticism and engender employee loyalty. Wanamaker, for instance, also took an early lead experimenting with employee support programs and initiated a number of benefits, including shorter work hours, early closing times on Saturday, and not opening on Sundays. Although Wanamaker rejected the idea that his programs were for show or welfare, he still advertised the benefits the store extended to its employees in full-page newspaper ads and in frequent cadet public appearances. He ar-

Figure 3.1. Wanamaker store school classroom, ca. 1890s. Wanamaker classrooms, camp programs, and marching bands were segregated by gender. In his new building, he dedicated substantial space for the school and physical fitness program.

gued that he had started the store employee programs because it was his "duty to the rising generations stepping upward through store-service."[36] Wanamaker imagined the school as his "garden" where he "grew" the virtue of his young employees.[37] Here was another way to reach a population that may not find connection in a church or YMCA. The program also benefited the store by molding his future employees from an early age. Wanamaker put it more succinctly when he told the young men of the store what he thought was important in life:

There seem to be just three things for you young men to have in mind. All of life may be grouped under these three heads:

1st: To honor the God who gives us the breath of life.
2nd: To protect and love our mothers. And
3rd: With love of country, to be patriots.[38]

Wanamaker and Race

However, the store school did not meet the educational needs of all employees. The education and support of black staff members were never priorities in the school programs. Of his thousands of employees, Wanamaker hired approximately three hundred African Americans between his Philadelphia and New York stores in the early decades of his business to operate elevators, serve at the dairy, scrub the floors, do the laundry, and work in the casual restaurant and in the more formal Crystal Tea Room.[39] Black employees garnered more attention when workers at the New York store formed their own employee association in 1911; the Philadelphia store organized the following year. They named their club the Robert Curtis Ogden Association (RCOA) to honor Wanamaker's New York business partner, who had a long record of supporting black education in the South.

Ogden had invested financially and personally in the education of southern blacks following the Civil War, inspired in part by his close friendship with Samuel Chapman Armstrong, one of the white leaders in black education. The two men met while still in their twenties in 1859 and forged a lifelong friendship. Armstrong was the son of missionaries and grew up in Hawaii. During the Civil War, Armstrong led a United States Colored Troop, an experience that generated his belief in black education. After the war, he signed up to serve in the Freedman's Bureau, a federal agency charged with assisting formerly enslaved blacks and impoverished whites. In 1868 Armstrong secured financial backing from the American Missionary Association (AMA) to purchase land in Hampton, Virginia, in the same region where he had worked for the bureau to start a school. The AMA had already underwritten a handful of educational efforts in the area, including the small salary paid to an educated and free African American woman, Mary Peake, who taught black Civil War refugees under an old oak tree.[40] With the support of the AMA and other organizations, the Hampton Normal and Agricultural Institute (now Hampton University) opened for teacher training.

Armstrong took the helm of the new school eager to put his educational theories into action. While many of the black schools started just after the war utilized a liberal arts curriculum, many more offered what was deemed to be a practical vocational education that emphasized the supremacy of whites in matters of political and economic leadership and the role of blacks as productive members of the working class.[41] Armstrong subscribed to this belief and developed a curriculum at Hampton where students received training for both teaching and vocational trades—a model similar to the program his father created for native Hawaiians.[42] The Hampton Institute trained African Americans as teachers to serve in black schools and to further black education. Students also learned vocational skills in a variety of practical trades. The vocational emphasis had a dual purpose. It was meant to impart the value and respectability of hard work in the teachers—values they could instruct their own students to accept.[43] It ingrained another lesson in students— that they were to be satisfied with occupations and social standing on the lower rungs of society. Required attendance at worship and strict behavioral expectations sought to make students into good Protestants with strong morals. Ogden joined the board of trustees of the school in 1874, and he took on the leadership of Hampton's board when Armstrong died in 1893. Through Ogden, Wanamaker developed his views on African Americans, which he translated into his employee programs.

Ogden also introduced Wanamaker to Hampton's most famous graduate and Armstrong's protégé, Booker T. Washington.[44] Washington came to Hampton as a young man, working odd jobs to earn his passage to the school. Armstrong was immediately impressed by the young man and decided to mentor Washington. The two men developed a close friendship. After graduation from Hampton, Washington attended seminary and then took a teaching position, first at Hampton and then at a newly opened school in Alabama that would become the Tuskegee Institute.

Washington became a popular black leader in the United States. In private, he supported black advancement and civil rights. In public, especially in front of white audiences, he delivered a message that eased nervous white leaders by advocating the idea that blacks were inferior and had a place in American society comfortably below whites in a supportive role.[45] He leveraged this accommodationist platform to raise funds for black education and causes among Northern white businessmen and industrialists such as Rockefeller, Carnegie, and Wanamaker.[46]

Wanamaker liked Washington and his message. They traveled in overlapping religious and political circles and often shared the same stage at Christian conferences. Wanamaker donated generously to Hampton and

Tuskegee and occasionally hosted Washington and his organizations in the store auditoriums. In 1905 Washington invited Wanamaker to speak at a meeting of the National Negro Business League (NNBL), an organization created by Washington in 1900 to support black businesses. Introduced to the gathering by Washington as a "Christian merchant," Wanamaker pompously told the audience that he came to the meeting "to see what kind of people are becoming business men of the country" and that "America is watching closely to measure your capacity for citizenship and the right to walk along with other men." He wanted to see whether they could measure up to white "American" standards, implying that white American standards defined citizenship. Wanamaker told his audience that he rejected the idea of giving extra support to blacks because they were barred from opportunity. He insisted, "You can't afford any longer to be the ward of the nation." In racism-denying language he would also repeat to his African American employees his "deep conviction that success or failure is not a matter of race, face, or place. It is a matter of grace." He said it was a matter of grace because he believed the prosperity gospel message that those who followed God and worked hard would be rewarded. It was a message that aligned with Washington's teachings. He contended that the struggles of black businesses had nothing to do with systematic racism—whites simply were doing business better than blacks. Wanamaker finished his condescending speech by explaining that "education, truth, and honor" belonged to black men as much as to whites.[47]

Even with his segregationist views, Wanamaker contested American racial norms. For example, Wanamaker's relationship with Washington caused a stir when the two dined together at a resort hotel that same year in Saratoga Springs. Sharing a dinner was only part of the perceived scandal. Newspapers nationwide picked up a rumor that Washington had escorted on his arm one of Wanamaker's daughters to the dinner table at the resort, and the next day dined alone with the young woman at lunch. Critics mostly attacked Washington for his part in the dinner party, questioning his fitness to be a leader of African Americans with what was deemed to be his attempt to act as a social equal with whites. The firestorm concerned Washington enough to hire a bodyguard for his return to Alabama in case of white reprisals.[48]

Ogden and Washington's philosophy on the potential of blacks permeated the views Wanamaker and his managers held about black workers and his ideas around vocational education. African Americans had a place at the Wanamaker store, but at the lowest ranks without hope for promotion. The limited and segregated education programs offered to African American workers included mathematics, public speaking, and separate physical fitness and music programs. Black employees were mentioned briefly, if at all, in store publications and only as an advertisement.

The Rule of Four

The inauguration of the JWCI compelled Wanamaker to formalize his store school practices, curriculum, and pedagogy. Harvey Freed, a principal of the JWCI, expressed the school's purpose: "The moral welfare of the students is of special interest," and that concern shaped the school's entire mission.[49] Employees under the age of eighteen entering the program were called "cadets," and they embarked on a rigorous curriculum of academic classes, moral education, and physical development in addition to their employment at the store. Poor performance in the JWCI could lead to termination, and disappointing work performance affected students' school assessments. Good performance opened access to promotion at the store.

For academic courses, Wanamaker hired a faculty of twenty-four part-time teachers, some of whom worked in the Philadelphia and New York public schools.[50] For boys and girls ages thirteen to fifteen, academic classes occurred two mornings per week before their workday began, with other mornings focused on music, military drills at special store events, and exercise.[51] Older boys took classes at night, in addition to chorus and band practice, with dinner provided by the store. Students received instruction in the basics—penmanship, spelling, writing, and arithmetic—subjects that supported the daily business of the store. Additional classes covered commercial law, geography, and other business school subjects.[52] Girls took courses deemed suitable for their gender and future work prospects, such as stenography, typewriting, and correspondence. Bookkeeping, drawing, French, and German were optional courses, although encouraged for employees who thought they might need those skills for their work at the store.

Wanamaker did not trust the young workers' homes or their churches (if they belonged to one). He felt that what the boys and girls absorbed at the store school could influence their homes; the boys' changed behavior would in turn encourage emulation by other family members.[53] A home visit became a part of the program. Store emissaries accompanied boys and girls to their residences to explain the JWCI's benefits and to assess the child's home situation. It was a clumsy attempt to surveil employees and their home lives. How these visits were received remains a question. In a move certainly reassuring to some parents and alarming to others, the parents were urged to allow their child to work for the firm until the child reached maturity in order to maximize the store's educational investment.[54]

The power of the school extended outside the classroom, making every interaction in the work life of a cadet a part of the educational process. Advancement at the store depended not only on job performance but on accomplishments in the classroom and physical achievements at the gym and, later, at a summer camp. The store school monitored pupils' progress with a report card, watching for proper behavior matched against a set of prescribed behaviors.

The report cards, called "Monthly Records," served to "discipline" the "raw recruit" and, through the child, potentially improve the parents too.[55] Cadets were charged with carrying their report cards on their person at all times, and they received both solicited and unsolicited marks in the classroom and at work.[56] A report card listed basic information about the employee-student—name, age, date of hire, and salary. The "Aisle Manager" graded the employee weekly on categories such as "Obedience," "Truthfulness," "Gen'l Deportment," and "Manners and Neatness," the very same values emphasized in a variety of Protestant organizations.[57]

Listed on the back of the report card was a set of rules, a different set for boys and girls, that outlined desired employee behaviors and appearance. One card listed sixteen rules for boys that admonished them to not run (instead they were told to "walk briskly"), to "be quiet," to be "clean and neat," and "don't slouch." Writing graffiti on store counters and walls,

eating on the sales floor, and sliding down stair railings happened frequently enough to require rules covering these infractions. Absenteeism
turned up as another recurring issue for young employees; they were
instructed to show up "promptly" and were shown how to communicate
necessary absences due to illness. The cards themselves were to be kept
clean and undamaged.[58] Brewer explained without irony that "the early
signs of progress" could be seen with "an increased average whiteness"
of the card.[59] The report cards thus were used to measure the interior
embodiment of moral values by the cadet and the cadet's care of his or
her monthly record card. The store demanded that parents participate
in the assessment process by signing the report cards each month after
reviewing them. Students who consistently received misconduct marks
on their card, called "bluies" by the children, or who demonstrated "a
lack of interest or a lack of improvement" over a six- to eight-week trial
period were let go from the store and school.[60] If a child passed the trial
period, they joined what Wanamaker liked to call his "store family."

The school adopted a four-pronged mission that closely paralleled the
YMCA's first mission to cultivate the mental, social, religious, and physical culture of young men.[61] Wanamaker called his mission the "Rule of
Four" and announced that it targeted for development the four quadrants of an individual—"strength, heart, mind, and will"—with the purpose of creating "fully rounded men and women."[62] Through the Rule,
he strove to reform the interior lives and exterior, physical presentation
of his employees. Wanamaker explained the school's mission as a way
to "enable its students, while earning a livelihood, to obtain, by text-
books, lectures, [and physical] drills" "practical and technical education
in . . . commerce and trade" and to engage in "personal development."
Through proper training, he planned to "equip them to fill honorable
positions in life and increase personal earning power."[63] It was an ambitious and paternalistic enterprise.

In 1896 the YMCA had introduced a triangle logo with "spirit, mind,
body" and described the unity of the three with "each being a necessary and eternal part of man, being neither one alone but all three." The
YMCA's logo was likely an inspiration for Wanamaker's Rule.[64] Wanamaker had already discovered the power of print. An avid advertiser, he
found printed materials useful for religious education. His acquisition

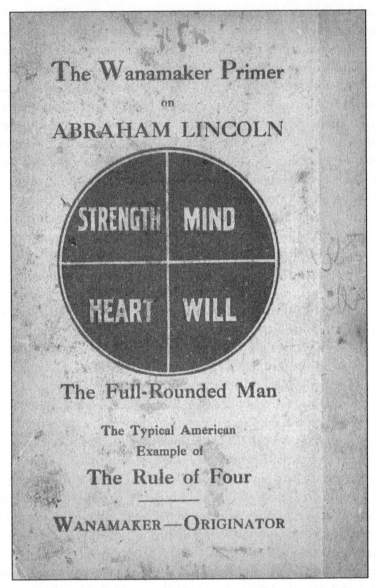

The Wanamaker Primer

on

ABRAHAM LINCOLN

STRENGTH | MIND

HEART | WILL

The Full-Rounded Man

The Typical American
Example of

The Rule of Four

WANAMAKER — ORIGINATOR

Figure 3.2. Back cover of 1919 edition of *The Wanamaker Primer on Abraham Lincoln* with the Rule of Four.

of the *Sunday School Times* in 1871 was the beginning of his publishing endeavors. Understanding the importance of quality curricula for children and young people from his work at Bethany, his press turned out a series of booklets, pamphlets, and small hardback books for use in the store classrooms and for the general public. Wanamaker commissioned publications from like-minded business leaders and reprinted texts that promoted the virtues he valued most. He saw the opportunity both to train his employees in his business methods and also to convert other business leaders to his "Golden Rule" approach. Wanamaker delivered lectures to business gatherings and invited like-minded speakers to give lectures to his employees. Using the publishing arm of his business, he compiled speeches, both his own and those of leaders he invited, into pamphlets that explained best business practices. Among these was a booklet called *Business Thoughts* by W. J. Johnston. Updated several times over the years, it included lectures, speeches, and quotes from businessmen and religious leaders such as the British evangelist Charles Spurgeon and his friend Russell Conwell.

Another Wanamaker friend, Elbert Hubbard, the founder of Roycroft, an Arts and Crafts studio and community near Buffalo, New York, had his story "A Message to Garcia" published by Wanamaker and distributed free to employees and shoppers in 1906. In "A Message to Garcia," Hubbard told the story of a soldier who was ordered to carry a message to Garcia, a rebel leader in Cuba during the Spanish-American War. It was a seemingly impossible task. The soldier did not ask how to find Garcia or where he was located. Instead, he performed his duty, locating Garcia and his troops in a mountainous area. Despite being behind enemy lines, he managed to deliver the message and return with a reply. Hubbard's essay admonished lazy and disobedient workers, lavishing praise instead on those who "carry a message to Garcia"—those workers who accomplish their tasks "without asking any idiotic questions, and with no lurking intention of chucking it into the nearest sewer, or of doing aught else."[65] In other words, workers who were obedient, hardworking, and unquestioningly loyal. It was a message that resonated with many Americans. Hubbard's piece later spawned several motion pictures and hundreds of reprints.

Outlining the themes, the *Lincoln Primer*, published in 1909, was a small hardback book and one of many primers Wanamaker printed to illustrate the Rule of Four. Using as an example the life of Abraham Lincoln from "his humble birth to his tragic death," the book highlighted and defined "strength, heart, mind, and will" through episodes in Lincoln's life. The importance of church was emphasized with a story about young Lincoln attending church, listening deeply to the sermon, and applying it to daily life. At the end of the book, excerpts from Lincoln's inaugural addresses, the Emancipation Proclamation, and letters he wrote during his presidency further exemplified the themes. The back cover depicted the Rule of Four in a circle divided equally into four quadrants to demonstrate the balance and equal attention the four rules demanded.

Another edition of the book modeled each of the four rules through short vignettes of boys and girls near the age of Wanamaker's young employees. The fourth quadrant, which emphasized strength, entailed more than the cadets' mental capabilities. Strong bodies and proper choices in life signaled strength. The stories showed how the Rule of Four affected daily choices and actions. In what would become a common approach in work with young people, the book finished by asking cadets to "make the pledge of four" to seal their commitment to achieving the goals. Reformers formulated pledges and oaths with the belief that making a pledge kept followers in line with espoused values.[66] Over the years, Wanamaker utilized this technique often, composing a series of pledges and oaths to guide the conduct of his cadets and employees both inside and outside the store.

Wanamaker Primers were part biography, part morality tale, and the books gave cadets clear examples of the Rule of Four. For example, a story about a fire in which a boy helped save his family demonstrated the importance of strength and courage. In the same primer, "heart" represented the four virtues, all of which were "links in the chain of success" and were named as "Purity, temperance, honesty, truthfulness." In a self-conscious moment, the text noted that the stories may sound like "a Sunday-school lesson," but, in reality, "it is a BUSINESS LESSON that all successful business men and women must learn."[67] Sunday school virtues and business lessons were the same.

Making Wanamaker Cadets

The military structure Wanamaker embraced was not a surprising choice given that the approach experienced surging popularity in the late nineteenth century. Military motifs infused British and American rhetoric, literature, music, and religion following the Crimean War (1853–1856), a series of bloody insurgencies that erupted in British colonial India in 1857 and 1858, the American Civil War (1861–1865), and during the expansion of the U.S. empire. Christian organizations found military language useful for describing their causes as battles of good against evil, with Jesus depicted as a military figure leading a Christian army.[68] William Booth, founder of the urban-focused Christian Mission in England, took the militaristic title of "General Superintendent" and called his workers the "Hallelujah Army." He renamed his organization the Salvation Army in 1878, the year before the group's arrival in the United States, and adopted military-styled uniforms that same year. Wanamaker became an avid supporter of Booth's Army, giving financial and personal support to the American branch. Dwight L. Moody promoted military imagery when he used it in his sermons on his revival tours in Great Britain and America. Hymn writers composed military-themed songs for worship with tunes suitable for marching, such as Wanamaker's favorite hymn, "Onward Christian Soldiers," a song originally written for English church children.[69] The military fever reached new heights through the buildup to the Spanish-American War (1898) and the well-documented escapades of Theodore Roosevelt's Rough Riders in Cuba.[70]

Many American Protestants found military-themed programs appealing because they felt that the format built character—a nebulous category that was never fully defined and yet emphasized a growing list of desired virtues and behaviors.[71] Soon, military designs served as the guiding principle for a profusion of new organizations from Boys' Brigades and the Boy Scouts of America to summer camps. Even some public schools incorporated military structures.

Choosing a military structure made sense for Wanamaker's educational goals and connected with the sentiments of service and patriotism. Regulations and self-control had long been hallmarks of Wanamaker's Sunday school classroom at Bethany. He believed that the military structure translated the moral values of "discipline, organization, precision and obedience" into a mental and physical regime. A store publication claimed that a military approach shaped a young man into "everything that is manly, loyal and upright; gives him the spirit of order, obedience, self-reliance, ambition and courtesy."[72]

"Discipline" was a particular favorite outcome of military training for Wanamaker. Cadet handbooks spent time explaining the purpose and importance of discipline, describing it as "a habit of obedience, in which the individual subordinates his own will to those of his superiors in rank," while cautioning that this obedience was done "without surrendering self-respect or individual rights." The store handbook proposed that discipline was "indispensable to the existence of a well-trained organization."[73] Its absence meant a lack of order and control and prevented the development of a "system" for work. Cadet training cultivated an "*Esprit de corps*" along with "pride of the organization," feelings the store wanted to encourage.[74] Military training also kept young boys (and girls) out of trouble, since the demands of regular military drills, exercises, and parades left little idle free time.

Organization was a positive by-product of military training. Wanamaker's cadet program corralled hundreds of young employees into a coherent hierarchy of military companies divided by rank, gender, and school grade. Adult employees served as "chiefs" of the cadet companies. Each company, from among their ranks, "elected their own military officers" who oversaw the day-to-day discipline of their charges and gave the employees a sense of empowerment.[75] To complete the entire program at age eighteen meant no less than achieving "manhood" or "womanhood," at least in the eyes of Wanamaker and his managers, and thus being poised for full entrance into the business world.[76] Wanamaker hoped that graduating cadets would stay with his businesses.

The JWCI took military training as seriously as it took academics. Wanamaker hired Colonel William R. Scott and Captain Percival C. Jones to establish the military side of the store's education. He also commissioned a series of manuals, books, and pamphlets to guide the cadets. A "Manual of Commands," issued in April 1916, one year before the U.S. entry into World War I, contained sixty-four pages of commands, songs, map-reading legends, and marching formations "compiled from the United States Drill Regulations" and other military manuals.[77] Cadet parents, as

Figure 3.3. Wanamaker stands with his cadets for a special, unnamed ceremony at one of the art displays.

well as other store employees, received a copy of the manual. The store expected cadets to review not only the store manuals but also the U.S. Army's *New Infantry Drill Regulations* and *Manual of Interior Guard Duty*.[78]

To carry out the military theme, Wanamaker equipped his employee-students with formal military uniforms. Custom uniforms made the cadets stand out as important members of the Wanamaker store. To nineteenth-century eyes, uniforms denoted service, patriotism, and commitment, thus making the uniformed cadets a public relations tool for the store.[79] They connected Wanamaker with the imperialist impulse that took hold of the nation at the turn of the century.[80] The uniforms erased visual class lines signaled by clothing among the cadets and in the process created an entirely new class that was tied neither to their family of origin nor to the larger society. Uniformed cadets took on a new persona; they became symbols of patriotism, orderliness, discipline, and precision—and the Wanamaker store.

The uniforms also served as liturgical garb for the various ceremonies and musical performances led by cadets. Although the cadets were young, their uniforms raised their stature in the world of the store by identifying them with leadership and demonstrating that they were acting in an official store capacity.

The wearing and maintenance of the uniforms was a serious business. Wanamaker provided detailed instructions for the care of cadet uniforms and produced detailed pictures to demonstrate the proper assembling of the uniform and its accoutrements. The uniforms did not take into account that children were wearing them; the children were, for instance, given white gloves with stern instructions that they "be kept spotlessly clean." This likely challenged the young employees and necessitated adding step-by-step instructions on how to clean parts of the uniform. For example, in a 1916 manual, cadets learned how to wash dirty gloves: "Put [the gloves] on your hands and wash with soap, the same as you would wash your hands. Rinse with fresh water and hang-up to dry." To protect the uniforms and equipment when not in use, cadets stored their equipment at Wanamaker's store armory.

Musical training formed another backbone of the cadet education program. From the earliest days at Oak Hall, Wanamaker began the workday with employee sing-alongs. At Bethany, he brought to worship congregational singing and started a church orchestra. For the cadets, Wanamaker encouraged music lessons and singing, which further underwrote the educational goals of precision, discipline, and teamwork. Cadets played bugle calls that signaled the beginning of the work day, when workers needed to take their stations, and when the doors of the store opened to the public. Cadets played taps to indicate the store closing time and played the bugle again to let employees know it was permissible for them to depart. Cadets marched in civic and store parades and played music at recreational venues—their public appearances were an advertisement for the store. As the cadet music program developed, Wanamaker and his managers used the cadets and employee orchestras for store musical programs and events to create structure for the musical and ritual life of the store.

Cadet marching bands were a visual and aural representation of Wanamaker's patriotism, a feeling he hoped to stir in his shoppers. Store youth, men, and women participated in a variety of musical education programs ranging from the standard military fare of drum-and-bugle corps to more formal employee orchestras and numerous glee clubs.

John Philip Sousa, leading the Military Band of the John Wanamaker Commercial Institute, Egyptian Hall.

Figure 3.4. Featured in the *Golden Book of Wanamaker Stores*, one of the JWCI military bands poses with famous bandmaster John Philip Sousa, who worked with the music programs at the store. As he did with many of the musicians featured at the store, Wanamaker helped make Sousa one of the most popular composers and band leaders of the day. Sousa, in turn, like other guest musicians at Wanamaker's, attracted large numbers of people to the store.

The military band consisted of seventy-five pieces, and the orchestra had thirty members.[81] To become a member of the band, cadets applied for the position after a study of basic music theory.[82] Employees took lessons under paid music directors and had access to practice rooms. African American workers also had a music program and performed on a routine basis at both stores. As was often the case in Wanamaker's vision, their musical groups were separate from those of his white employees. In the Philadelphia store, African American workers had a seventy-nine-piece band led by a professional director.[83] The New York African American band won many awards.

Wanamaker believed that his employees benefited from the music they played. In turn, in a belief that the right type of music uplifted customers, cadets gave regular music performances and concerts. Wanamaker felt that music served a higher purpose: to elevate listeners morally and give inspiration.[84] Music was only one element in a comprehensive program.

Wanamaker Bodies

Coupled with the popularity of military themes was a growing perception that middle-class white bodies were losing physical strength. Industrialization and urbanization contributed to an emphasis on skill-based labor, shifting away from the physical, manual labor of an agrarian nation. American Protestants worried over the weakening of white male bodies with the paltry physical demands of white-collar jobs and the ill effects of urbanization.[85] In some cases, Protestants feared that "over-civilization" caused weakness.[86]

American church leaders were concerned about men disappearing from the pews and from church leadership, leading to what some felt was a "feminization" of Protestant churches.[87] They also perceived white masculinity as under siege by an influx of immigrants and African Americans moving north. Aptly called "muscular Christianity," the movement arose to address these concerns. With roots earlier in the century, muscular Christianity found traction in Protestant churches and parachurch organizations from 1880 to 1920, spinning off dozens of clubs, camps, sports, and institutions to build muscles and bodies.[88] It was a reassertion of a romantic view of manhood that harkened back to an imagined past of knights, chivalry, and physically powerful men.[89]

Thomas Wentworth Higginson, writer, minister, soldier, and abolitionist, had captured the emerging disquiet in an article published in the March 1858 issue of the *Atlantic Monthly*, which still reverberated in the late nineteenth century. His lengthy and popular article "Saints and Their Bodies" moved from warnings to practical advice about the proper care of boys' and men's bodies. Starting with two examples, he upbraided sedentary boys, whom he described as "pallid, puny . . . lifeless," while he praised boys who were "ruddy, the brave and the strong." He wondered why the pallid and puny boy was thought to represent a minister in popular culture while the ruddy and strong boy was "assigned to a secular career!"[90] He argued that religion was perceived as weak and effeminate—it was losing its virility—while work and life outside the church reflected strength and vigor. Higginson complained that Protestant men were becoming associated with weakness and softness while Roman Catholic immigrants through hard physical labor were seen as virile and robust. Pushing for a reversal of this trend, he declared, "We distrust the achievements of every saint without a body." Not only was physical weakness unhealthy, but "physical health" was "a necessary condition of all permanent success."[91]

Higginson noted the importance not only of physical activity but also of fresh air. He implored boys and men to "meet Nature on the cricket ground or at the regatta; swim with her, ride with her, run with her"; doing so would allow "your heart of manhood" to be "born again."[92] Strong bodies would represent a strong church and would better spread Christianity at home and abroad. By the end of the nineteenth century, Higginson's advice took hold, mostly "in response to middle-class white men's concerns about teenage boys of their own social class" and prompted a shift among Protestants away from a negative view of sports.[93] Groups such as the YMCA, the Businessmen's Revivals, Sunday schools, and Boys' Brigades, as well as the ministry of Dwight L. Moody and others, took up the mantle of muscular Christianity, generating a variety of approaches for strengthening Protestant men and their bodies.

Through the proper training of his employees' bodies, Wanamaker hoped to translate Protestant values into embodied knowledge.[94] For example, students were instructed that "strength is about health" and the "development of the physical body." In order to properly cultivate health, boys and girls should eat "in moderation," rise "with the sunrise" and sleep "with the sunset," and "breathe fresh air as much as possible."[95] Cadets were taught the four virtues in the classroom and training field.

To further support the health of his workers, Wanamaker opened a medical department in 1906 with physicians, specialists, dentists, nurses, and chiropractors to care for employees' medical needs as well as to regulate and measure their bodies.[96] Good health, he believed, equaled good morals.[97] The medical offerings did more than add a much-needed convenience for employees. On-site medical care also cut down on absenteeism. Claiming an illness no longer served as an excuse to stay home from work. Caring for the health of employees also helped to shape and monitor the wholesome bodies Wanamaker wanted on the sales floor. Employee manuals, such as *Safeguards and Aids to the Health and Well-Being of Employees*, covered everything from diet, sleep, dental care, eating habits, and exercise to bathing frequency and women's menstruation.

Camp Wanamaker

Concerned that his young employees lacked a healthy place for vacation and play, Wanamaker augmented his store school with the purchase of five acres in the town of Island Heights, New Jersey, in 1898 for a summer camp.[98] Such camps first appeared in the United States starting in the 1880s, part of a larger movement that began decades before as a way to fortify urban children with the benefits of fresh air, exercise, and camp discipline. Wanamaker extended the military format of his store school to the campground, placing him squarely within the growing trend among boys' camps developing all over the country, and in particular on the East Coast.[99] He started the camp "to develop in a boy manliness, loyalty, uprightness, obedience, self-reliance and courtesy."[100] Wanamaker's store general manager, Franklin Brewer, spoke of the challenge of consistently facing the "problems of the discipline and development of our young people." He explained that the Commercial Institute summer camp took "raw recruits" whose "characters are forming"; at a young age their "faults" and "defects" were correctable under the charge and expertise of the Wanamaker store programs.[101]

Wanamaker liked the idea that his young workers would have the opportunity to experience the restorative power of the ocean as he did every summer at his summer home some distance away on Cape May, New Jersey. While it was touted as a perk for the employees, it also gave Wanamaker's education programs an advantage. For two weeks, unhindered by family obligations, the children and youth of the store were completely immersed in the store's curriculum. As with many of the employee programs, African Americans were excluded from the camp.

The development of a summer camp reflected yet another growing anxiety of the late nineteenth century: urban dwellers' lack of connection with nature. The location of the camp gave cadets the opportunity to bathe and swim in the ocean and take in the fresh sea breezes. Wanamaker had been on the leading edge of the moral character training movement with his store school, and now he joined the burgeoning crusade to bring boys and girls into the outdoors through a summer camp experience. Wanamaker held the first camp in 1900, and by 1904 he had constructed a central building that hosted a mess hall, classrooms, and shelter for the cadets when rain dampened their outdoor activities.[102] The Wanamaker Camp building became known as the Barracks.[103]

Attending the summer camp at the Barracks was required for boys under age eighteen who were employed at Wanamaker's. While the camp did not solicit a fee from the boys' families, first-year employees attended camp without pay. Those who stayed among the ranks of the cadets received a full two weeks' salary for their camp "vacation" time in Island Heights. Camp became an option for Wanamaker's female cadets three years later, although they enjoyed a less rigorous schedule than the boys and slept in the Barracks rather than in tents, since it was felt that girls could not withstand the elements the way boys did. Girls' families received extra assurances that they were separate from the store's boys, just as they were in the JWCI classrooms. They rode on a special train accompanied by additional store staff.

Every summer, the youths arrived in the once-sleepy Methodist enclave of Island Heights in reserved train cars from Philadelphia and New York City, participated in the annual parade of hundreds of boys and girls in spiffy uniforms marching in step from the train to what locals cheekily named "Camp Wanamaker."

Camping with Wanamaker

The first bugle call sounded at 6:55 a.m., breaking the ocean lullaby. The boys stirred in their cots, two tucked in each tent lined up in a series of "company streets" skirting a parade ground. A cool morning breeze carried the scent of pines and salt, and the promise of abundant sunshine. Staked "in a most healthful place near the ocean and among the pines" on the highlands overlooking New Jersey's Barnegat Bay, campers enjoyed stunning views and fresh air.[104] Many of the youths looked forward to their two-week summer camp—miles away from the grime and noise of the city and their daily lives as clerks, cash boys, and stock boys in Philadelphia and New York City. Reveille followed first call—one of the numerous musical signals meant to transition the boys, ranging in age from thirteen to eighteen, from activity to activity in tight military precision.

Each day began with camp maintenance followed by an afternoon packed with boating, fishing, swimming, military drills, field sports, dress parades, and army calisthenics. Worship was the focus of Sundays, the only day formal camp activities were not scheduled. The stringent regimen for the two-week summer camp included donning stiff uniforms with white trousers and long-sleeved navy blue jackets topped off with white gloves and tidy caps. Regular marching drills sought to develop in the cadets a "muscle memory" for discipline, order, and obedience.

A group of twelve Methodist ministers and businessmen had founded the town of Island Heights twenty years earlier. Shaped by temperance concerns, they wanted the town to be a wholesome Christian resort for Methodist camp meetings. The community took off, necessitating an extension of the nearby railroad to bring summer visitors to the enclave.[105] Long an admirer of the shore's benefits, Wanamaker owned homes on Cape May and nearby Bay Head. The town's dedication to religious purposes likely attracted Wanamaker, since its values aligned with his own. He had founded Cape May's Sea Grove Association in 1872 with a group of Presbyterian businessmen who wanted to establish a Christian summer community by the sea. Because of Island Heights' history, Wanamaker felt that it made a good place to further cultivate the virtues and values he wanted to instill in his young workers. Moreover, Island Heights' proximity to other fashionable shore resorts linked the camp with other middle-class and upper-middle-class enclaves. It also gave Wanamaker another opportunity to advertise the merits of the social experiments he was conducting with his employees.[106]

The Barracks camp experience started long before the cadets arrived at the shore. Employees met at the store armory to don their formal uniforms, gather camp kits that they purchased from the store (at a discount), and, for those in the military band, collect instruments. John Wanamaker frequently addressed the campers before they left, presenting them the store flag to be flown over the encampment. Near the end of the encampment, Wanamaker and lead staff came to inspect the cadets at Island Heights. Fully assembled and properly dressed, the cadets marched out of the store and down the street to the train station in a spectacle of military precision in their "picturesque combination of blue coats, blue hats, white trousers, white gloves and smartly cut leggings."[107] They incarnated Wanamaker's values—discipline, trustworthiness, and obedience.

Arriving at the Barracks, campers erected rows and rows of tents for their stay, creating "streets" in the process that surrounded the central focus of all military-style camps, a parade ground.[108] Over two hundred "waterproof" tents with board floors were arranged into seven company streets, with small tents of seven by seven feet for cadets; officers enjoyed more spacious accommodations of tents nine by nine feet. Despite all the formal rules and the watchfulness of officers and commanders, cadets engaged in after-hours mayhem frequently enough to prompt the installation of electric lights on the campgrounds. Camp officials reported that the electric lights improved discipline "one hundred per cent."[109]

The orderliness of the camp not only represented the military design but also invited the cadets into a utopian world of orderliness far removed from the pandemonium of city living. In many ways, the camp structures resembled those of the Methodist camp meeting in Ocean Grove, New Jersey, a village north of the Barracks. When not bathing or playing on the athletic fields, cadets performed military drills on the parade ground, and the band entertained evening guests in and around Island Heights. Each two-week camp received an official inspection by store managers and by Wanamaker, who arrived with great fanfare. Through their activities and behavior, the boys and girls performed their education for store leaders.

Strict rules were in place from the beginning. Behavioral guidelines and camp regulations demarcated the line between good and bad behavior.[110] Wanamaker hoped that what was taught at the camp would adhere to his "little soldiers." The summer camp promoted "nature," as another way of beckoning campers' potential for moral perfection, if only they would follow the rules. With a firmly regimented day Wanamaker attempted to contain the temptations of boyhood: rowdiness, immorality, and laziness.[111] Adult camp leaders recruited staff commanders and officers from their own ranks to keep the boys in check; they acted as role models, teachers, and guards. Their vigilant attention helped the boys refine their behavior and presentation of self.[112] There were consequences for improper conduct. A trial court convened daily to review the cadet's infractions before several camp officers.

The camp emphasized exercise in addition to discipline. The youths engaged in field sports, baseball games, and "rambling" hikes. The military drills, parades, and marches promoted orderliness, but they also contributed to physical fitness. For the boys and young men, the store charted physical measurements regularly to quantify the youths' progress. Boys were encouraged to monitor their charts for improvements. Advisors tweaked the program to obtain the best results for the young bodies put in their charge. Compulsory swim lessons were provided for those who could not swim to maximize the benefit of bathing time and its exercise merits. Wanamaker firmly believed that the training he offered made "better men physically, better men economically, and better men morally" and that these efforts would improve the "morals, ethics, mental ability and physical strength" of his workers.[113]

The rigor of the camp could be interpreted as stifling, and no doubt was for some of the cadets. Cadet yearbooks tell another side of the story not easily visible in the list of rules, regulations, and inspection parades. The store youths who went camping had fun. In the evenings, campers performed plays and musicals, entertaining one another with stories. Cadets were playful with one another, gave each other nicknames, and engaged in friendly competitions. Yearbooks commemorated each academic year at the store and summer camp season. One Wanamaker Cadet, Lillie Rubin, remembered the camp as "a noble undertaking" for the store, while another cadet, Ida Mellor Brooks, recalled the camp as "a most pleasant place to be," where "we would have watermelon parties on the beach and parade in the marching band." She thought of it as "a pleasant experience" that she "treasured all her life."[114] In an interview later in his life, Donald Gapp, a dress-shirt salesman, spoke of the years he attended the camp, noting that his "memories are very fond of that place" where he spent "the best two summers."[115] Over the years, an active and devoted alumni and alumnae club regularly fed the nostalgic memories of summer camp days through reunion dinners and dances.

At the outbreak of World War I in Europe, Wanamaker's camp shifted from fun and games to focus on military readiness. Although professing a desire for peace, Wanamaker took every opportunity to present the boys (and girls) of the store as "military ready." When the United States finally entered World War I, Wanamaker turned over his campground to the U.S. Army for training troops. Wanamaker encouraged store employees to enlist by paying their salaries while they fought in the war.

As the sections of his new Philadelphia store building went up, moving the project closer to completion, Wanamaker expressed his confidence in the store school and summer camp during a speech at a Founder's Day celebration: "It seems to me that a tremendous responsibility rests upon employers toward their intelligent, painstaking employees, who spend their lives year in and year out under the same roof." Underscoring the seriousness of this responsibility, he explained, "No ship sails without a compass. The Pilot and the Course are guided by it, and its ship moves safely though the passengers are unconscious of the controlling power."[116] The compass was no less than God, and Wanamaker himself. With conviction, he told the crowd that he felt like the new building was a church of sorts, "a great cathedral of magnificent opportunity," and he hoped that his employees would help him to fill it.[117] To meet this goal, he continued to expand his educational efforts.

Wanamaker's provided a comprehensive approach to employees' lives, supporting the development of their "strength, heart, mind, and will." The education, music, and health programs, among other services designed to promote this development, went far to squelch worker unrest and disloyalty, though Wanamaker also forbade the unionization of employees in his stores. He publicized the positive effects of his extensive services, claiming, "These exercises are quickly seen to have marked effect on the bearing and physical development of the young people with Health Lectures by the Store Physician."[118] Marking a new era in his educational organization, Wanamaker enlarged the education program by chartering a school in the spring of 1916 to replace the JWCI. He named the entity the American University of Trade and Applied Commerce. Construction of the new store building in Philadelphia allowed Wanamaker to augment the store school. Reserving valuable sales floor space in the new building for the university, Wanamaker constructed fifteen classrooms, a series of faculty offices, and music practice rooms.

As the centerpiece of the school, Wanamaker fabricated a replica of Princeton University's stately wood-paneled faculty room from Nassau Hall, the school's historic building. Princeton was Thomas and Rodman's alma mater. The replica sent a message to his employees that they were as important to him as his own family, and it visually and materially linked their education to one of the great Ivy League universities. The elegance and formality of the room also continued the nutritive work of discipline, trustworthiness, and moral behavior through aesthetics.

However, not all of the extravagance for the store school was inside the building. Perched on top of the new thirteen-story department store was what Wanamaker termed "a gift to clerks." For his seventy-seventh birthday, he opened a rooftop athletic center boasting an outdoor cinder running track; squash, volleyball, and tennis courts; an indoor exercise space with a full gymnasium; bowling alleys; and shuffleboard tables.[119] Staff trainers led classes and coached the store athletes on proper form. The athletes were also supported by Wanamaker's medical department, which routinely measured the physical progress of his cadets. In addition to building an athletic center as part of his store, Wanamaker also sponsored the creation of a gymnasium at Bethany Church.[120]

To give his store's athletic center a touch of sophistication and an association with leisure, he named it the Meadowbrook Athletic Association, after the name of his son Thomas's country mansion.[121] The New York store employee club was off-site in a nearby building and received the name Millrose, after Rodman's country home. Wanamaker established an intramural league where teams from the two stores competed against each other for trophies and bragging rights. The 1916 edition of a yearly store publication, *A Friendly Guide-Book to the Wanamaker Store*, extolled the merits of the "inner life of [the] store," sharing that "one of the ideals of the Wanamaker business has long been the training of its employees to greater usefulness and self-development."[122] The guide declared that Wanamaker's was more than a department store because its owner was concerned with the "modern, educational, social or industrial conditions" and the formation of his employees' minds, bodies, and spirits.

The Millrose Club initiated an annual indoor track-and-field competition starting in 1908 and held at a New York armory. The last event of the annual competition was a one-and-a-half-mile race; it was reduced to one mile in 1925 and dubbed the "Wanamaker Mile." The event drew larger and larger crowds and forced a move to Madison Square Garden, where the games were held for many years. The Wanamaker family's interest in athletic development extended far beyond their store employees. In this same period, Rodman invested heavily in raising the status of amateur athletics. In 1916 he gathered a group of thirty-five prominent golfers to discuss the professionalization of the sport, resulting in the creation of the Professional Golf Association (PGA). To encourage friendly competition, Rodman donated a silver trophy, the Wanamaker Cup, weighing twenty-seven pounds and standing two feet tall, along with a cash prize, for a yearly golf championship. The Wanamaker Cup is still awarded at the annual PGA Golf Championship.[123]

Store Family

Wanamaker had started addressing his employees as his "store family" at Oak Hall. It was a natural shift in language that captured the long-term relationships he maintained with employees, and it hinted at the relationship he craved. With the growth of the business, Wanamaker redoubled rather than jettisoned "store family" terminology when addressing his mushrooming workforce.[124]

In the hierarchical universe of the business, Wanamaker was the father figure in the store. It was a familiar model to his employees—a mirror of the ideal Victorian family.[125] Other corporations and large businesses in the same period adopted family language to describe business relationships and to encourage loyalty. Wanamaker's regular presence on the sales floor and the longevity of his leadership made the analogy not so far-fetched. A hands-on employer, he walked the sales floors on a routine basis, to observe store displays, customer behavior, and interactions between employees and customers. He carried a little notebook where he recorded notes for improvement. During the week, he watched sales numbers and made suggestions on discounting stock to make room for new merchandise.

Wanamaker positioned himself as a father who watched over his children. He frequently wrote personal notes and letters to his employees encouraging them with bits of religious wisdom.[126] The store school and cadet program reinforced Wanamaker's role as head of the family and what he called, at the end of his life, his "store army." He inspected his troops several times a year and watched their scholastic and physical progress through his store programs. The continuity of his leadership added to his stature. He stayed at the helm of his business for sixty-one years, until his death. Wanamaker's birthday and the anniversary of the store were celebrated every year, even after he died.

Evidence shows that Wanamaker held a great affection for his employees, and many employees shared this affection.[127] He gave pensions to long-term employees and offered other benefits—although a partial profit-sharing plan was short-lived. Over the years, he introduced a number of employee-friendly measures. Wanamaker shortened store hours on Saturdays and in the slow summer season; keeping to his Sabbatarian commitments, he never opened on Sundays; and established employees enjoyed a two-week vacation. An employee dining room and reading rooms gave workers access to healthy food and a place to rest.

Wanamaker liked to gather his employees for special events and commemorations, where he would deliver speeches on the successes of the store and the importance of the employees to those successes. He sponsored numerous employee clubs and societies and attended picnics and dances. Every year he hosted employees at his country home. By 1911, over four hundred employees had worked for him for more than twenty years. A large number of the employees stayed their entire careers with his massive enterprise.[128] He rewarded long-term employees' work anniversaries with watches and souvenirs.

Wanamaker's consistent use of "store family" language denoted a perceived deficiency in the lives of his employees, and perhaps his own. Bringing his employees from working-class backgrounds into his "store family" signaled to them that he expected a lot from them, as much as their own parents had. His standards were high, and they necessarily supported his business success and moral behavior. He wanted employees who were truthful, abhorred deceit, and shared "his contempt of the sloven and slacker."[129] He wanted them to be moral and to be like him, or at least how he perceived himself to be. In making the employees his family, Wanamaker indicated a lack in his own life. His son Rodman moved to Paris as an adult, to return only when his older brother Thomas died unexpectedly. Wanamaker's wife, Mary, spent months at a time in Europe either chaperoning one of their daughters at society events or taking spa treatments for her health. His workaholism kept him at his stores or at Bethany—away from his family—for most of his waking hours.

But not everyone was content with their placement in the "store family." In 1906 Wanamaker attended a service at a local African American church where some of his black employees attended. After the service, the pastor invited Wanamaker to the front of the church to hold a public conversation about black employee concerns. The pastor conveyed that many black employees believed they had lost jobs and promotions at the store because of the color of their skin. Wanamaker rejected the claims, confidently telling the gathering that "some of you would say that the color of your face had lost you the position" but "you would be wrong." He explained, "There is no question here of race, of face, or of place, but purely a question of grace, that is to say of aptitude and capacity." He claimed that black employees "will always be welcome to a position but to have it is not all; you must fill it. If, upon trial, we see that you have asked for a place in which you cannot successfully hold your own, we are obliged to discharge you, just as we should do in the case of a white man." It was the same argument he had made at the African American business gathering. Wanamaker did not explain that he believed African Americans were not the same level as his white employees. He continued, "Believe me, we are your friends, and if an injustice should be done one of you, we should not stand behind any one answerable to us or within the limits of our influence, who had dared be wanting in respect or fairness towards one of your number."[130]

Despite Wanamaker's impassioned speech, he was wrong. African Americans were viewed as inferior by Wanamaker and his managers and systematically kept out of sales clerk positions. The attitude lingered at the store long after Wanamaker's death. In the March 22, 1947, issue of the *Chicago Defender*, a story ran about a Wanamaker employee, J. Harry Scroggins, who had worked at Wanamaker's for fifty-six years and retired at age seventy-five.[131] At the age of twenty, Scroggins was hired at Wanamaker's in Philadelphia as an elevator operator. Outside the store he had been active in local affairs, serving in the Pennsylvania National Guard and as a YMCA secretary. For fifty-six years, he faithfully worked at the store and was never promoted. The *Defender* quoted another newspaper story about Scroggins, indicating that for African Americans, "once an [elevator] operator, always an operator." This was the reality of Wanamaker's and the other department stores that hired blacks in Philadelphia and New York. There was no chance for promotion.

Despite Wanamaker's declarations of fairness, his department store did not hire blacks as salespersons, managers, or other administrative positions until the 1950s, when they did so in response to the Committee on Racial Equality's (CORE) activism and a Philadelphia city council ordinance that addressed integration in Philadelphia department store sales forces. The store met the push to integrate sales positions with intense resistance, claiming that hiring African Americans would scare away customers—they meant *white* customers.[132]

Not invited to attend the employee school, summer camp, or athletic competitions, black workers were provided with a watered-down and separate education program. Nonetheless, here, too, Wanamaker's concern for employees' moral interiority and physical bearing surfaced in the courses available to African American employees: "reading, . . . music, athletics, thrift, and the up building of character."[133] African American employees held regular store-sponsored social events that were well attended. Black newspapers spoke favorably of working and shopping at Wanamaker's for the most part, especially in comparison to other stores that would not hire black employees, let alone serve black customers.[134]

Though Wanamaker's may have been an easier environment to navigate than other stores in Philadelphia, it was not a progressive haven for Philadelphia's African Americans. Wanamaker did not see his black workers as equal to his white workers. As a result, he focused the majority of his educational and morality efforts on the white workers, children, and youth. African American workers would see their humanity presented in patronizing and demeaning ways by the in-store minstrel groups.

Wanamaker supported minstrel troupes at his stores. The groups consisted of white employees who rubbed burnt cork over their faces and hands and performed skits and musical numbers in "blackface."[135] The cadet yearbooks reproduced photographs of the store minstrel groups, complete with blackface makeup. Outside work, white clerks also frequented nearby minstrel shows located a couple of blocks from the store. Even Wanamaker's store restaurant made appearances as the "set" for a popular skit performed by the group.[136] These performances were one of the many ways employees were encouraged by one another and by store management to assert whiteness as a shared identity to the exclusion of African American employees.[137] In major store publications, black employees were never included in photographs.

* * *

In the last year of his life, Wanamaker gathered his boy cadets about him after a return from a long trip. He solemnly told them, "The best people that we have in the store, in all its history, are the boys that have grown up in it." And then, in a fatherly tone, he instructed them, "If you go to church, go to learn more. If you go to Sunday School, study your Bibles, and believe that God, who keeps the sun rolling and the moon shining, must care a great deal more for a boy that he has made a man in his own image. The Heavenly Father loves all that He made and keeps His eye on us."[138] While maintaining that his employees were free to follow their own religious creed, Wanamaker dispensed his religious views in theological language and through moral enculturation that evoked his middle-class Protestant values. Those values were themselves grounded in what it meant to be white in a rapidly changing culture shaped by an influx of immigrants and the early stirrings of the Great Migration of African Americans to Northern cities. Wanamaker believed that the moral ambiance of his store radiated from its architecture, the education of the store guest, and, in particular, his business system, all of which were rooted in his own personal character as a widely known "Christian man." The store employee was a key purveyor and exemplar of this morality. Wanamaker wanted to foster in his employees' exterior and interior lives the very moral ambiance he was trying to bring to Philadelphia. They were his liturgists and models of Christian taste.

His impulse to offer education to his employees was a mix of his religious mission and business practicality. Wanamaker mobilized his business resources to reach an audience otherwise not touched by other entities, and this mobilization also assured that his hiring pipeline kept a steady supply of suitable workers flowing. Wanamaker Cadets served as ritualists for the store and walking advertisements for the Wanamaker brand and Wanamaker values. By starting a school within his store, he trained hundreds of young men and women in his principles—and created an army ready to evangelize for his way of doing business.

4

Sermons on Canvas

Art goes hand in hand with commerce.
—John Wanamaker

On a bitterly cold night in 1907, flames curled outside the windows of Lindenhurst, John Wanamaker's country home near Jenkintown, Pennsylvania.[1] A watchman discovered the fire and acted quickly, warning the slumbering servants inside. At a Walnut Street townhome in Philadelphia, the phone rang, and Wanamaker received the terrible news: Lindenhurst, the home of his massive art collection, was on fire. Only six years earlier, the country home and art collection of his eldest son, Thomas, burned to the ground after an alleged lightning strike.[2] Soon, firefighters, a class of men Wanamaker had worked hard to reform from their nefarious ways during the Businessmen's Revival, arrived on the scene only to be thwarted by the frigid temperatures—all nearby water sources were frozen, including the lake Wanamaker had created to help if a fire should ever break out.[3]

The house contained over eight hundred treasures: art, books, antique furniture, pianos, a pipe organ, glass, rugs, tapestries, and statuary from around the world. Wanamaker "directed by phone the work of the rescue," giving instructions on what art pieces to save first.[4] Fortunately, many of the paintings and statuary resided in an adjacent gallery wing, one of two additions built to house Wanamaker's growing appetite for art. The gallery's location allowed firefighters, servants, and neighbors to save hundreds of paintings before the aggressive flames reached them.[5] Larger paintings, too heavy to carry, were brusquely cut from their frames, rolled, and pulled out of the building. But not all the art could be saved. Smaller and lighter pieces of art exited first, and, in the rush to save as much as possible, rescuers unceremoniously dropped Wanamaker's valuables onto the snowy lawn. The art "lay in heaps, and crowds of persons . . . tramped among them unhindered."[6]

The fire drew spectators from a wide area to watch the "remarkable" sight of the great house with its turrets and porches in flames.[7] "A score of persons seated themselves in beautifully carved and upholstered chairs and divans saved from the house and comfortably watched the splendid spectacle."[8] The chill of the night did not interfere with their voyeurism. "They were so near to the fire where they sat that the flames kept them warm."[9] As the night wore on, the scene grew more bizarre; the *New York Times* reported, "A piano lay on the ground in the rear of the art gallery, and some boys drew discordant sounds from it by striking the keys with their feet. A superb bronze figure 'Le Bucheron,' ('The Wood Chopper,' by Chambard) lay prone on its back in the snow near heaps of books, rugs, cut glass, pictures."[10]

Significant pieces disappeared that night—but not in the flames. Some witnesses helped themselves to the art. "Many persons openly carried off books, cut glass, and various other objects" to decorate their homes or to sell.[11] In different circumstances—had the spectators paid for the art treasures or viewed the pieces in his department store art galleries— the dissemination of the items would have pleased Wanamaker. But the onlookers—especially the ones who carried off his treasures—were not the kind who likely shopped at Wanamaker's emporium or spent time browsing his art displays. They probably missed the significance of the pieces carefully collected by Wanamaker not only for his pleasure but for the education of his store guests.

When hearing the extent of the losses that February night, the sixty-nine-year-old Wanamaker lamented to the *New York Times*, "It is a terrible thing to think a collection of a lifetime swept away."[12] Later, he wrote privately in his diary, "It will be a blessed thing for us if all our fires are in this world and not in the next."[13] He reminded himself that the material was transitory, and yet he regularly relied on its power for his religious work. The surviving artwork would eventually be displayed again in the private sanctuary of a rebuilt Lindenhurst and again for the public in his department store art galleries that were under construction.

Wanamaker had enthusiastically embraced a notion growing in esteem among Protestants that proposed a connection between the visual and the moral. He believed that art was a tool to shape the morality and taste of his customers.[14] He asserted that "art in its highest sense is the expression of ideal beauty."[15] Wanamaker believed, as English art critic and tastemaker John Ruskin did, that art and beauty stirred religious faith, and he quoted Ruskin often in store publications.[16] For Wanamaker, promoting aesthetic beauty and art served a religious purpose as a moral influence that had the power to change people. To collect art, and then share it, was another motor in his moral evangelizing machine.

The Art of Taste

The Wanamakers—John and his two sons Thomas and Rodman—obsessively collected art, although the father's motives were sometimes different from those of his sons. John's sensibilities were influenced by an emerging Protestant aesthetic, one rooted in architecture and fine art and one that, he believed, held didactic potency. He bought the paintings not only for his pleasure but for pedagogical purposes. As a collector, he enjoyed a variety of forms of art, and, by curating it, he hoped to engage people in a discourse of good taste that was, in his mind, cultivated and that reinforced moral living. Although he thought of taste, beauty, and morality as universal qualities and standards, they were socially constructed categories rooted firmly in white, emerging middle-class Protestantism and shaped by people like him.

John Wanamaker's foray into serious art collecting launched the same year he opened his Grand Depot. He had traveled to Paris that year to glean merchandising ideas from the French department stores like Le Bon Marché. During his research trip Wanamaker attended his first art Salon in a city and a country that he grew to love.

During the nineteenth century, Paris lured Americans with its wide boulevards, beautiful buildings, and an electric art scene. In its recovery from the Franco-Prussian War and the devastation of the Paris Commune, France's capital reasserted itself as an authority on good taste in fashion, art, and culture.[17] Visitors thronged the Louvre and other museum spaces scattered across the city and visited the many expositions and commercial art galleries. American artists flocked to Paris, entering its art academies, opening studios, and exhibiting their work to an extent that many Americans considered Paris the capital of American art.[18] Wanamaker and his sons joined other wealthy Americans who attended the Salons and purchased mass quantities of art for their collections. Not only did art collecting raise the Wanamakers' status among their peers, but it also helped to establish them as American art connoisseurs in a league with even more affluent Americans: John D. Rockefeller, Henry Clay Frick, and J. P. Morgan.

Although the Wanamakers viewed art in a variety of venues, John Wanamaker's favorite was the official Paris Salon sponsored by the French government and later one of its prestigious art academies. A juried event, the Salon supported international "academic" artists who had gained admission into the selective constellation of *academie* artists by offering them an opportunity to exhibit their work where thousands of visitors would experience it. The Salon galleries hosted art of a wide variety of subjects, which were displayed from floor to ceiling and side by side. Artists jockeyed for jury medals and prominent display locations.[19] Illustrated catalogs further disseminated the artwork by offering facsimiles of featured pieces.

Wanamaker started purchasing paintings from the Paris Salon and other exhibitions in 1893. The official Salon served as the primary source for his contemporary painting purchases. Over the years, he expanded his consumption of art and fashion to London. Except for the years of the Great War, his trips to Paris and various Salons became an annual affair where he would spend hours studying the art, speaking with the artists, and deciding on his purchases.

Occasionally, the Wanamakers served as patrons to Salon artists like Mihály Munkácsy, Frederick Carl Frieseke, and Henry Ossawa Tanner. Support came in the form of purchasing artwork, commissioning special pieces, and paying expenses.[20] Paintings and sculptures by the Old Masters also appealed to Wanamaker, but most were not available for purchase. Pieces that were available were gobbled up by an increasingly competitive group of American millionaires. To feed his longing for classic art canonized by European museums, he commissioned copies and reproductions—sometimes of entire collections.[21] If a statue in the Louvre appealed to him, Wanamaker, like other wealthy American art patrons, had it copied, sometimes in plaster, sometimes in bronze, and added to his collection.[22] Copies gave Wanamaker and other American collectors access to "the aura associated with original works of art."[23] He was particularly attracted to Old Masters' depictions of Bible stories. When the opportunity arose, he purchased what he believed to be original classic paintings, only for his heirs to discover after his death that many of these paintings were forgeries or misattributed to the wrong artist.[24]

* * *

France, especially Paris, had seduced the Wanamakers in the 1870s. Family members made frequent trips for personal pleasure and store business. *Les grands magasins* of Paris had served as one of the muses for the Wanamaker store. In general, Americans had fallen under France and Europe's spell of art, architecture, and fashion. For John Wanamaker, France possessed "artistic inspiration that belongs to no other nation." Starting at the Grand Depot and expanding over the years, Wanamaker curated French goods and art as the major source for the refinement and good taste that he sold at his stores and that decorated his homes.[25]

Rodman Wanamaker shared his father's passion for France. Without the duty to take over the business as the second son, he moved to France in 1889 with his new wife of French descent, Fernanda, and spent the next decade living in the capital running the Wanamaker Paris office and living a European aristocratic lifestyle. Rodman and his wife participated in the dinner parties, art scene, and social whirlwind of the American colony in Paris. They summered in Biarritz, mingled with aristocracy, and at some point, befriended Great Britain's Prince of Wales.[26] As the head of the Wanamaker Paris office, Rodman sought out merchandise, furniture, antiques, and art to funnel back to the family stores. His activity did not go unnoticed. The French government honored him with the Legion of Honor medal for his support of French trade with the United States, his commitment to French art, and his role as the president of the American Art Association in France. Later, France would recognize the senior Wanamaker by making him an officer in the Legion of Honor in 1911 to honor his hefty investment in French art and the aid he sent after the Great 1910 Flood, when the Seine River inundated much of Paris.[27]

The Wanamakers had an insatiable appetite for art. Every year, they sent to the United States crates packed full of hundreds of paintings, art objects, sculptures, and originals and copies of masterpieces to join their personal collections, to go on display at the store art galleries, or to be sold at the store. In 1902 alone, Wanamaker purchased the entire collection of well-known Czech artist Václav Brožík's 300 paintings in

Paris and an additional 118 watercolor paintings on a trip to London.[28] Evidently, he was troubled by the opulent nature of his purchases, describing the acquisitions as an occasion when he "fell from grace."[29] His 1903 trip turned out to be only slightly more moderate: he returned from Paris with 250 paintings. Sheepishly, in a diary entry, Wanamaker worried that the Salon invoices would arrive in Philadelphia before he could personally explain the purchases to his sons.[30] In addition to their own shopping sprees, the Wanamakers hired art agents to search for and obtain paintings, rare books, and sculptures for their collections.[31]

To house the regular inflow of new art, the Wanamakers built massive art galleries at their country and city homes and created viewing galleries in their Philadelphia and New York City department stores. Paintings and sculptures also appeared in window displays, store model homes, and special fashion and history exhibits. John Wanamaker's church, Bethany, hosted his art on its walls for what he felt would be the betterment of church members. When Wanamaker joined the Masons late in life, he stocked the Philadelphia Masonic Lodge with artwork and rare books. These multiple exhibit spaces not only enabled Wanamaker to collect more art but also allowed him to deploy art as a "civilizing force" for moral character formation in multiple locations.

Moral Art

The idea of artwork as a moral instructor was a rather astonishing development in the nineteenth century. At the beginning of the century, Protestantism was often at odds with art. A change took place in the early decades of the century when Protestants discovered that pictures were powerful helpmates in missionary efforts and in religious education, so they adopted images as a standard pedagogical tool.[32] Historian David Morgan has traced how, from the 1820s through the 1890s, the use of images rapidly expanded, in part because of advances in technology that made the reproduction of quality images affordable.[33] Wood-engraved illustrations first appeared in Bible tracts, almanacs, and school primers, followed by picture cards and books. Not only did church leaders quickly adopt images in their religious work, but they also sought cheaper and more efficient reproduction methods.[34] The adoption of religious fine art reproductions in Protestant circles took longer.

Fine art was initially seen as a corrupting influence, with seductive qualities much like theater, sporting events, gambling, and other forms of entertainment. Religious art repulsed some Protestants with its depiction of Catholic iconography and practices. Gazing at a painting of Jesus was thought of as dangerous ground—it smacked of Catholicism. They feared that viewing Catholic art would cause them, inadvertently, to commit "idolatry," one of the popular charges against Catholics.[35] Anti-Catholic and nativist movements further sowed negative views.

Art began to gain reverence in Protestant circles in the 1840s when American clergy and their wealthy parishioners, especially Presbyterians, Congregationalists, and Unitarians, flowed into Europe in larger numbers and experienced its famed museums, great cathedrals and their catacombs, roadside shrines, and ancient abbeys to take in the sumptuous Catholic images and spaces.[36] Many of the churches and buildings were ruins, crumbling from the ravages of time and war. This gave the old buildings an alluring quality that drew American visitors, prompting European cities and towns to preserve and restore the edifices for the booming tourist trade.[37] American Protestant tourists wrote about their experiences and produced a large corpus of travel journals that often relied on religious language to describe encounters with Catholic art and edifices, demonstrating a simultaneous romantic magnetism and fearful repulsion. To commemorate their tours, they brought home with them reproductions and engravings of art pieces.[38]

A curious tension appeared as Catholic immigrants poured into the country and Protestants vilified Catholic practices while at the same time being drawn to historic Catholic art and architecture.[39] Many saw within medieval Christianity's art and architecture a unity, simplicity, and cultural authority that they perceived to be slipping away.[40] Helping to usher in this transformation were the writings of English art and culture critic John Ruskin; his American disciples James Jackson Jarves and Charles Eliot Norton; Elbert Hubbard, the founder of the Roycroft Arts and Crafts enclave in New York; and Congregationalist minister Horace Bushnell.[41]

Ruskin's first book, *Modern Painters*, which deeply influenced British and American thinkers, reached American audiences in the summer of 1847 and was widely circulated by the 1850s. His book taught American Protestants to see art not as an enemy but as an ally by "shifting the criteria of artistic judgment from the sensuous, which was suspect and unfamiliar in America, to the moral."[42] Art was not a dangerous foreign "other"; rather, it was deeply rooted in religion, morality, and nature. His work, extended by Jarves and Norton, helped drain European religious art of its negative Catholic associations by aligning Catholic art with Protestant moral values and a romantic, premodern, and simpler form of Christianity. Contemporary Catholics crowding into American cities were not associated with this form of Christianity by Protestants; rather, they were a people who had lost touch with their "purer" medieval past.[43]

Ruskin and other cultural critics made it possible for Protestants to find meaning in Catholic church interiors, crucifixes, and Madonnas without fear of contamination because they signified something else.[44] "Beauty" usurped cleanliness as an ideal; although the two would remain intertwined, beauty had the power to evoke morality.[45] For others, the opportunity to immerse themselves in beauty helped salve nerves rattled by the pressures of the industrialized world. Protestant collectors by this time had moved past their earlier rejections of Catholic art, and many, especially the wealthier collectors, now sought Catholic pieces for their collections.[46] Images of Madonna and Child were particularly attractive.[47] Leading art critics and magazines of the period fueled the desire by associating the experience of aesthetic beauty with the cultivation of morality. Beauty transformed into a socializing and sanctifying force.

Horace Bushnell's book *Christian Nurture* arrived the same year as Ruskin's *Modern Painters*. A favorite among Protestants, the book was revised by Bushnell in 1861 for a new generation of readers. Character formation had slowly developed into a focus of religious educators as views of children and domestic life changed.[48] Bushnell, among a growing body of Protestant leaders, instructed that the formation of character occurred both through explicit teaching and through a subtler, unconscious form of nurture. This marked a move away from a focus on sudden conversion experiences to a more organic, slower process that happened over time in the family home and at church. This shift aligned with a developing class consciousness and the belief that the people one associated with, how one dressed, and how one looked had the power to shape one's character.

For followers of Bushnell, the goal of religious education changed from saving souls from damnation to fostering the "self realization" of human society.[49] Henry Frederick Cope served as a spokesperson for this new trajectory in education: "Hence the aim of every religious institution should be the development of character to fullness and efficiency under the best social conditions."[50] Thus for Cope and others, human society would improve through education. This idea was taken further by art lover and writer Augustine Duganne. He promoted art as a force for "moral refinement" and urged readers of his 1853 pamphlet *Art's True Mission in America* to see art as a way to lift up American society by experiencing beauty.[51] Art had a moralizing power, whether it was a landscape or a religious painting.

The practice of collecting and displaying art among private collectors, which had developed before the Civil War, became a marker of good taste by the end of the war.[52] Art and artists were seen as respectable and as tools for reform.[53] Inspired by Ruskian ideas on art and later his ideas on architecture, and shaped by Bushnell's call for nurture, clergy and tastemakers began promoting art as a complementary path to moral improvement.[54] With advances in technology and a new perspective on religious fine art, reproductions of paintings provided a focus for devotion and religious education in late nineteenth-century Protestantism.[55]

Rising naturally out of his work with the YMCA and Sunday school, Wanamaker's Ruskian turn to "Christian nurture" in his department store was not a big leap. Wanamaker looked for aesthetic models that drew out religious and moral sentiments from viewers. He too believed in the moral influence of art and pictures. It is likely that he first encountered didactic images in the Landreth Sunday school he attended as a boy. Later, as the founder of a mission Sunday school, he found images a useful tool for leading his growing school. An early adopter of didactic imagery, he regularly used illustrations at his Sunday school, such as the printed "blackboard illustration" method in which an image and words embellished the Sunday lesson by providing a visual element.[56] He had purchased the *Sunday School Times*, to make illustrated content more readily available for Bethany and other congregations.[57] Following Bushnell's emphasis on character formation and developments in religious education, Wanamaker actively participated in the groups made up of leading religious educators.

The *Golden Book* reflected Wanamaker's philosophy of art and subtly raised the tension between beauty and fashion. It declared, "The truth is, that the quality of art comes out in everything we do. Whatever is well done, with sincerity and love of the work and of feeling for beauty, is art." Beauty needed sincerity and intentionality. "Whatever is badly done, with pretense and half-heartedness and clumsiness, is far from being art. It is not only the person whose soul sings through his lips, or who puts his thoughts on canvas with a brush, who is an artist. The vehicle of expression does not matter. It is the spirit that counts."[58] It was a sentiment Wanamaker applied to his store's educational efforts, from his historical displays to thoughtful home décor; for him, the "right" material was indeed an expression of the spirit. He believed that "art in its highest sense is the expression of ideal beauty."[59] He agreed with other followers of Ruskin that beauty possessed the power to stir religious faith: "The greatest art originated in and reinforced religious faith."[60]

Just as illustrations in Sunday school lessons instilled religious teaching, Wanamaker believed that fine paintings, sculptures, and artifacts held power in their beauty, simplicity, and message. But Wanamaker held a more liberal interpretation of what constituted religious art. Carefully curated pieces that illustrated landscapes, village scenes, or a young girl sitting under a tree all displayed the values Wanamaker hoped to foster in his store guests. He argued for the importance of a painting to "preach a sermon." Nonetheless, his measure of a painting remained whether he liked it.[61] He preferred art that he deemed beautiful and that he thought could teach a lesson.[62] Sometimes the message was overtly religious—images of the Virgin Mary and baby Jesus or of Christ's crucifixion. Seeing no problem or conflict with this criterion, he held himself up as the arbiter of the taste he hoped to cultivate. All the same, Wanamaker straddled two worlds in his art collection. A leader in a growing trend in Protestant aestheticism, he embraced aesthetic beauty in his public religious expressions at his store and at Bethany.

The Conquerors

One of Wanamaker's early significant purchases from the Paris Salon was the controversial painting *Les conquérants* by Pierre Fritel. He first saw the painting on his visit to the Salon in 1892. It was exhibited prominently where another grand-scale award-winning painting, Georges Antoine Rochegrosse's *Le mort de Babylone* (The fall of Babylon), had hung the year before, adding to its prestige.[63]

Les conquérants startled Salon goers. A monumentally sized canvas of sixteen by twenty feet, Fritel's painting depicted a tightly clustered group of horsemen—two of them riding chariots—galloping down a wide, endless valley lined with scores of naked, white, presumably dead bodies, some of them children, in a devastating uniformity. The figures riding the horses were some of the most well-known conquerors from history. The central figure was a toga-draped Julius Caesar, with Rameses II and Alexander the Great alongside him in their chariots. Riding next to them, but slightly behind, were Attila the Hun, Charlemagne, Genghis Khan, Tamerlane, and Napoleon in his famous bicorn hat. They were the historic conquerors of Europe, Africa, and Asia. Marching on their heels, an immense army carried the conquerors' standards and sharp spears with red shafts reminding viewers of their killing power. A large crimson cloth standard fluttered in a breeze at the center of the painting, high above the conquerors' heads. The faces of the accompanying army were obscured by murky shadows of dust and darkness, while an ethereal and mysterious light illuminated the bodies along the road.

The art magazine the *Collector* described the astonishing nature of the painting as "something more than forcible—it is horrible." And yet, despite its horrific topic, the author argued that it somehow "exerts an indescribable spell over the morbid or cynical side of our nature." Viewers were mesmerized by the painting, which was simultaneously repellent and magnetic. The magazine proclaimed that it was "neither conventional nor commonplace" and surmised that it "will be awarded a medal."[64] It was.

Wanamaker purchased *Les conquérants* a few years later, in 1899, at the recommendation of the Hungarian artist Mihály Munkácsy, an artist who created two of the most beloved paintings in Wanamaker's collection.[65] *Les conquérants,* now called *The Conquerors* for an American audience, appeared to be a curious purchase for a man whose passion for the military went as far as dressing his youngest employees in military uniform and calling them "cadets." He did not see a conflict.

When Wanamaker began featuring *The Conquerors* at his department store, viewers of the painting had assistance with interpretation, as they did with many of the store's art and holiday displays through the years. Booklets, formal presentations, and speeches attempted to guide shoppers' experiences of the disturbing painting. In 1905 the store newspaper, the *Wanamaker Herald*, included a special booklet grandly titled *A Message to Mankind*. The booklet argued that the importance of the painting rested not in in its horrific display of the conquerors marching through the bodies. Rather, the painting's most distinguishing characteristic was its "meaning and message." It claimed that the painting "images an idea" and that it was "an embodiment of history—the splendors of human ambition, and side-by-side with these their appalling cost in human blood."[66] Not shying away from religious overtones, the *Herald* explained, "It is the most powerful sermon ever preached on canvas against the lust of conquest . . . and the sermon is as pointed in the new century as in the old."[67] Human ambition was splendid and dangerous at the same time. The painting served as a warning to viewers about greed.

Sharing a similar point of view on the value of work and the dangers of ambition, Elbert Hubbard delivered a speech on *The Conquerors* at the store. He shared with the audience the first time he saw the painting at the top of one of the great staircases at Wanamaker's in Philadelphia. Describing each of the emperors and their achievements, his speech turned somber and he asked the audience the question, "What have they conquered?" Then he explained, "The irony of it, men, male men have endeavored to conquer the world since the days of old, but every man who endeavored to conquer is riding to his own funeral." Addressing the ills of individual ambition, Hubbard told those gathered, "The world will not be conquered by man or woman; it will be conquered by the Blessed Trinity of Man, Woman, and Child." The painting, for Hubbard, spoke for the need of "the spirit of co-operation" over and against the individual. The wrong kind of ambition was dangerous.

Ministers found *The Conquerors* a provocative example and referred to it in their sermons—frequently enough that Wanamaker collected the sermons. Henry Fosdick, the prominent liberal minister of Riverside Church in New York City, reflected on *The Conquerors* in his famous essay series originally printed in the *Ladies' Home Journal* and later turned into the popular book, *Twelve Tests of Character*.[68]

The painting was also used to address the tragedy of war. During the decade of the Mexican Revolution, the *New York Times* reproduced Wanamaker's painting in the November 3, 1912, edition with the following headline: "A Picture That Pleads the Cause of Peace in These Days of War," using it as a commentary for "The Price of Glory." The *Times*'s description of the painting lifted parts of Fosdick's essays without crediting him, explaining that the painting warned against "ambition" and describing it as "the desire to overtop our fellows, to have more than other people have, to be more than other people are." Ambition, the article noted, "has left a bloodstained trail across history." Fosdick and now the *Times* declared that everyone possessed ambition; it was a "primitive instinct ingrained by immemorial necessity passed from the jungle into history." However, as *The Conquerors* depicted, "the consequences were terrific" for pursuing the wrong kind of ambition.[69]

Throughout the decades that it was on display at the store in Philadelphia, *The Conquerors* was often hung in common spaces and was moved to one of the store's two concert halls for special viewings. It remained a staple display piece until the devastation of World War I, when it went into storage on the upper floors of the store and was largely forgotten, only to make a brief reappearance in 1938 to honor the women who led the Transcontinental Peace Caravan that crossed the country in a two-month period.[70]

Store officials considered putting the painting back on display in 1948 in the Grand Court to support peace, although they determined that it was too gruesome for the upcoming Republican and Democratic conventions meeting in Philadelphia. At that point, the painting had not been on permanent display in twenty years. In its heyday, it drew large numbers of visitors, and, many years later, customers who remembered the picture still asked to see it.[71] A letter written to the store in 1965 inquiring about the painting received the reply that the store took it down because it was deemed "too controversial."[72] Years later, the painting was discovered hanging from the rafters on the top floor of the store.

The Conquerors was but one of the paintings that drew crowds to Wanamaker's. At the beginning of the twentieth century, art collections at department stores successfully competed with budding American art museums, drawing thousands of visitors to view art during shopping excursions.

The Rise of Museums

Cities in the early half of the nineteenth century focused on creating cultural institutions ranging from historical societies, libraries, and theaters to art unions, art academies, and lyceums.[73] Art museums were late arrivals, not fully emerging until the last half of the century. To the majority of nineteenth-century Americans, fine "art remained something suspicious and European" and suffered from a lack of popularity, slowing the creation of public art museums.[74] European art faced enduring associations with decadence and a lack of morality. Scholar Lawrence Levine describes the development of American museums as moving from the "general and eclectic to the exclusive and specific."[75]

Early American museums originally focused on entertainment and education for the lower classes. Dime museums offered lessons on natural history and scientific curiosities, along with the entertainment of the bizarre or grotesque, "where one could usually find, along with the bones of the woolly mammoth and the miniature steam engine carved from a cherry pit, the most lifelike waxwork tableau of some celebrated criminal in the act of committing his most celebrated crime, with the very hatchet or the very knife."[76] Museums were primarily collections of the strange and curious of scientific interest, often alongside examples of art. This was true of Charles Peale's famous museum of natural objects and paintings, which opened in 1786, and of the Columbian Museum of Boston, which opened in 1795.[77]

These incipient museums inspired the provocative innovator P. T. Barnum to open his famous American Museum in 1841 in New York City. Barnum's menagerie featured "the natural science collections of several other earlier museums" sitting next to relics from the Holy Land, among other things.[78] Barnum's museum was wildly successful, so much so that he struggled to control the crowds of visitors. When his museum accidentally burned down in the summer of 1865, he quickly rebuilt a grander version to maintain his lucrative enterprise.

Two types of museums acted as models for American efforts. European fine art museums, with their core art treasures derived from nationalized royal, ecclesiastic, and aristocratic collections, resided in converted mansions and palaces.[79] The other type of museum concentrated on education, with collections more broadly defined than fine art; they centered on manufacturing and craftsmanship. These museums arose out of the great exhibitions and continued the tradition of displaying a variety of textiles and ceramics while positioning themselves as arbiters of good taste for visitors as well as retailers.[80] The South Kensington Museum in London (now the Victoria and Albert Museum) exemplified this model.[81] Following in the footsteps of the 1851 Crystal Palace Exhibition, it opened in 1857; the museum developed displays on "good taste," and, in an adjacent area, showcased a curated room of "bad design."[82] Following this example, the Franklin Institute of the State of Pennsylvania for the Promotion of the Mechanic Arts was founded in 1824 by William Keating, a professor at the University of Pennsylvania, and Samuel Merrick, a clerk. They created the institute to teach people about the advances and developments in mechanical sciences through exhibits, classes, and a comprehensive library.[83]

Several fine art museums opened in 1870 in Boston, New York City, and Washington, D.C., and attempted to emulate European collections.[84] However, without the historical advantages of European museums' royal or aristocratic collections and buildings, fledgling American art museums gravitated toward education and the display of contemporary art.[85] The United States' first international exhibition in Philadelphia, the Centennial, ushered in an early attempt at establishing an art museum. In addition to erecting temporary structures, fair planners included a provision for constructing a permanent building, Memorial Hall, to house the fair's art collection. Items were purchased from fair exhibitors to populate the new museum's collection, but the space mainly showed European and Japanese examples of industrial, home, and decorative art objects, much like the collections in the South Kensington Museum. Another museum opened in the city in 1897. Called the Philadelphia Museum, most people knew it as the Commercial Museum. It was started by William Wilson, a botanist, after he visited the Columbian Exposition in Chicago. Thrilled by what he witnessed in Chicago, Wilson wanted a place to house the exhibits from the 1893 fair and from future world's fairs to educate Americans about other countries and the possibilities for business. To stock the new museum, he had twenty-five boxcars transport items from Chicago's exposition. Each year, he added more to the collection from fairs held around the world.[86] But the Franklin Institute and the Commercial Museum were not fine art museums, and it would be some years before Memorial Hall took on this role. When Philadelphia's first art museum finally emerged, it concentrated less on fine art in its earliest days and would not augment its fine art collections until the 1920s.[87] While Wanamaker supported, financed, and provided leadership to the fledging Philadelphia art institutions, he also felt he could be more successful with offering fine art to the community.

At the outset, American department stores did a better job than smaller museums. While museums emphasized the education of the masses, they had trouble reaching them. Stores promoted themselves, like the exhibitions, as a place of culture and learning as well as fantasy. Displaying art furthered this goal.[88] Department stores successfully democratized art by appealing to diverse audiences. Stores combined the attractive characteristics of world's fairs and early museums. For visitors, a department store furnished a broad range of curated decorative household goods, textiles, and the latest fashion—all available for purchase and with no admission charge.

Many of the department store founders collected art and deemed their stores a perfect place to display their personal treasure troves, while some presented rich historical and scientific displays.[89] Le Bon Marché and Selfridge's attracted visitors with their inventive displays of art and technology—Harry Selfridge famously suspended the plane that Louis Blériot used to fly across the English Channel.[90] Marshall Field's collections earned his store the moniker of Chicago's "Third Museum."[91] Morton May of May Company displayed over twelve hundred sculptures from his Greek and Roman collection in a Washington, D.C., store. Yet the dominant and earliest American department store maestro of art display was John Wanamaker. Most department store art galleries did not take off until after the turn of the century.[92]

Buying and displaying art in his store more extensively and earlier than his counterparts, Wanamaker introduced a wide range of people to the fine arts with eye-catching and well-designed displays.[93] By creating his own public art galleries, Wanamaker presented himself as having the authority to curate artwork that was morally uplifting and in good taste. It also communicated what he valued in art.

Wanamaker hung his first painting in the men's tailoring department in his first store, Oak Hall. The Chestnut Street branch of John

Wanamaker & Co. featured a collection of paintings on the walls. In 1881 Wanamaker carved out a devoted space in the Grand Depot for a store art gallery. He added the feature to his New York branch when he purchased it in 1896. With the construction of the new flagship store in Philadelphia, Wanamaker committed a huge amount of floor space to form a series of art galleries large enough to hold a significant portion of his collection, including his most treasured pieces. By 1914, he added additional gallery space in his New York City store.

Wanamaker continued to scatter art pieces throughout the store, as in the case of *The Conquerors* and large statues. For example, he placed two bronze lions from Paris at the entrance of his millinery department in 1904 in the partially finished building. A sculpture of Joan of Arc graced the Market Street entryway to the store. For the celebration of Joan of Arc day, the statue moved to anchor various displays. In 1924 the statue appeared in one of the Wanamaker store windows surrounded by French flags.[94] Copies of statutes from the Louvre were found throughout the store.

Wanamaker bragged that his art galleries outstripped American art museums. While his claim could appear to be mere braggadocio, he was addressing the real differences between early art museums and the capabilities of his art galleries. For a time, his claim was true. The display of his art collection on the higher floors of his store was meant to do the work that Wanamaker felt museums were failing to do: to bring in a large variety of people to experience the edifying power of beautiful and inspiring curated art.

Wanamaker regularly advertised his store's connections with the Paris Salons, telling his customers, "Probably no other store in the world . . . has gone to the Paris Salons and purchased the pictures best worth having to decorate its walls."[95] Not only did he acquire a fine collection of paintings and art objects, but he also rotated the artwork to alleviate the potential for boredom and added educational exhibits to the rotation. Special exhibits enabled him to entice visitors with a menu of new visual experiences. Those wanting to see the famous paintings of Europe only needed a trip to the store, where he arranged "reproductions of all the beautiful Nattier portraits in the galleries of Versailles."[96] Invitation-only dinners served as another way to present the art treasures. The store also

Figure 4.1. French Revolution store exhibit, one of the hundreds of educational exhibits Wanamaker offered in his store over the years. French history was a regular theme of these displays, reinforcing the connection between the store and French goods and refinement. Other exhibits were scientific in nature. For example, Wanamaker displayed the newly discovered element radium in exhibits in 1904 at both his New York and Philadelphia stores.

printed yearly catalogs of its art shopping sprees, with black-and-white reproductions and descriptions of the pieces on high-quality paper.

Wanamaker boldly called his store a "sight teacher of history, industry and the arts."[97] To accomplish this goal, he rebuilt historic structures in the store, antique homes, old-fashioned sweet shops, and a reproduction of a Philadelphia shop and cottage.[98] Wanamaker also curated special collections of fine art, objects, and reproductions for the public's education. One of the first themed events occurred in 1895 when Wanamaker celebrated "Monarchs and Beauties of the World" by exhibiting more than six hundred photographs of France, hundreds of miniatures, dozens of paintings of rulers, and a reproduction of the world's largest diamond in what Wanamaker claimed to be "educative exhibits of art and life and history."[99] Another display featured the life and military career of Napoleon. This instructive presentation traced Napoleon's early life in poverty, placed on view how his signature had changed over time, and illustrated his experiences on the military battlefield.[100] Napoleon's rags-to-emperor story mirrored Wanamaker's own rag-to-riches biography.

The Philadelphia art museum's location and admissions charges also contributed to Wanamaker's feelings of superiority. Situated in Fairmount Park, far from the city center, the museum was inconvenient to visit. Wanamaker's art galleries did not charge admission, arguably offered better art in this period, and were located near several convenient transportation options. Wanamaker actively competed with local art museums by advertising that his store was "open to all for the coming" and that he had converted his stores into "vast public museums."[101] Indeed, he bragged that his store art galleries welcomed more visitors than most state or local museums. They even, he argued, beat New York City's Metropolitan Museum of Art, which in 1910 claimed nearly a million visitors while "the attendance at Wanamaker's reaches many millions of visitors!"[102]

The Art of Display

Long a leader in department store merchandise display, Wanamaker pioneered a new attitude in art display with the help of his son Rodman, his close associate Robert Ogden, and his store art directors. While other department stores developed picture galleries as a place to display art for sale or as a sampling of the store owners' private collections, Wanamaker did both. Lithographs, paintings, and art objects for sale were found in other parts of the store scattered throughout model home galleries, situated in display windows, leaned against walls and cabinets, or displayed in the model rooms of the furniture store.[103] Reproductions of paintings from his collection appeared on Crystal Tea Room menus, Bethany church programs, store publications, and souvenirs.[104]

Wanamaker's display techniques for his fine art differed from the those of the great exhibitions and art museums, in which curators crammed multiple paintings into the available wall space and clustered sculptures in the center of packed rooms. While he employed a similar approach in his home galleries, like the one at Lindenhurst, where the size of his collection necessitated using every available inch of wall space, he took a different tack for his department store. In the store, there was ample room to give his curated collection of artwork dedicated space. Wanamaker and his team avoided visual cacophony by hanging paintings individually or, in the case of smaller pieces, in groups of no more than two, one above the other.[105] Nearly all the paintings were hung at eye level, inviting an intimacy with the paintings. Tracts of blank wall between frames and individual lamps isolated the paintings in a pool of light to define and focus visitors' viewing.[106] This display technique also heightened a sense that the paintings in the gallery were important for the viewer to see without distraction.[107] Small brass plaques identified the title and artist of each artwork. Overall, gallery visitors encountered less visual clutter than they would find at the Philadelphia Museum of Art or New York's Metropolitan Museum of Art in the same period.[108]

Set apart from the hubbub of the busy sales floors, the store art galleries provided a quiet oasis on the upper floors of the thirteen-story building, granting shoppers a quiet place of contemplation inside a commercial and urban world.[109] The Philadelphia galleries occupied parts of the seventh and eighth floors, and over the years moved to make room for special exhibits and additions. On the eighth floor a gallery was placed near the entrance of the store's elegant Crystal Tea Room and was dubbed the Rendezvous. Elegant chairs and cushioned benches scattered throughout the area invited visitors to linger among paintings and served as a comfortable spot to wait for friends before entering the Tea Room. A reserve gallery operated on the ninth floor. Large oriental rugs softened footfalls and added a touch of elegance to the gallery.

The main galleries consisted of six rooms where hundreds of paintings hung on the walls, and elegantly draped islands were set up in the middle of larger rooms to accommodate more art. Wanamaker had the artwork mostly organized by country of origin, following the pattern of his personal galleries, with sections labeled Italian, English, French, Flemish, or Dutch. Special areas mixed artwork for drama. The reserve gallery served as a home for his largest paintings, among them Munkácsy's, and as an overflow space for the treasures picked up during Parisian shopping sprees. Bronzes and statuary had their own gallery. By 1926, the reserve gallery housed ninety-five paintings.[110] Other paintings in the room focused on Christian themes: Benjamin West's *Christ Blessing*

Figure 4.2. The Rendezvous art gallery. Sometimes referred to as the furniture store in archive photos, this art display was more likely Wanamaker's Rendezvous art space outside the Crystal Tea Room.

Little Children, a fifteenth-century Flemish painting titled *Portrait of a Lady*, H. O. Tanner's *Behold the Bridegroom Cometh*, *Virgin and Child and St. John*, and a painting called *Italian Interior of a Cathedral*.[111]

Ornate metalwork gates marked the entrance to the main galleries. The gates framed the galleries as liminal space set apart from store business and demonstrated the paintings as objects of high value, needing to be locked up in the interior of the store.[112] Moving past the iron gates, visitors first encountered a succession of religious paintings and objects that positioned the gallery experience as a reverent and religious one. The first visible painting, *The Holy Family* by the School of Pietro Perugino, showed Mary and Joseph and the baby Jesus. Next to the painting stood a magnificent six-foot-tall reproduction of the great Strasbourg Cathedral Clock.[113] The clock depicted the four "ages" of humankind—childhood, youth, adulthood, and old age—four times an hour. As the clock tolled the quarter hour, the clock sprang to life when a small door above the clock face opened and figures representing Jesus's twelve disciples emerged. Each disciple turned to Jesus as a cock crowed three times—a reference to Peter's denial of Jesus in the Gospels.[114] Two angels at the front of the clock represented Judgment Day. Wanamaker had created a place where everyday time was suspended—it was the time of the ages, and it was holy time. The gallery featured a mixture of paintings from the Salons and Old Masters (sometimes copies). Landscapes and portraits were displayed next to Madonna and Child paintings and depictions of New Testament stories. One area of the gallery displayed Lely's *Lady with Curls*, Bylert's *Lady with White Collar* and *Woman in Orange Dress with Parrot* next to Carlos Dolci's *Madonna and Child* and Gainsborough's *Landscape with Cattle*. Another wall placed together Revez's *Husking Corn*, Fortuny's *Religious Procession*, and Weenix's *Sheep and Shepherd*.[115] Religious paintings were sprinkled among depictions

Figure 4.3. Art gallery display. There was a separate gallery for sculptures. Paintings and sculpture pieces were also used throughout the store for window displays and decoration. Wanamaker's art display techniques were a forerunner of today's fine art museums.

of everyday life and beautiful landscapes. Statuary punctuated open floor space in the gallery.

Although the Wanamaker store galleries moved from time to time as departments were added or rearranged, the pictures cycled regularly between his homes and church. For many years the main gallery resided on the eighth floor just outside Wanamaker's office. If store guests harbored any doubt of the importance of the galleries to Wanamaker, their location offered a firm answer. In the middle of the art gallery was a door marked "Founder's Office" with Wanamaker's portrait hanging beside it.[116] On one side of his office door was a work purportedly by Titian and on the other side were three religious paintings—two depicting the Virgin and Child and the other depicting Mary and Joseph's flight into Egypt from the Gospel of Matthew.[117]

Wanamaker did more than display paintings and art; he also wanted to instruct the viewer and did so by providing educational booklets that explained prominent pieces of art. One booklet counseled visitors to the galleries, "The Wanamaker Picture Galleries bid you welcome at all times. They are in close relation with the Paris Salons, and with all art centers, and always have something new to show you." In case a visitor was uncertain of the importance of what they were viewing, they were told, "Art students and collectors might seek the country over in vain for a better exemplification of all that is authoritative or representative in art than is yearly gleaned from the two Paris Salons by the Wanamaker Store; and its gleanings, of course, take in other fields as well."[118] The paintings were important, and, by proxy, the store guest was important by viewing the paintings. The art displays were then advertised, with large exhibits accompanied by interpretative booklets "explaining the significance of the art."[119] Featuring quality reproductions of the art on high-quality paper, the booklets allowed shoppers to continue their relationship with the paintings at home for further study and contemplation.

Department Store Christ

When the fire broke out at Lindenhurst, Wanamaker's summer home, on that frigid night in 1907, the first art pieces saved by his butler were the two gigantic paintings *Christ before Pilate* and *Christ on Golgotha*. To save them, the butler cut the canvases out of their frames, rolled them, and carried them outside to safety (likely with help). They were Wanamaker's most precious possessions and, at the time, two of the most well-known paintings in the world created by the prominent Hungarian and Catholic artist Mihály Munkácsy. Brought to the United States with great acclaim, Munkácsy's work would become some of the best-known art to American audiences in the nineteenth century.[120]

The two paintings that Wanamaker purchased depicting Jesus's Passion, *Christ before Pilate* and *Christ on Golgotha*, proved to be some of the most dramatic additions to his art collection. Wanamaker acquired Munkácsy's *Christ before Pilate* in 1877 and *Christ on Golgotha* in 1888.[121] He paid the highest price ever paid for a painting in America at the time, explaining that he found the paintings particularly moving.[122]

Munkácsy's improbable rise to stardom in the art world started in 1870, when his painting *Last Day of a Condemned Prisoner* won a prestigious gold medal at the Paris Salon that year. Orphaned at an early age, Munkácsy first apprenticed under an itinerant painter before studying at the Vienna Academy in 1865. Following his time at the academy, he traveled to Dusseldorf to study with Ludwig Knaus, a well-known genre painter.[123]

A visit to Paris in 1867 introduced Munkácsy to realism—an approach to painting that emphasized painting everyday life instead of romantic and idealized pictures. He used the new style for his medal-winning painting. Two years after his successful debut at the Salon, he moved to Paris and married the widow of the Baron de Marches. The marriage opened aristocratic circles to him, where he excelled in charming the Parisian elite. Casting himself as a mysterious figure and artist, he continued painting and produced *Milton Dictating Paradise Lost to His Daughters* in 1877 and sold it for the hefty sum of thirty thousand francs to the art dealer Charles Sedelmeyer, who would later sign him to an exclusive contract. For the next twenty years, Munkácsy painted across several genres including landscapes, historical subjects, scenes of wealthy domestic life, and portraits. His works were cherished among well-heeled collectors in the United States and Europe. Bouts of ill health and mental instability that had plagued him all his life finally took their toll, and in 1896 he was committed to a mental institution, where he died four years later.

Despite his success in France, Munkácsy did not achieve celebrity status on both sides of the Atlantic until the 1880s, when he painted two enormous canvases that depicted scenes from Christ's Passion. The art dealer Sedelmeyer helped secure a studio space substantial enough to hang a painting of nearly three hundred square feet.[124] The first painting, *Christ before Pilate*, went on display in 1881 at Sedelmeyer's home in Paris after the Salons rejected it as a late entry. The painting immediately garnered high acclaim.[125]

In *Christ before Pilate*, Munkácsy captured the story told in all four Gospels of Jesus's trial and sentencing before the Roman prefect, Pontius Pilate. While the Gospel accounts conflict on the details of the story, Munkácsy created a large-canvas depiction of the story. His version portrays Jesus standing in a gleaming white robe before an enthroned Pilate in Herod's palace. Pilate, also in white, is the other central figure in the painting. Playing to a desire for historical paintings of Jesus, and of a Jesus who was not effeminate, Munkácsy found a middle way with a historical narrative painting that featured a strong yet tender Jesus—a popular combination in the late nineteenth century.[126] Depicted as European, Jesus stands against the backdrop of a Middle Eastern crowd representing the Sanhedrin. The painting features an animated crowd scene of men and a lone woman holding a child. The facial expressions and body language of the crowd are clearly visible and tell the story of a variety of reactions to Jesus's trial and death. The actions performed by the people in the crowd invite viewers to identify or reject the emotions on display.[127] The men in the painting appear angry, agitated, thoughtful, and worried, while the woman holding the child shows sympathy. Striking in its use of shadow, the otherwise dark painting gifts a glimpse of blue sky and Jerusalem beyond the immediate scene. Though Munkácsy was Catholic, both scenes fit well into the Protestant repertoire of Jesus images by illustrating a Bible story and not focusing too much on the body. Sedelmeyer took the painting on a tour of the European capitals, which reaped more praise and acclaim for the painting and its artist.

Munkácsy finished his second work, *Christ on Golgotha*, in 1884. A powerful painting in its size, scale, and storytelling, it depicts Jesus's last moments on the cross before his death. Using more vibrant colors in this painting, Munkácsy employs bright blues and reds to direct viewers to take in different parts of the painting's story. Jesus, illuminated from a heavenly light above and draped in white, hangs on the cross while three grief-stricken women (Jesus's mother, Mary, as well as Mary Magdalene and Salome) gather at his feet and a disciple stands nearby, aloof. One woman motions to a young man with a ladder, desperate to take Jesus off the cross, while two Roman guards watch the scene unfold from different vantage points. The two thieves hanging on crosses frame Jesus's broken body and provide contrast with their slack bodies and bowed heads. Jesus's face looks skyward toward a heavenly light; his body, despite its abuse, glows. Some members of the crowd cry out, others look on in awe, while others turn their backs or appear indifferent, and one man runs away.

Christ on Golgotha debuted on Good Friday, again at Sedelmeyer's home, but now in an addition built for the sole purpose of displaying the two mammoth canvases together.[128] Unbelievably, *Christ on Golgotha* eclipsed the first painting in praise and renown. Once again, Sedelmeyer arranged a major tour, making the painting and its author one of the most famous pairs in Europe. With the European capitals conquered, Sedelmeyer turned his attention to the United States and began planning what would prove to be by far the most successful presentation of the paintings to an enthusiastic and broad audience.

Sedelmeyer decided to launch an American tour in New York City. Finding the right venue to display the paintings posed a challenge. Eventually, he secured the Twenty-Third Street Tabernacle, a space in the city with a conflicted past. Originally an armory, the building was rented by the Reverend Albert Benjamin Simpson in 1881 to open what he called the Gospel Tabernacle, an outreach church to immigrants and the working class. The congregation left when it outgrew the armory.

Following this, a controversial businessman and showman, Salmi Morse, had secured the Tabernacle to perform a ten-act play he wrote on the end of Jesus's life, titled *A Passion Play: A Miracle Story*.[129] After being run out of San Francisco, in part for the play's content, Morse decided to try New York. Investing a large sum of money to renovate the Tabernacle for his production, he suggested that it would become a "shrine" once he presented the play in the space.[130] City authorities refused to issue a theatre license, and shortly afterward, Morse mysteriously turned up dead. The space became available for rent again.[131] When Sedelmeyer secured the Tabernacle to display Munkácsy's paintings, art historian Laura Morowitz explains, it was essentially an exchange of Morse's Passion play for another—in this case, Munkácsy version.[132] It was also the replacement of one business proposition mixed up with religion for another.

Munkácsy and his paintings arrived in New York City on November 14, 1886. The New York press greeted them at the dock. Crowds clamored to see the paintings and paid an admission fee for access. The reviews were mixed. While some visitors reported religious experiences while viewing the mural-sized paintings, a New York Times reporter warned that the paintings showed evidence of business taking over religion. Charging an admission fee struck the reporter as incongruous with the subject of the painting. The association with commerce hung over the popular and profitable religious paintings from the beginning. But the crowds came anyway to spend time studying the stunning paintings, and religious leaders who viewed the paintings went on to write about them. Many attendees traveled from afar to see Munkácsy's masterpieces. Wanamaker was one of them.

When Wanamaker visited the paintings, he arranged to meet Munkácsy. From their meeting, they forged a friendship that lasted the rest of Munkácsy's life. Wanamaker commissioned the artist to paint a portrait of one of Wanamaker's daughters. Later, the store hosted Jan Munkácsy, the painter's nephew, a violin virtuoso.[133]

In 1888 Harper's Weekly featured a full-page advertisement selling copies of Christ before Pilate. The advertisement boasted that to buy a copy of the famous painting was to own a reproduction of a $120,000 painting—a startling sum in 1888 and arguably the most ever paid for a painting in the United States—and to have a reproduction that "dense crowds" in Europe and the Americas lined up to view.

Clergy testimonials bolstered the importance of the artwork and were published in an accompanying booklet to demonstrate the paintings' religious merit and authenticity. The Reverend Charles P. Deems claimed, "The face of Christ is a stroke of genius," and the eminent Presbyterian New York City minister Reverend Henry J. Van Dyke said, "The picture of 'Christ Before Pilate' . . . is potent, intense, throbbing with life."

Readers were told that the sales of the image had been high and that it would make "a beautiful holiday present."[134] Ferdinand French, an associate superintendent for Bethany's Sunday school, wrote a multipage essay on the paintings, possibly as a teaching tool for Sunday school students who went to the store to see the paintings. French presented a brief history of the paintings and the painter, claiming that Munkácsy's artwork emerged from his brush after careful study of the "word of God." "No one has any knowledge of the face of our Lord Jesus Christ," even painters.[135]

Wanamaker purchased Munkácsy's paintings in 1887 and 1888, for what was claimed to be the highest sum paid for a painting at the time. The claim would become a part of the advertising. Wanamaker extended the public tour of the paintings; he sent them on a tour of sixty-two churches in the United States.[136] Again, admission was charged to view the paintings. Wanamaker said that the admission covered the cost of the tour and was split with the hosting congregations.[137]

After the tour, Wanamaker installed the paintings at Lindenhurst for his personal viewing. They became his favorites, and when the house burned down in 1907, he was most concerned that those two paintings be rescued. Following the fire, Wanamaker had them restored to their original size and, perhaps in a move to protect them, installed them in the art galleries of his Philadelphia store. At times, he had to defend or at least explain his display of the paintings in his store to friends who worried about mixing sacred art with the commercial world.[138]

The elder Wanamaker preferred a devotional setting for the paintings and refused to display them in the Grand Court. Instead, customers would be directed to the quiet of the art galleries for viewing during the Lenten and Easter seasons. They were hung in a large room, the Munkácsy Gallery, on the ninth floor. The paintings were placed at eye level, from floor to ceiling giving viewers the impression they could walk into the painting and be among the spectators surrounding Jesus before Pilate or at the foot of the cross where Jesus was crucified. It was a room Wanamaker was known to visit alone at the beginning of the business day to spend some time contemplating the last days of Jesus's life.[139]

* * *

Munkácsy was only one of several artists that the Wanamakers befriended and supported. Henry Ossawa Tanner had moved to Philadelphia when he was twenty-one to train with Thomas Eakins and was one of the first African Americans to attend the Pennsylvania Academy of the Fine Arts. He left Philadelphia for Paris in 1891 and began submitting his work to the Paris Salon. Rodman Wanamaker likely met Tanner in 1895, when Rodman served as the president of the American Art Association of Paris and the artist joined the organization.[140] John Wanamaker had also sponsored Tanner's teacher Thomas Hovenden.[141]

In the summer of 1896, after six months of painting, Tanner completed his dramatic painting *The Resurrection of Lazarus* and was later awarded a medal at the Salon. The painting attracted Rodman Wanamaker's attention when he saw it at the artist's studio. Rodman noticed what he called an accidental "Orientalism" in the composition.[142] Rodman's use of "Orientalism," according to art historian Anna Marley, "was most likely referring to the work of nineteenth-century French painters . . . who used architectural elements and ethnic details derived from their travels in North Africa and the Near East to depict aspects of native cultures in their paintings."[143] The success of *The Resurrection of Lazarus* led Rodman to sponsor a trip to the Holy Land in 1897, where Tanner was to research the landscape, architecture, and atmosphere of the Holy Land to incorporate into future biblical paintings.

Only the year before, in 1896, Rodman had convinced his father to make a six-month pilgrimage to the Holy Land. The trip had a profound effect on John Wanamaker. It kindled within him deep emotion, so much so that on his visit to the Holy Sepulcher he bribed the tomb's attendant to leave, and, he recalled, "Yielding to an irresistible temptation, I stretched myself out on [Jesus's] tomb."[144] Perhaps Rodman believed that a similar trip for Tanner would put the artist in touch with the deep emotion his father experienced. Tanner's trip followed the route most American tourists took by traveling to Cairo, Jerusalem, Port Said, Jaffa, Jericho, the Dead Sea, and Alexandria.[145]

Rodman financed a second trip for Tanner in 1898 and 1899, allowing the artist to draw inspiration for what would be a series of religious paintings that elevated his career. Tanner returned to Paris, purchased "oriental" objects and costumes from the estate of Mihály Munkácsy, who had recently died, and began to paint a series of religious paintings that secured his reputation as an in-demand religious artist. The Wana-makers purchased many of the paintings inspired by Tanner's Holy Land trips and displayed them at both of their department stores. Among the works of art displayed were Tanner's *Christ and His Mother Studying the Scriptures, Christ Washing the Disciples' Feet, Mary Magdalene Returning from the Tomb,* and *The Holy Family.* Other pieces by Tanner hung in several of the Wanamakers' homes.[146] The largest canvas Tanner painted, *Behold the Bridegroom Cometh* (also called *The Wise and Foolish Virgins*), had been commissioned by Rodman and was displayed in both stores.[147]

* * *

While the Philadelphia store had Munkácsy and Tanner, New York had the paintings of James Tissot, at least in reproductions. A French artist famous for his paintings of everyday life, Tissot changed his artistic direction when he experienced a moving vision of Jesus at the Church of Saint-Sulpice in Paris during Mass. After the experience, he decided to create an illustrated New Testament. Like Tanner and other artists before him, he traveled to the Holy Land in an attempt to make his paintings historically authentic; the trip resulted in a collection of 350 watercolor paintings picturing key moments in the biblical text. The watercolors went on tour in Europe, premiering in Paris in 1894, and in the United States as other epic pieces of religious art did throughout the late nineteenth and early twentieth centuries, drawing eager crowds. The Wanamakers were not able to purchase Tissot's collection. The Brooklyn Museum acquired the complete collection of Tissot's paintings in 1900 after a community fundraising effort through subscription.[148] The Wanamaker store instead exhibited high-quality reproductions of the paintings in the art gallery.

Tissot's project resonated with the Wanamakers the way Tanner's work had. They named their New York store art gallery the Tissot Art Gallery and made a deal to publish the artist's epic series in a deluxe four-volume set: *Tissot's Life of Christ.* While not the first to publish the series, Wanamaker made it accessible by offering financing. To make the extravagant purchase possible—volumes ranged in price from thirty to fifty dollars—Wanamaker invited shoppers to join the "Wanamaker-Tissot Club" and to buy the volumes in monthly installments. It was a popular item. Purchase of a Tissot set was newsworthy in small towns, with local papers reporting the arrival of each volume, usually obtained by the local minister.

Advertisements stressed the authenticity of the pictures as a central selling point, emphasizing that it had taken Tissot ten years to complete the paintings and noting his status as "a devoted believer," ignoring the fact that Tissot was a committed Catholic. His travels to Syria and Palestine, to places where Jesus had "walked and talked," lent weight to the authenticity of his paintings, depicting the "Holy Land" as a place suspended in time. Tissot's artwork, the advertisement claimed, recorded "the men, women, and children" and "the rocks and hills, mountains, valleys, lakes, stream, villages and roadways that Jesus knew," making them accessible to viewers of his paintings.[149] The concept of authenticity invited the viewer to make an emotional connection with the story of Jesus.

Jesus in the Grand Court

After his father's death, Rodman initiated a new Lenten-Easter tradition at the store. An Episcopalian who had heartily embraced the Gothic Revival movement's penchant for opulent interior decorations to communicate spiritual emotion, Rodman moved Munkácsy's two famous paintings into the Grand Court during the four weeks of Lent leading up to Easter. To make the paintings stand out in the visually busy Grand Court, store designers hung dark navy velvet curtains along the walls just above the court's arches, suspended above the first floor on opposite sides, forming an informal trinity with the Great Organ. Given the history of the paintings' public consumption, they continued to have a profound effect on visitors wherever they were located. At the ground level, large standing markers gave a brief history of each painting and of Munkácsy's life. Two allegorical shields ringed in lights, symbolizing the Bible, hung on either side of the paintings, and a line of silk pennants adorned the sides of the court. The placement of the paintings in the court invited shoppers to enter the story of Jesus's last days and last breath.[150]

A store advertisement for the "pre-Easter season" displays of *Christ before Pilate* and *Christ on Golgotha* in the final days of World War II utilized gothic typeface. A backdrop of the Great Organ's pipes reminded

Figure 4.4. Munkácsy's *Christ on Golgotha* in the Grand Court. After Wanamaker's death, the Munkácsy paintings were displayed on either end of the Grand Court during the weeks of Lent. Munkácsy's other painting, *Christ before Pilate* (not shown here), was hung on the opposite end of the court. A variety of flags and standards were used in holiday and patriotic displays. The lamp shades above the merchandise counters say "EASTER He is risen! Alleluia!"

readers of the popularity of the paintings and how "thousands" came to the store to see them every year. The advertisement noted that it was "an impressive sight to watch those gathered in the Grand Court" to see the paintings with "respectful mien" and an "attitude of reverence." The writer of the ad interpreted this outlook as being generated by the universality of the paintings. Who were these visitors? "Some come to study the technique of the artist," but the majority "come because these paintings arouse some inner emotion, thought or feeling," and "offer inspiration." As a result, viewers "gained spiritual enrichment." The advertisement promised visitors to the store and its famous painting that those who came to visit and took a moment to look at the painting would participate in sending a communal "silent prayer" that had the power to break through the "shadows" and bring forth peace.[151]

Although there appear to be no extant letters to the Wanamaker store from the early days expounding on the power of the paintings, letters from the 1940s and 1950s demonstrate how customers who viewed them in the Grand Court were moved by the painting. One visitor from Ohio wrote to the store after his visit to see whether he could acquire reproductions of the paintings and a biography of the artist.[152] Another visitor, Walter Galbraith Dunlap, conveyed how popular the paintings were. Dunlap's letter, which was written in the 1940s, demonstrated how the paintings in a public commercial space still managed to operate as religious devotional objects: "Each year thousands of people pause, as they pass through the Grand Court of Wanamaker's Store in Philadelphia, at Easter Time, and stand in wonder as they view the two great paintings of Munkácsy—Christ Before Pilot [sic] and the Crucifixion." Dunlap observed that the shoppers who stopped to view "the magnificence of the artistry" did not do so by happenstance. Instead, they made a pilgrimage:

> They are people who annually make a special trip to the store to see again the paintings and draw anew some message, some inspiration from their grandeur and solemnity. . . . Perhaps here too we can make a grand venture in Faith—that somehow out of all the turmoil of the age, out of all the depths of degradation to which man seems to have sunk, we can look out from the Court of Pilot [sic], across the ghastly hill of Calvary to the hope and sunlight of a distant Easter. To an Easter where the best that we can be will triumph over the worst that we often are.[153]

Surrounded by the latest in fashion, Dunlap had described a religious experience—one he felt confident those around him who gazed in the same direction shared. Wanamaker may have disapproved of the paintings hanging in the Grand Court, but Dunlap's meditations validated much of the religious work Wanamaker did inside his store.

William F. Hamill Jr. reached out to the president of the store in April 1950 to share his Lenten experience of the Munkácsy paintings, calling them "beautiful murals." Hamill visited the paintings regularly each Lenten season. Standing in the busy Grand Court, he would steal "a few moments in Silent Meditation and prayer." He wrote, "I have overheard many awed comments on these pictures, many of them indicating a new appreciation and inspiration to faith and understanding in Christ." He asked that the pictures remain in the Grand Court for "inspirational effect," noting that it was a time when all needed inspiration, whether "Catholic, Protestant and Jew." If the store allowed the paintings to remain for a bit longer, Hamill believed the store would reap "the gratitude of hundreds of thousands of Christians and Americans."[154]

Writing a reply, the next day, John E. Raasch, president of the store from 1947 to 1966, agreed with Hamill that the paintings were powerful, and, in a statement that echoed John Wanamaker, he said, "More and more do we realize that the salvation of the world rests in the spiritual and not the material." However, Raasch worried that the power of the paintings of Christ's final days would be lessened if the store displayed them all the time. He explained, "The impact that these pictures make during the Lenten Season, when the minds of many people are most receptive to spiritual suggestion," was a phenomenon he was "loathe to interfere with." Because of that, he felt it was important to remove the paintings "immediately after Easter," as had been the store's long custom.[155]

A retired Presbyterian minister from Ohio sent a note to the store in March 1958 after a visit to Philadelphia for the funeral of his youngest brother. The Reverend William Waide went to the store to view the Munkácsy paintings he recalled having seen twenty years earlier. He described the experience as "a great privilege and a great blessing" and asked whether the artist had created a "statement" on "the various characters" in the paintings and who they "were supposed to represent and the feelings and attitudes he sought to depict."[156]

Word spread about the annual display of the paintings. A letter dated March 28, 1965, from the Reverend M. L. Heerbotha, a Lutheran minister from St. Louis, asked whether the paintings were still displayed during Lent. He hoped the store could send a brochure about them; if they were still displayed every year, he expressed a desire "to come see it sometime." The minister had heard about the paintings or perhaps had seen a reproduction of them in a Sunday school newspaper or magazine article. "From all I have heard and read about this masterpiece," he wrote, "it must touch the viewer deeply. Your firm is to be commended very highly for giving such a positive witness for salvation through Christ."[157]

An employee, a woman named Evelyn B. Conner, drafted an introduction for the paintings that she delivered on a routine basis.[158] Once she shared the history of the paintings, she asked customers to "pause for an extra minute" on their next visit to the Grand Court and "offer these three short prayers":

> FIRST—A prayer of thanksgiving for such an artist as Munkácsy who gave us these magnificent paintings.
>
> SECOND—A prayer of thanks to the John Wanamaker Store for their great generosity in sharing them with us every Eastertide.
>
> THIRD—(and most important), A prayer of thanksgiving to our HEAVENLY FATHER for having HIS SON to die upon the cross, that we might have the light of CHRISTIANITY throughout the world.[159]

For Conner and many customers over the years, the paintings were more than holiday store decorations. They gave a focus for prayer and meditations on Jesus's life, death, and the possibilities of his resurrection during the Lenten season.

Although some visitors felt uncomfortable with the lavishly decorated court surrounding the paintings. Jean Shyrock of Philadelphia sent a letter in May 1965 to Wanamaker's great-grandson, who served as the chair of the store's board, to give advice on how the Munkácsy paintings should be displayed. Shyrock had visited the store for the explicit purpose of viewing the paintings and had heard Evelyn Conner's presentation on the "details of these superb works." Yet she found the decorations distracting and recommended that the store "let the paintings alone dominate the Court during Holy Week, but *without* any decorations in the Court." Such a presentation would be more appropriate for the "most solemn week of the Christian calendar." As she explained, "there should be nothing to divert the spectators' attention from the tragic event that gave us the enduring meaning of Easter."[160] The store did not heed Shyrock's advice. Nearly every year, the Easter decorations in the Grand Court grew more extravagant. The Munkácsy paintings reconstituted a retail space into a sacred one.

* * *

As the ashes smoldered at John Wanamaker's summer home, exhausted servants, firefighters, and neighbors gathered the scattered artwork that escaped the fire and spectators and gently placed the pieces in the home's carriage house and other outlying buildings to protect them from the elements and looting. Watchmen were posted to guard the art from further theft.[161] Most of the paintings were moved out over the next few months, while china, crystal, and art objects remained in storage. But the Lindenhurst fire would not be the last conflagration. Six months later, the carriage house mysteriously burned to the ground, consuming the part of the collection that still awaited removal to more secure quarters.[162]

John Wanamaker's department store art galleries were his own art Salons, which he and his sons juried through purchase and presented to the public as examples of good Protestant taste, gentility, and inspiration.[163] As generations had traveled to European art galleries especially in England, France, and Italy to acquire taste and culture, the Wanamakers brought a European art experience to Americans to give them taste and culture in the confines of his store. After the death of his father, Rodman maintained the practice of buying pictures from the Salons every year and putting them on exhibit complete with an accompanying catalogue.

The art critic John Ruskin and minister Horace Bushnell had promoted a way to view beauty that gave religious meaning to his art collecting. Wanamaker put these ideas into action as ministers and other leaders had in their institutions. The religious art in his collection could act as a portal for devotion. He felt that the right kind of art stimulated morality, instilled civic responsibility, and cultivated virtue in its viewers.[164] Wanamaker took seriously the power of beauty conveyed through art to edify people. He gave himself large doses while sharing his work with the people he cared for the most. He displayed the same art that he surrounded himself with, edifying those at his Philadelphia and New York City department stores and in the halls and meeting rooms of Bethany Church. His two most famous purchases had an even broader audience as they were paraded across the country in a multicity tour. Believing he had moral authority, Wanamaker used his taste, which was tied to the popular taste of America's wealthy elite, to elevate the taste of others and was a part of a larger movement that sought to curate and "sacralize" particular musical and cultural forms.[165] By displaying art in the space of his stores where goods were for sale, he also made consumerism, by association, a cultural act.

Shoppers and employees responded to the art in multiple ways—some with deep religious devotion. Others were oblivious to the images of Jesus in the court or in the galleries in a rush to complete their shopping errands. Just as the lines between department store and sacred space slipped during the holidays, the art galleries invited a multitude of responses and prepared shoppers for the possibility that the experience could be a religious one.

Wanamaker acquired art to uplift himself, and he displayed and sold reproductions of art in his store to sell refinement to the American upper and middle classes. Fashion and taste were for sale and could be purchased. Wanamaker served as a curator of that taste, which was defined in his advertisements and displays. They encapsulated the respectability proffered by his involvement in Protestant Christianity, whether by closing stores on Sunday or being known as a leading Presbyterian and temperance movement figure in Philadelphia. Wanamaker sought to use art and beauty to influence the moral character of his shoppers and staff. Wanamaker's massive art collection and its use and display in his home, church, and the department store during his lifetime and after his death were key elements in his religious work.

5

Christian Interiors

To give people the things they want is not enough for the Wanamaker Stores. . . . They must be a leader in taste—an educator.

—John Wanamaker[1]

On Christmas Eve in 1911, John Wanamaker stood in the middle of the colossal atrium of his new store building. He was now seventy-three years old and had been in business for over fifty years. He looked up to take in the sweeping marble-clad seven-story space and the series of skylights crowning the top that brought natural light into the heart of the store. At night, the latest technology in electricity kept the store brightly lit for late shoppers.[2] Corinthian pilasters, crowned in gold, framed the hall, giving it the appearance of a great temple—a flourish of beauty in the heart of a commercial building. Standing in the center of the store's atrium, Wanamaker, like many of the shoppers milling around him, gazed at a feature unique to his store: a three-story golden organ, the largest in the world, topped by a trumpeting angel.

On that night, as for years to come, the Grand Court filled with the sound of Christmas carols sung by thousands of shoppers, reading the words to the beloved hymns in their Wanamaker Christmas songbooks. As Wanamaker stood in the center of the elaborately decorated bustling hall, "Oh, Little Town of Bethlehem" permeated the Grand Court and spilled out into the depths of the store, christening the new space with the story of Jesus's birth. Wanamaker recalled that moment in his diary: "I said to myself that I was in a temple," a sentiment quite possibly shared by the thousands who thronged to the store that night to sing carols and make last-minute Christmas gift selections in his elaborately decorated space. He then offered a gesture of humility: "but may I never say, 'I built it!'"[3]

Earlier that same year, Wanamaker had penned a letter to his son Rodman, full of memories of the beginning of his department store.

He confessed, "fifty years are crowding upon me." He reminisced, "I see again the first morning when I swept the shavings and blocks that were about the front door [of the Grand Depot]. . . . And the procession of the years before that, beginning at Oak Hall with its little square box of a store . . . the rapid extensions of the old Grand Depot building. . . . It was splendid." By this point in his life, Wanamaker had survived the death of three of his children, witnessed the destruction of his beloved summer home, faced down several economic calamities, and lived through a disappointing stint in politics. Finally, the new building he had long ago dreamed of was almost finished. "All these things," he wrote, "fill me not only with wonder, but with great thanksgiving that I have been permitted to toil so long." He paused as he often did at major turning points in his business and gave thanks to "the Heavenly Father to have permitted me to live to see so much of His hand of love toward me in the things that are surrounding me to-day."[4] He saw the building as a sign of God's endorsement of his business and religious activities.

Construction of the last of the three sections of the building had been completed in July 1911. That summer, another celebration ensued. In the store's atrium, the installation of the mammoth organ was nearly finished and now functioning. Shoppers were invited to witness the first playing of the instrument on July 22 in a dedication ceremony for "The Reigning Monarch of All Instruments." Giving the organ an even more regal aura, the dedication of the organ and its first playing were timed to coincide exactly with another event across the ocean—the coronation of King George and Queen Mary of England.[5] As the processional at Westminster Abbey in London took its first steps to the sound of the church's organ, Wanamaker's instrument roared to life backed by a 550-member chorus singing "Zadok the Priest" and "The King Shall Rejoice" to celebrate the king and queen's crowning and the first music of the Wanamaker organ. The Wanamaker Cadets marched in a parade down the center of the Grand Court that day, in what would become a standard practice for store events and rituals.

In late October of that same year, the store family of 6,500 employees gathered to celebrate the building and Wanamaker's fifty years in business. The employees processed down the center of the new building before a reviewing stand, singing "Onward Christian Soldiers." That same evening, they put on a pageant of the origin story of the store and its place in the history of Philadelphia—a history that was retold repeatedly in store literature.[6] Linking the store's history with that of city and nation was one of the many ways Wanamaker and his employees crafted the civic identity of the store.

Concluding the year of celebrations, the ceremonies reached a crescendo with the formal dedication of the new building on the last day of December. A chorus, now one thousand voices strong, sang several compositions commissioned for the occasion. The store organ thundered alongside two cadet bands and the store employee orchestra. During the event, President Taft delivered a speech to the packed room that acknowledged the store's role in the city as edifying public space. He told the audience, "We are here to celebrate the completion, in its highest type, of one of the most important instrumentalities in modern life for the promotion of comfort among the people" and "for the betterment of the condition of men."[7] Taft revealed that even he was affected by the space: "No one can stand here in this presence, in this magnificent structure without being awe-inspired."[8]

The Great Civilizer

Monumental in design on the outside, the interior of Wanamaker's department store sought to ignite wonder in those who came inside. Wanamaker cajoled shoppers from the comfort of home with advertisements promising not only a cornucopia of tantalizing merchandise from all over the world, but also an education in the latest home and personal fashion, technology, science of living, art, and music. A simple trip to find the perfect pair of red leather gloves trimmed in mink afforded a woman (or man) the chance to hear a lecture, attend an organ concert, tour a tastefully decorated model home interior, or spend a quiet half hour in the store's art galleries gazing at copies of works from Old Masters and the latest contemporary paintings from the Paris Salons. Capping a visit, a shopper could dine in one of the store's luxuriously appointed fine restaurants. Visiting Wanamaker's was not limited to shopping; it offered an educational experience.[9] Other department stores in the early twentieth century offered similar delights of music and art, leading them to be described by some as more of a "club house" or an "amusement place" than a retail store.[10] While the French and

German department stores inspired his choices with their jaw-dropping interiors, Wanamaker took a page from his YMCA work and used these attractions to woo customers for his intertwined purposes of selling and shaping people's taste—an effort that had religious import.

Wanamaker promoted his stores as "centers of learning" and "an ever-changing educational museum" for the "multitudes" of shoppers that came every day.[11] The changing nature of the displays was meant to keep customers' interest but also offered something that museums and great exhibitions could not—a curated cult of the new, displayed more enticingly, and for sale. Wanamaker wanted people to linger not only to buy, but to learn. He explained that the goal was more than the freedom to browse. As he explained, "One's eyes are the great gateways to knowledge," and thus "in Wanamaker's everyone is free to look, to see, to learn and to enjoy without feeling any obligation to buy."[12] At least according to store literature, learning was equal to buying. Wanamaker's heavy use of store floor space for cultural offerings suggests that he meant it.

The interior provided a feast for the eyes like many of the department stores of the day; however, Wanamaker took care to construct his store's central space to echo a great church. If his intention proved too subtle for the everyday, during Christmas and Easter the store often took on the appearance of a Gothic cathedral. For his purposes, Wanamaker reached beyond the buying appetites of the consumer. He wanted to stir their souls and invite them to reach higher moral fortitude. The beautiful interiors of the store and the lavish music programs called the customers to participate in a sensory education in visual and aural aesthetics.[13]

Music permeated the store. It echoed out of the two exotically decorated concert venues, the Egyptian and Greek Halls. The store employees' orchestras, bands, and choruses produced music for concerts and ceremonies. And music poured out of the heart of the store into nearly the entire building through the centrally located Great Organ. Wanamaker created his store as a place to shop and for the burgeoning white middle and upper classes to receive an education on taste.[14] The store's anniversary *Golden Book* unabashedly asserted, "Commerce is the great civilizer."[15] The store's atrium, the Grand Court, served as Wanamaker's principal pedagogue.

Atriums, rotundas, and grand halls were common in early department store buildings to allow natural light to permeate the depths of the store. Wanamaker's architect Burnham employed the feature in all of his department store designs.[16] He felt that light was necessary not only to demonstrate the quality of goods but also to make the space uplifting. The Filene's and Gimbels buildings contained atriums, while Marshall Field's Chicago State Street store boasted two—with one seven-story atrium sporting a dazzling Tiffany iridescent glass dome ceiling.[17] But Wanamaker's atrium dwarfed them all. A glass rooftop that admitted sunlight floated over the Grand Court seven stories above the Tennessee marble floor. Graceful vaults covered in decorative tile stretched overhead. Lining the five floors that opened to the court were stout, curved balustrades with broad tops apt for leaning, which allowed customers to view the court from multiple perspectives. The Grand Court's open design allowed it to be repurposed for a variety of store events. Indeed, only a few other American commercial buildings—a handful of new bank buildings in major cities—competed with Wanamaker's Grand Court in 1911. Only large churches, courthouses, and train stations offered similar stately spaciousness.

While the atrium was unusual in its breathtaking size and décor, Wanamaker made it stand out in other ways. He gave his atrium a name, the Grand Court of Honor, a gesture to its hoped-for significance. Its name was derived from the 1893 Columbian Exposition's central open area of lagoons and pedestrian promenades, the Court of Honor. In Chicago's White City, the spectacular Court of Honor functioned as the central axis of the extensive fairgrounds, linking the most prominent buildings with one another in a harmonious vista decorated with theatrical statuary and water features. The exposition's court drew the fair's variety of buildings into a unified whole.

Wanamaker's Grand Court functioned similarly. Connecting the multi-staged building project, it was the heart of the store and the locus of store ritual. It gave shoppers a breathtaking perspective that hinted at the store's size from inside. But the Grand Court did more than knit together parts of the massive building: it provided a place to display goods and a large flexible civic space repurposed for ceremonies, concerts, religious events, and holiday celebrations.

The Great Organ and the Eagle

Burnham and Wanamaker designed the interior of the new store down to the minute details, adding fluted columns, tray ceilings, intricate moldings, sweeping staircases, rich fabrics, elegant lighting, marble, mosaics, tile, and decadent wood paneling throughout the store's public rooms to reflect the latest in elegant interior design. Specially themed rooms took on an additional opulence. Among these were the multi-story Egyptian and Greek concert halls and a group of adjacent smaller rooms—the Byzantine Chamber, Louis XIII and Louis XIV Suites, Empire Salon, Art Nouveau Room, and Moorish Room. The rooms that sold women's dresses, Little Gray Salons, were outfitted to look like a collection of small Parisian luxury shops. Nearly the entire store was a spectacle of refinement.

Shining and gleaming with the latest in building design, the store felt different with its climate-control systems that circulated cool or warm filtered air as needed. The ventilation systems fostered an atmosphere that was meant to be refreshing to shoppers (and those who worked at the store) as they came off the buzzing city streets into a well of calm and beauty. The multitude of services offered to customers—or store guests, as Wanamaker liked to call them—unburdened them of hats, coats, and packages. Thoughtful touches aimed at customer comfort and delight were spread throughout the building. But easily the most seductive part of the building was the Grand Court.

For customers entering the store through one of its majestic colon-naded entries that suggested an ancient Greek or Roman temple, the Grand Court, located in the center of the store, was easy to stumble into, and the wide marble arches beckoned customers into the vast open space. Its size alone supplied drama. The elegant architectural details gave the room a palatial feel, drastically different from many stores that felt confined and cluttered. A store publication described the role of the Grand Court as "an imposing and artistic center for the store, binding all the rest together around it, and creating a certain atmosphere that the most remote corners of the store feel bound to reproduce."[18] The Grand Court served, too, as the spiritual center of Wanamaker's store.

Two features dominated the immense court and communicated Wanamaker's commitments—a colossal bronze eagle sculpture and the majestic organ, both from the 1904 Louisiana Purchase World's Fair in St. Louis.[19] The Grand Court was connected to the great exhibitions, and the eagle was another link between the store and the fairs. Wanamaker purportedly purchased the mammoth eagle to serve as an example of fine art statuary along with the statues of Joan of Arc, the reproduction of Diana de Gabies, and the Polyhymnia scattered throughout the store.[20] No small addition to the Grand Court, its procurement necessitated reinforcing the atrium's floor to carry the weight of the 2,500-pound bronze sculpture and its large 4,500-pound granite base.[21] The placement of the eagle in the center of the court created other roles for it. Visible from the edges of the court and from the floors above, it drew shoppers into the heart of the store. For some, it was a curiosity, while others came to view it as a familiar friend. As with other public bronze sculptures, shoppers and their children could not resist touching the eagle, making its tail feathers and talons glow from the caresses of millions.

The eagle signaled to customers the store's patriotism. Frequently photographed surrounded by American flags and the organ, it represented God and country, powerful symbols of a blossoming Protestant civil religion. Ever present during the concerts and public functions, the sculpture provided orientation in a sea of people, and, perhaps because of this, the eagle quickly became a symbol of the store, much like the exterior grand clock at Marshall Field's. Generations of Philadelphians made the eagle their rendezvous spot, making the phrase "Meet me at the eagle" a well-known shorthand for a convenient place to meet in central Philadelphia. The eagle was something to see and somewhere to meet.

The eagle also drew attention to the other occupant in the Grand Court imported from the St. Louis Exposition, the Great Organ. If shoppers initially missed the organ, the eagle's gaze drew their eyes to look at it towering above. From the beginning, organ music held a significant place in the life of Wanamaker's stores. He installed his first organ at the Grand Depot in 1876 in a period when the popularity of organs was on the rise in home parlors, stunning new and remodeled churches, and concert halls and outdoor tabernacles like the one at Chautauqua, New York. A gorgeous instrument, the Grand Depot organ provided a visual and aural focus in the converted train shed. Covered with intricately carved wood paneling and topped by an angel holding a torch, the organ offered a focal point for special store events and a backdrop for decorations. Other early department stores followed suit and installed their own instruments for musical concerts and entertainment. At the turn of the twentieth century, organ music began to fall out of favor in shopping settings, even while it experienced a resurgence at movie theaters, concert halls, and churches. But organ music held a significant place in the life of Wanamaker's store as early as the Grand Depot.[22]

For years, the business day at the store began for employees with an optional time of singing, inviting employees to "come when you like and enjoy it."[23] To aid this exercise, Wanamaker produced employee songbooks that included Christian hymns and patriotic tunes.[24] In a 1917 *Employee Songbook*, Wanamaker explained to them why he felt this was important: "Starting our days in this business place where thousands are employed and thousands more come and go, with hundreds" of joined voices singing, "smoothes out the wrinkles, clears out the cobwebs and sweetens the spirit at the beginning of the day."[25] He believed that "music inspiration should be a part of the daily lives and work, as well as a form of relaxation and amusement."[26]

The construction plans for the new Philadelphia store originally included two large organs for the store's Egyptian and Greek concert halls. The plan shifted sometime in 1907 when it was decided that a large organ would be installed in the Grand Court. Originally, elaborate decorations dominated the Grand Court design. The decision to add an organ to the court led to a dialing back of the decoration scheme. The decision was an unusual choice in 1911 and a major change to the space. Two explanations for the decision to add an organ circulated. One story gave the credit to Rodman. By this time, he had moved back from France and was participating in the day-to-day management of the two stores. Wanamaker had encouraged his son to take organ lessons, and Rodman had grown up playing the organ at Bethany.[27] It was during "one of [Rodman's] routine tours of inspection" of the new store as it was under construction that he saw "the possibilities of the Grand Court as a music center" and exclaimed, "I want the finest organ in the world built up there above that gallery!"[28]

Mary Vogt, one of the longtime store organists, told a competing story. She suggested that the idea of placing a magnificent organ on the second level of the Grand Court materialized after the devastating fire at Lindenhurst in 1907 destroyed the two-manual Roosevelt organ that John Wanamaker had installed for Rodman on the landing of Lindenhurst's grand staircase.[29] Since construction of the new store was still ongoing, Vogt claimed, Wanamaker decided to build an enormous organ in the court to honor his only surviving son.[30]

Whether for sentimental or visionary reasons, the Great Organ in the Grand Court carried several associations. It connected the store with many middle- and upper-class homes where parlor organs were standard and occupied a prominent place. Home organs also were read as a sign of a family's religious devotion and social status.[31] The size and location of the Wanamaker organ visually aligned it with theatre-style Protestant churches of the period that were busily adding gigantic organs to their sanctuaries and prominently placing them in the chancel in the front of the church, elevated above the first floor with an eye-catching array of pipes soaring upward.[32] Bethany Presbyterian was one of these churches.

The choice to place an organ in the Grand Court posed challenges. An instrument needed to fill not only the court but the surrounding floors opening to the atrium. Was it possible that a single organ could be built with enough power to manage the job? Research revealed that the cost of building an organ from scratch was unmanageable, and it would take years of construction to complete the project.[33] The Wanamakers began searching for a large organ to buy for the court and discovered that the 1904 St. Louis Exposition's Festival Hall concert organ lacked a home. The Festival Organ was supposed to be sold by the end of the fair; however, no one had stepped forward to purchase it.[34] Wanamaker had heard the organ play during his visit to the fair and was delighted when he discovered that the instrument sat in storage awaiting a buyer. He sent his "organ man," George W. Till, to inspect it and, after receiving positive reports despite some damage from disuse, purchased it for a heavily discounted price.[35] Till arranged for the delicate transport, while Wanamaker made it into a traveling advertisement for the new store. Eleven freight cars carried their musical cargo across the country with each car displaying a muslin sign declaring, in capital letters,

"ST. LOUIS WORLD'S FAIR ORGAN / JOHN WANAMAKER PHILADELPHIA." Once again, a piece of one of the Great Expositions had found a home in Wanamaker's store.

Installation of the organ began in the fall of 1909 while the last phase of the building was still under construction. The Festival Hall organ's original façade was an unimpressive wall of pipes in a plain case. Wanamaker arranged for a new case and exterior pipe display with the building's architect, Daniel Burnham. Reminiscent of a church organ, the new composition placed an ornate Renaissance-style tower in the center, flanked by two smaller towers. Crowning the central tower, a life-size angel balanced her delicate feet on an orb as she blew two horns. Behind the angel, 22-karat gold leaf gilded the visible pipes, and an ivory case hid some of the instrument's apparatus.[36]

Though workers had toiled nonstop to finish the organ in time for the store's dedication, the organ's first playing in July of 1911 ended up a disappointment. The organ was not fully complete, and it was obvious that, despite its immense size, it did not have the power necessary to fill the court and surrounding floors with sound. Those in attendance described the sound as "puny."[37] For two years, workers had manipulated the instrument's pipes to fit in hidden rooms around the court. To increase the organ's power, they needed more pipes. Rodman Wanamaker hired an in-house crew of specialists to begin the expansion. Making the organ powerful enough for the Grand Court required sacrificing additional centrally located retail floor space to the organ. A workshop was opened on-site, and work commenced even as the organ became a central part of the store's daily life. The project unfolded over a twenty-year period with a series of major enlargements in 1914, with the addition of four thousand pipes, three thousand more pipes added in 1917, and an ongoing series of enhancements and tweaks that stopped in 1930, long after John and Rodman had died.[38]

Making the organ larger did improve its voice and volume. It also gave the store ongoing bragging rights for the world's largest organ—and it was promoted as such, even when that was not entirely true. In the end, the organ contained approximately 28,500 pipes with 461 ranks.[39] Called the Great Organ, it merited its own guidebook discussing the sound, beauty, number of pipes, stops, pedals, and other trivia for interested customers.[40]

The installation of the organ had been a gamble. In the end, it made an impression aurally and visually. Perched high above the ground floor, its lustrous golden beauty sometimes eclipsed the merchandise by drawing customers' gazes.[41] In an area that held well over fourteen thousand people, Wanamaker and his team of workers used the organ as the ever-present accompaniment to ceremonies, musical extravaganzas, and holiday events, with the organ jumping back and forth from concert instrument to religious instrument, depending on the occasion.[42] A professional organist was hired and a daily recital schedule was developed, except on Sundays, when the store was closed. Some customers timed their visits to the store just to hear the organ play, while others were surprised by the massive instrument thundering to life.[43] Certainly, there were customers who avoided the store when the organ played.

Any doubt store guests had of the organ's status as a quasi-religious symbol would have quickly evaporated when they read the essay by French writer Honoré de Balzac on the guidebook's opening page. First included in the 1917 booklet, "The Organ" became a mainstay in the guidebook. Balzac's essay majestically described it as "the grandest, the most daring, the most magnificent of all instruments invented by human genius" and "a whole orchestra in itself." His tone turned religious when he explained that the organ is "a pedestal on which the soul poises for flight forth into space . . . to cross the Infinite that separates Heaven from Earth!" The organ served as a tool for prayer; "nothing save this hundred-voiced choir on earth can fill all the space between the kneeling men and a God hidden by the blinding light of sanctuary." Above other instruments, Balzac claimed, the organ produces music that is "strong enough to bear up the prayers of humanity to Heaven." Exclusive to no faith, the organ's prayer is "upspringing with the impulse of repentance, blended with the myriad fancies of every creed." The Balzac piece ends with the startling assertion that from "the chanting of a choir in response to the thunder of the organ, a veil is woven for God."[44]

While Balzac's essay implied the spiritual and religious significance of an organ, Alexander Russell, professor of organ music at Princeton University, wrote an essay describing playing the Wanamaker organ during a two-week period as a guest musician in which he more explicitly evoked the divine.[45] For Russell, something magical happened when he played at Wanamaker's. In an organ guidebook, Russell shared the experience of playing a Bach chorale: "As the melody of the superb hymn poured forth, the angel's trumpet seemed to be sounding and the great Court became a temple." He confided, "I had a sensation too often denied the performer; a delightful thrill, cool and exhilarating, passed up and down my spine. . . . The effect was electrifying."[46] This experience was more than a moment belonging to his imagination. When he finished his recital, he turned to look down into the court and discovered, "Below were crowds of people, standing and sitting everywhere. Above, the balustrades of five galleries were lined with crowds. . . . The sound of the organ had created this great audience."[47]

Russell had found that the organ's power cut across class lines, drawing listeners together and, as Wanamaker hoped, elevating them. Since the organ was placed in a centralized location, it was hard to avoid its sound. Many sought it out, attracted by the music. The guest musician Russell, in the same piece, recalled the daily visits of a bank clerk, motor salesman, and engineer who sometimes phoned up requests to the organist. Russell reflected, "They may not be on the subscription books of the opera or of a symphony society, but they know who Schubert was because they asked for him."[48] But Russell also received less lofty requests that he cheerfully played despite the incongruence. He explained, "In ten days, I played over one hundred different compositions, varying from the classics to 'I Hear You Calling Me.' Antithesis, do you say? Perhaps, but I believe that the sun-god of music shines in the little valleys as well as on the great mountains." He smugly added, "Not every one can live on a mountain."[49] Later in the essay, Russell appeared to understand Wanamaker's mission for the store organ. He closed with this claim: "This great organ creates music-lovers, not once in a while, but every working day in the year. It brings music into the daily life of the people."[50] The first store organist, Dr. Irvin Morgan, had a similar observation of the organ's musical effect on people. He noted the positive reaction of store employees, "I have seen them raised from nervousness and weariness in their work to cheerfulness and confidence in a manner that nothing else would produce." He, like Russell and Wanamaker, understood the organ as a "refining influence" on the class of people who were employed at the store.[51]

Music had always been a central component in the store's life. Wanamaker, and now his son Rodman, routinely commissioned pieces of music as they did with art, and developed a robust music program organized around the cadets and the Robert Ogden Association's bands, orchestras, and choruses. An organ concert was given several times a day. More music poured out of the Greek and Egyptian Halls and the Crystal Tea Room.

Music was everywhere at Wanamaker's and other American department stores. As historian Linda Tyler notes, "Department stores were not merely centers of buying and selling, but also grand theaters of cultural expression and consumer manipulation. Music played a prominent role in this new drama of consumption."[52] Other stores also created employee bands and music groups, much like Wanamaker's, while Strawbridge and Clothier, another Philadelphia store, maintained a large touring chorus, as did Chicago's Marshall Field's. Such efforts sought to reap not only goodwill but also higher sales. Used to draw customers into the stores, music productions most often accompanied sales events, holidays, and the premiere of new fall and spring fashion collections.[53] Wanamaker's organ consultant and sometime guest organist launched a new program for the store when he suggested the Grand Court host an after-hours concert. In March 1919, when the store closed, workers moved in to remove the display cases on the ground floor and add thousands of chairs on the main floor and the six floors of balconies. It was a startling transformation. The Philadelphia Orchestra and its famous conductor Leopold Stokowski played that night to an audience of twenty thousand. Charles M. Courboin was the organ soloist for the successful night, which began a new tradition. Over the years, star organists, popular composers, and musicians, including Richard Strauss and John Philip Sousa, played at Wanamaker's. The music Wanamaker promoted had cultural authority and contributed to shifting the canon of tasteful music and art in the United States.[54]

By the early twentieth century, store music productions earned prominence by tapping "well-known artists" to give special concerts no longer tied to specific retail events.[55] Retailers also tested the practice of having hidden musicians throughout the store play background music for shoppers. It soon became a best practice, with the virtues of music for shoppers and employees extolled by *Dry Goods Economics* and other professional retail magazines.[56] Wanamaker led the way among retailers, becoming what Tyler describes as "the most ambitious and audacious of music impresarios among American merchants."[57]

The Grand Court took on many guises depending on the event and decorations. For day-to-day operations, it provided bright, ample space for merchandise in glass-and-wood display cases. For special music concerts, patriotic extravaganzas, and holiday presentations, display cases were rolled away to make room for the crush of the crowd or, for more formal events, chairs. The open floors above became viewing galleries from which to witness the pageant of activity below and around the store.

Holidays and Holy Places

Wanamaker's store became famous for its sumptuous holiday decorations, especially for Christmas and Easter.[58] The practice of decorating the store lavishly for religious holidays began at the Grand Depot. As Wanamaker built out the store, the holiday decorations grew more dramatic. In 1893 Wanamaker purchased the Westinghouse lighting column he saw on display at the Columbian Exposition and put it in the central aisle of the old store. Installed in time for Christmas, it showed off the latest technology from the exposition and was also employed for a different purpose. The column stood in the center of the building with twenty-six hundred lamps, whose light traveled from the base all the way to the top "when it shoots off into forked lighting to the four points of the compass, emptying into revolving spheres" that whirled and flashed. The light then faded, only to repeat once again. Wanamaker's designers built a Christmas display around the column and wrote a new interpretation of the light and buzz of the machine. Store literature described the forked bolts of light emanating from the column as symbols of the "Bethlehem light; hidden sometimes by the traditions and misconceptions of men." The column showed "the heaven, the light which lighteth every man."[59]

In 1894 store decorators constructed a "winter fountain" in the transept of the center aisle of the store. The fountain, covered in lights and greenery, featured a large twenty-four-foot basin and at its center a statue of "winter," a woman in a "loosely flowing robe" who held "above her head 240 jets of water" that shoot into the air, with the water coming back down around the statue. A dome lit the water with colors moving from red to purple to orange, a series that the *Watchman* interpreted as sacrifice, passion on the cross, and a crown of glory.[60] Angels made a regular appearance at the Grand Depot; dozens of angels with outstretched wings perched on the balconies surrounding the depot's organ at Christmas and Easter. But decorations at the Grand Depot frequently looked cluttered, with statues, garland, and special exhibits crammed into the limited open areas of the store. The new building with its expansive Grand Court furnished a larger canvas for Wanamaker's team of designers to adorn.

Turning the Grand Court into a cathedral for Christmas was a natural choice. In many ways, it already resembled a church with its seven-story ceiling, marble floors, sweeping archways, and large pipe organ. Over the course of the first decade of the new building, the Wanamaker art department designers slowly built out the cathedral composition, adding layers of details onto the previous year's design. As the decorations grew more complex, an outside firm was hired to create some of the decorations. Around 1919, a full-scale Gothic cathedral plan emerged in the store and became an annual tradition. In the decades that followed, the store would bring together elements from European Gothic cathedrals, at times, authentically reproducing a particular element such as a rose window from the Reims Cathedral, a place Wanamaker had visited. The Grand Court's cathedral was not the first dalliance by the Wanamakers with Gothic architecture.

Appropriation of medieval Catholic architecture and art was a part of a larger movement by Protestants to reinterpret them as quintessentially Christian. Since the 1830s, Protestants had been actively stripping away Catholic associations and recasting Gothic architecture and art as symbols of a nostalgic "premodern" time of Christian unity, simplicity, and authority.[61] Cathedral design tapped into a larger trend that began in the nineteenth century. The aesthetic and material desires of Protestants had found expression in architecture. Starting in the 1840s and continuing in a series of waves stretching into the first part of the twentieth century, a Gothic Revival in architecture took hold in the United States.[62] Pioneered by Anglicans in England and adopted first by American Episcopalians, soon Unitarians, Presbyterians, Methodists, and Congregationalists were raising scaled-down Gothic cathedrals across the country. This trend was meant to move away from regional particularities to a universal and romantic Christianity rooted in an interdenominational

Transept in the Old Philadelphia Wanamaker Store.

Figure 5.1. Interior view of a crowded John Wanamaker's Grand Depot transept decorated with hundreds of angels for Christmas. Shoppers and employees fill the floor space and surrounding galleries. The basic structural elements of the transept became a part of the design of the Grand Court. Eye-catching and religiously themed decorations were used for holiday displays from the earliest days of Wanamaker's business. The Depot's organ pipes are visible on the right of the picture. Musicians stand on a balcony in front of the organ; the arrangement was replicated in the Grand Court on a larger scale.

Protestant ethos. Its participants found within the beautiful lines and ornate design the values and ideas of Protestantism. Churches across denominations embraced the ornate style. The Gothic style thrived in Philadelphia with two churches leading the revival—St. James the Less and St. Mark's.[63] Both were Episcopalian congregations founded within a year of each other and served Philadelphia's established and emerging upper class.

Rodman Wanamaker had become deeply invested in the Gothic Revival movement starting around the time of his marriage to Fernanda. The year after Rodman graduated from Princeton, he married Fernanda de Henry (sometimes spelled de Henri) in the church where she was baptized and confirmed, St. Mark's Episcopal Church. Although the couple moved to Paris for a decade, their ties with home remained enduring. Fernanda served on the church's altar guild, and she was deeply attached to her home congregation.

His father and family visited often, and Rodman and Fernanda traveled back to the United States too. The rhythm of the bicontinental lifestyle came to a sudden halt when at the age of thirty-six Fernanda fell gravely ill and died. Rodman was devastated. He returned to the United States and, in his grief, found solace in Fernanda's church, the site where they had married. Rodman's return to Philadelphia came just as the Reverend Dr. Alfred Mortimer was settling in as new rector of St. Mark's. Devoted to High Church ritual complete with incense and rich fabrics for vestments, Mortimer envisioned a decorated interior that aided the worship and ritual experience of the church.[64] Under his leadership, the congregation's membership expanded rapidly with many of Philadelphia's wealthiest residents as its members. With Mortimer's encouragement, the congregation answered his call for enhancing the church's interior and ritual pieces. New flooring was installed, and the altar was covered in marble. He believed that beauty and refined decorations heightened emotion in the worship.

Mortimer guided Rodman's donations. Within two months of her death, Rodman and the church had agreed to the addition of a "Lady Chapel" for his sweet Fernanda. He committed to more than the structure; he also promised to furnish the chapel with an elaborate altar and communion ware. Underneath the altar, a crypt was built. Fernanda, who had been buried at the churchyard of St. James the Less, was moved to St. Mark's upon completion of the crypt.

Rodman loved beautiful objects and continued to make substantial contributions to St. Mark's on and off over the years, stopping for a time when he remarried, only to resume after his divorce. He made a name for himself as a benefactor through a series of grandiose and extravagant donations to Anglican churches. He gave Westminster Abbey a jeweled processional cross and the royal family's estate church a bejeweled Bible. In 1901 he donated two large Louis Comfort Tiffany stained-glass windows, "The Word" and "Contemplation," in memory of his wife to the American Church in Paris.[65] Through donations like these, he took on the role of European aristocracy who bestowed treasures to the church.[66]

The Lady Chapel was Rodman's first Gothic memorial structure. The sudden death of his brother Thomas Wanamaker in 1908 spurred Rodman to undertake another project. This time he involved his father in constructing a family mausoleum. They chose the churchyard of St. James the Less, Fernanda's first resting place before she was moved to St. Mark's crypt.[67] None of the Wanamakers were members of St. James. In consultation with the church leadership, Rodman hired a local architect, John T. Windrim, to draw the plans for the Wanamaker mausoleum. Windrim was familiar to the family. He was their choice to design the Wanamaker branch of the Free Library of Philadelphia in the Grays Ferry neighborhood, and the new Lindenhurst after it was destroyed by fire. However, Windrim did not have free rein on his design. The Wanamakers' decision to locate the mausoleum at St. James the Less came with some restrictions. The Gothic design of the structure needed to complement the church building, one of the finest examples of English Gothic architecture in the United States—it was a replica of a thirteenth-century church from Cambridgeshire, England.[68] To ensure accuracy, English-born and trained architect Henry Vaughan of Boston, who later went on to design other famous American Gothic churches, including the Washington Cathedral and three chapels of St. John the Divine, consulted on the project. The Wanamaker Tower was built during the same period the Wanamakers constructed their new store building in Philadelphia, and was completed in 1908. Dedicated to Thomas, who had died the year before, the tower accommodated two small chapels and a crypt. The bell tower received a fifteen-bell carillon in 1915.[69]

At Christmas and Easter, Gothic architecture brought the Grand Court's church-like qualities to the fore. In the Grand Depot, Wanamaker had celebrated Christmas in its religious vein with music and decorations in the middle of his commercial empire. He continued the tradition in his 1911 building with intricate designs executed by his able designers that sought to create a Protestant Christmas experience—carefully crafted and staged to please a broad audience and symbolize Protestant Christian unity.

Wanamaker's store holiday displays proselytized thousands of shoppers on how to decorate and on what the focus of Christmas ought to be. Embracing the neo-Gothic movement's fascination with a medieval aesthetic, the Wanamakers instructed their decorators to design Gothic cathedrals with dazzling shrines devoted to the story of baby Jesus. Here, the authenticity cherished in Tanner and Munkácsy's paintings was left behind for a sensual and highly imaginative concoction of shining, flowing fabrics, sparkling jewels, stunning paintings, and colorful light, all with the Great Organ visible in the background, filling the building with the sound of church at appointed hours. Symbolism was everywhere, telling a number of stories all at once.

The Wanamaker cathedrals required a guidebook and signage to decipher the rich symbolism. The religious meaning of the holiday was not discreet at Wanamaker's; rather, images of the Christ child in his mother's arms, paintings of the Magi, and biblical quotations conveyed the season's Christian focus.[70]

For the 1926 Christmas, a collection of twelve murals depicted "The Progress of Civilization" through images of twelve countries. The series began with Egypt, followed by Judea, and culminated, not surprisingly for Wanamaker, with France and America. Highlighting the importance of the store's Christmas decorations, the guidebook noted that "there is no place, save their own hearthstones, where the public feel more completely at home than in this vast and hospitable hall." The store's opening and closing each day was marked by the singing of "beloved Christmas Carols" where "all listen" and "many join the singing." The publication pointed out various Christian symbols: "The five-pointed stars signify 'The Creator'" and "the stars with seven points symbolize 'The Perfect Number'" while the "twelve-pointed stars are 'The Disciples.'" Backlit in a stained-glass window was "The White Cross of Light," the cross repre-

Figure 5.2. Wanamaker's Grand Court at Christmas time, ca. 1920s. Many of the decorations were used year after year in the displays as more pieces were added.

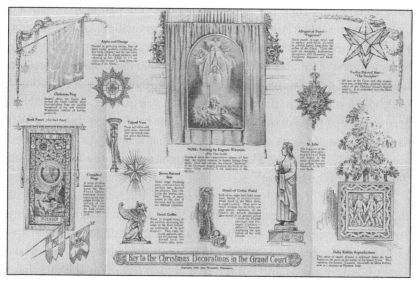

Figure 5.3. "The Grand Court at Christmas" guidebook. A key to the symbolism of a Wanamaker Christmas Cathedral. On the inside cover, the booklet quotes Wanamaker: "I said to myself, I was in a Temple."

senting God and the Holy Spirit. Twelve statues of the disciples, made to look like carvings that belonged in a European cathedral, appeared year after year in different places in the Grand Court. Store guides named each disciple and explained the symbolism of what each held in his hands or what stood at his feet. Byzantine columns glittered with gold and paste jewels at either end of the court. Framing the entrance into the court, twelve large crosses stood surrounded by red lights and emblazoned with the first two letters of the name Christ in Greek. Salon paintings made appearances in the court if they matched the theme. For instance, *Les rois mages*, from the 1924 Paris Salon, was displayed when the Magi were a central element of the year's theme.

The next year, for the 1927 Christmas, the Wanamaker cathedral shared some of the same elements from the year before and added special Christmas flags of blue and silver, and a collection of Crusaders' flags to represent the seven campaigns to retake the Holy Land from 1096 to 1370. Gracing the arches in the court, "flashing clear-blue stars" represented "The Creator," and a collection of twelve batik panels represented the twelve months. Four other panels illustrated "the Elements—Earth, Air, Water,

Fire." Allegorical panels finished in an antique gold patina and encircled by lights represented "Antiquity, architecture, navigation, Old Testament, New Testament, and Paganism," among others. A rotating collection of reproductions of knights and military regimental flags, hand-painted on silk, added a layer of romance and mystery to Grand Court decorations.[71]

People responded to the decorations with solemn awe. A store advertisement noted that "many men remove their hats" when they visit Wanamaker's Grand Court at Christmas and that visitors are "transported out of a hurly-burly world" and "are caught up with the radiance and symbolism" of the holiday.[72]

At the center of the Christmas display was the Nativity—the Christ child cradled in a manger dramatically lit by a beam of light streaming down from the ceiling.[73] Later, Wanamaker commissioned a French artist to paint a large, eye-catching canvas with the baby Jesus and Mary surrounded by angels and bathed in a golden light. For the merchant and at least some of his customers, the message was clear.[74] Christ was at the center of Christmas and at the center of the commercial world of his department store. But this space, like all sacred space, was contested.[75] Some non-Christians felt excluded, as did those who abhorred the placement of a Christmas spectacle in a store; yet thousands did respond to Wanamaker's call to share the holidays with him, and for many it became a part of their Christmas tradition to participate in the department store's festivities in the Grand Court, creating a ritual and religious association with the space.

Singing Christmas carols transformed into a Philadelphia holiday staple starting in 1918, when Wanamaker invited shoppers to sing Christmas carols at the end of the shopping day in the weeks leading up to Christmas. Thousands gathered nightly in the Grand Court, clutching their store-printed souvenir songbooks, which Wanamaker first printed in 1918. Each songbook opened with an edifying message from Wanamaker to the carolers. In the first songbook, the message inside the cover framed the songs as anthems proclaiming the glory of God:

> Glory to God! "the sounding skies
> Loud with their anthems ring—
> peace to the earth, good-will to men,
> From heaven's eternal King!"

The following year's edition carried the title "Christmas Carols in the Grand Court" and opened with a theological poem:

> Lie circles widening round
>   Upon a clearer, blue river,
> Orb after orb, the wondrous sound
>   Is echoed on forever:
> Glory to God on high, on earth be peace,
> And love toward men of love—salvation and release.[76]

Carols for 1919 included "Good Christian Men Rejoice," "Joy to the World," and "Once, in the Royal City of King David," as well as "O Come, All Ye Faithful."[77] Emphasizing religious hymns over seasonal tunes, Christmas caroling at Wanamaker's was a Protestant Christian event. Even as the songbook grew over the years and patriotic songs were added to the repertoire, the last hymn was always "Onward Christian Soldiers."[78]

Wanamaker thought of Christmas as far more than a holiday for making money, although he did realize that it was one of the most lucrative seasons in the life of his store. He resisted candy-coating the holiday and persisted in conveying his Christian devotion. In another undated Christmas songbook, he plainly articulated his belief: "For thousands of years the expectant world waited for the Christmas that came with its wonderful gifts over which the angels sang 'peace on earth, good will to men.'" Wanamaker did not want shoppers to confuse his store's grand decorations with another understanding of the holiday. He attested, "Christmas is a man born, not a sentiment." Suggesting a way to align oneself properly with the intent of Christmas, he instructed shoppers, "To get right with Christmas would make men right with one another in this old world, almost falling to pieces. Let us pay real tribute to Christmas."[79] The "real" Christmas was the one Wanamaker presented—it was a mix of Jesus and the popular medieval aesthetic of the neo-Gothic movement.

Easter received similar treatment at Wanamaker's, and the store sometimes outstripped local churches' efforts to celebrate the important day in the Christian calendar.[80] One store advertisement told shoppers to visit the store during Easter for "spiritual refreshment and happiness"

Figure 5.4. Munkácsy's *Christ before Pilate* Easter crowd. During the holidays, Wanamaker's Grand Court filled with people for the special ceremonies, organ and other musical concerts, and at Christmas time for caroling. The eagle sits in the center of the crowd and a decorative placard shares information about the painting and the artist.

that could be found among the sea of flowers in the Grand Court. Simply by "standing in the Grand Court," shoppers received reassurance that "it would be impossible to fail to receive a sense of immense blessing that Easter time again confers upon the world" and that at Wanamaker's they would find "the true Easter spirit."[81]

Every year, the Grand Court was awash in decadent arrangements of Easter lilies, angels, palms, educational displays of glittering ecclesiastical vestments, and stunning tapestries.[82] Embellished lampshades that hovered over store counters in the Grand Court proclaimed, "He is Risen!" and "Alleluia!" At Wanamaker's, Easter constituted flowers, spring fashion, and Jesus's resurrection.

In 1893 a lawn of green grass was cultivated along the arcade leading from Chestnut Street, and "cherry-trees and apple-trees" appearing to

Figure 5.5. As with the Christmas displays, Wanamaker's Easter needed interpretation as well. Here is an interpretative placard from 1932 explaining the intricate Christmas symbolism throughout the Grand Court. The angel statue appears to be presenting the placard to viewers. Munkácsy's *Christ before Pilate* can be seen in the right-hand corner of the photograph. The Easter lampshades and the biblically themed shields used for many years are also visible.

be in full bloom decorated the pastoral scene. On balconies above, boys working for the firm sprayed "the perfume of apple blossom down upon the people and the trees." The *Store News* likened it to walking through a place where "the perfume of mothers' prayers"—and thus home— misted down on the shoppers.[83]

Lent had a place at the store festivities as well. Prior to 1922, during the forty days leading up to Easter customers were specifically invited to the store's art galleries for quiet contemplation of two Munkácsy paintings depicting Jesus's trial and crucifixion. After John Wanamaker's death, the paintings moved to a place of prominence in the Grand Court during the Lenten season.

Civic Virtue

For national holidays and special events, the Grand Court served as a patriotic ritual site. Flags were a constant presence at the store. Clusters of American flags trimmed the store entrances, hung from the building, adorned the Great Organ, at times surrounded the eagle, and were ceremonially carried through the store by cadets. On the announcement of the armistice in 1918, hundreds of American flags were displayed in the store. In addition, Wanamaker and his son Rodman had custom flags created for store events and special anniversaries. Each of the different branches of the Wanamaker Cadets had their own flags that were used for store ceremonies.

Store newspaper advertisements publicized the public rituals. Frequently, the celebrations and commemorations extended over the entire day to give shoppers ample opportunity to experience the store's ritual offerings. Ritual schedules were listed with times and descriptions in newspaper advertisements announcing the schedule of mini-concerts featuring the store's bands, chorus, and the organ, making it possible for a shopper to encounter a part of the celebration throughout the day.

An example of a special ceremony was the one following the death of former president Theodore Roosevelt in 1919. A solemn tribute took place in the court, with Wanamaker's military band and his cadets serving as the liturgists for the ceremony. The court, decorated in flags, included a display of Roosevelt's picture and a program for the event to start at two o'clock sharp. In crisp military fashion, the liturgy unfolded:

1. Chopin's funeral march
2. Cadets march in to the beat of the drum
3. Present arms and three rolls of the drum
4. *Lead Kindly Light*, Brass Quartet
5. One minute of Silence
6. *Taps*
7. Cadets march out.[84]

Different versions of the liturgy would be repeated throughout the day, cycling through the store's military bands, orchestras, and other musical options Wanamaker's had through its employee programs. Patriotic events peppered the schedule of the Grand Court with the ever-present Wanamaker Cadets always ready to lend an official and military flair to the proceedings.

Just as the organ maintained a religious tone in the Grand Court, so Wanamaker found a way to keep a patriotic and civic tone in other parts of the building with the installation of a series of plaques mounted on the store's pillars and walls. The messages conveyed the civic virtues Wanamaker held most dear to those who paused and read the signs. In case someone missed them, store guides discussed the plaques and their meaning. They included excerpts from some of the same speeches found in the booklets that Wanamaker distributed to shoppers, including George Washington's Farewell Address and Lincoln's Gettysburg Address. In addition, one plaque displayed Henry Lee's oft-quoted eulogy of the first president, "First in War—First in Peace—First in the Hearts of His Countrymen."[85] Linking his methods of retail with the founder of Philadelphia, Wanamaker installed a plaque honoring William Penn with a quotation from his Philadelphia Elm Treaty: "We are met on the broad pathway of good faith and good will so that no advantage is to be taken on either side, but all shall be openness, brotherhood and love."[86] Nearby, Ulysses S. Grant's plaque offered a series of quotations from his presidency, about the Civil War, and regarding his visit to the store in 1877.[87] Wanamaker had mapped the history of Philadelphia and the

United States onto the history of the store. He had turned the ground floor into a patriotic museum.

On the side of the court where President William Howard Taft had stood for the dedication of the store, a brass star marked the spot on the marble floor, with a plaque explaining the star's significance. For Wanamaker, an active Republican, Taft's visit was a significant nod to his efforts for the Grand Old Party, as well as a symbol of shifting attitudes about the interaction of politics and business. For Wanamaker, civic virtue was intertwined with moral virtue. To be a virtuous individual was to embrace civic virtue. One needed to be moral to be a good citizen. Wanamaker himself joined the ranks of great men he had chosen to be honored on the columns with a plaque reiterating his own words on the store's cornerstone: "Let those who follow me continue to build with the plumb of honor, the level of truth, and the square of integrity, education, courtesy, and mutuality."[88] The plaques complemented the pictures hanging in his personal office upstairs, where images of Ulysses S. Grant, Theodore Roosevelt, and Abraham Lincoln decorated the walls, along with copies of the Gettysburg Address and other American history memorabilia.

In 1881 and in the following years, Wanamaker distributed booklets to shoppers with a copy of the Constitution, the Bill of Rights, Lincoln's Gettysburg Address, and George Washington's Farewell Address. There was no charge for the booklets as long as customers vowed to read the entire contents and sign a pledge on the back cover to seal the promise that they had read the words.[89]

John Wanamaker, whose birthday and store anniversaries received ceremonial attention every year while he was living, remained a part of the store's ritual rhythm after his death. For many years, on his birthday employees would place one of the several oil painting portraits or a bust of "The Founder" in front of the eagle. Flags representing both stores, the Wanamaker Cadets in New York and Philadelphia, and other groups clustered behind the painting along with bouquets of flowers and wreaths laid as offerings to the dead merchant.[90] With each year, the displays became more ornate.

Such religious and patriotic festivals and adornments in the Grand Court could easily be dismissed as pandering for sales, and some customers may have taken the plaques this way. Yet Wanamaker made

Figure 5.6. Every year following his death, Wanamaker's birthday was celebrated in the store. His portrait was placed in the Grand Court in front of the eagle. Flowers and other offerings from the Wanamaker Cadets and employees were placed next to and at the foot of the portrait. The celebration shown here was in 1930, eight years after his death.

these efforts sincerely, hoping to share a bit of his wisdom with those who came to shop with him. They translated his Protestant Christian ethos into the commercial space in a new way. He hoped that shoppers took home with their merchandise the markers of good character and morality—the virtues of a genteel Protestant Christianity.

* * *

In the spring of March 1922, Dennis F. Crolly, "a stranger," sent a letter to Wanamaker to express gratitude for the store's interior. The new building was ten years old now and still dazzled. Crolly commented on the "myriad clustered lights" and how they beautifully played off of the "crystal glass and burnished metal and polished wood; and bewildering variety of articles." Beautifully lit and displayed merchandise caught his eye, and so did the art. Crolly mentioned "the pictures; the sculptures; the tapestries" and asserted that "whoever planned the storescape and set the seal of beauty on it deserved the holy name of artist." For him, the Wanamaker store was a place of "sheer beauty" that evoked delight. Crolly observed the crowd in the Grand Court, a "moving, busy, happy, smiling, chatting throng," and noted how the people gathered there "gave it all a soul." What he saw before him was what he called "the ideal represented in the living reality," an ideal that "edified the Anglo-Saxon." He went on to say that he had heard that Wanamaker was "a great merchant." Now that he had visited the store, his admiration had increased. Crolly ended his letter declaring to Wanamaker, "You are a great man."[91]

Wanamaker wanted his store to do more than sell goods. Art and commerce went hand in hand, and his success beyond mere consumerism. He sought to use his store interior to foster a particular Christian vision of community deeply steeped in Protestant middle-class values and a form of Christian taste. Wanamaker wanted to awaken his customers' souls and invite them to reach a higher morality. To acquire Christian taste was to appreciate beauty, which Wanamaker believed would lift the spirit closer to God, and to embrace the values of trustworthiness, simplicity, control, discipline, and balance, which he thought could be nurtured by one's physical environment and material practices. In other words, to embrace Christian taste was not only to gain an aesthetic education but also to experience moral uplift. Wanamaker pursued this commitment most intentionally in the Grand Court by creating a space that was both beautiful and awe-inspiring. He shaped it into a sacred space through architecture, rituals, and performances. These Christian and civic expressions created religious sensations cultivated by fusing religious symbols and sentiment with spaces and practices of consumption. His displays contributed to the creation of civic Christian holidays.

Teasing out the values of morality, orderliness, and discipline that Moody's revival had emphasized, Wanamaker merged them with Bushnell's Christian nurture and Ruskin's promotion of beauty as he designed the interior of his building to generate emotions in his shoppers. One of the aspects Wanamaker loved about the type of revivalism the Businessmen's Revival and Moody were known for was the controlled, disciplined, and balanced stirring of emotions. By designing and creating the interior of the Wanamaker Building, Wanamaker sought to continue what had started on that site over twenty-five years before when Moody and Sankey had captivated thousands on his future sales floor. The new building was its own form of religious excitement, controlled and disciplined through granite and communicated through its interior design. The spacious Grand Court, the enormous organ, the musical performances, the fine art, the holiday displays—all this and more communicated to shoppers a message of morality and hope and possibility. Wanamaker had created a Protestant temple in the middle of his Philadelphia department store empire. He peddled more than just merchandise. He presented to shoppers a cultural education and a place to publicly celebrate the holidays.

Shoppers heartily responded, making Wanamaker's department store a part of their holiday traditions and cultural excursions.

Conclusion

The store is a personification of ideals.
—Wanamaker Store Guide

A light snow fell in the early morning of December 14, 1922, on the gathering crowd waiting outside Bethany Presbyterian Church. They waited for the casket of John Wanamaker to make its way from his mansion on Walnut Street to the church he had founded.[1] Wanamaker had died at home two days earlier at the age of eighty-four. Never retiring from his business or church, he had been at work just days before he took to his bed with a bad cough, as he did nearly every December, but this time he did not recover. The *Philadelphia Inquirer* announced his death the next day on the front page, declaring, "World's Greatest Merchant and Philadelphia's Leader in Business, Philanthropy, Religion and Civic Effort Ends Brave Fight for Life."[2] Wanamaker had outlived all but one of his siblings, his wife, and three of his children, including his oldest son, Thomas, as well as a daughter-in-law. Of his children, his son Rodman and two daughters, Minnie and Lillie, remained.[3]

At 9:20 a.m. the doors of Bethany opened, and an estimated twenty thousand people solemnly processed past Wanamaker lying in state. The church overflowed with people and the heavy scent of more than two hundred floral arrangements. At 2:00 p.m. the funeral began, and many Philadelphians paused in their work or closed the doors of their businesses to remember the great merchant for a five-minute silence. The Philadelphia Stock Exchange stopped trading at the time of the funeral.

The Wanamaker's stores had shuttered their doors and draped the windows in bolts of black fabric, casting the business in mourning. Retailers in Philadelphia and New York took out large advertisements in local newspapers to honor Wanamaker and his contributions to retail. Countless city and service organizations passed resolutions recognizing his philanthropy. Telegrams and letters of condolence poured in from across the globe; those sending messages of sympathy included mere acquaintances, people who had shopped at his department stores, and powerful intimates such as Commander Evangeline Booth of the Salvation Army and President Warren G. Harding.

Wanamaker's final resting place was not Philadelphia's Laurel Hill Cemetery, where many of the city's elite went for their eternal slumber. He was not buried in one of the historic Presbyterian cemeteries either. Instead, Wanamaker's casket was interred in a place that echoed the Christmas cathedral he had constructed in his store; he was buried in a large English Gothic-revival bell tower mausoleum in the quiet churchyard cemetery of the English Gothic-styled St. James the Less, an Episcopal church.

The outpouring of grief at Wanamaker's funeral demonstrates that he was more than a successful businessman and the founder of a large Sunday school and church. People lamented his passing because he had changed the emotional and material landscapes of their lives. Wanamaker led and supported dozens of civic programs aimed at improving the urban world and its inhabitants. Through his church and stores, he opened up new and beautiful spaces in the middle of the city that focused on service and moral reform.

Wanamaker had changed the way people shopped, dined, and spent their free time. He had entered people's homes through the goods he sold—the fashions they wore, the furniture they selected, the art they hung on their walls—and the newspaper editorial advertisements he wrote six days a week. He had made fashion, music, art, history, and refinement accessible. He crafted public celebrations that were Christian and patriotic. He tried to make his store a "temple of culture." He provided educational opportunities and a path to bodily improvement that offered upward mobility for some of the thousands of young men and women who worked for him, while at the same time reinforcing racial and gender hierarchies that stymied the potential of African Americans, women, and immigrants. Wanamaker had consciously and unconsciously defined what it meant to be a valued American citizen—Protestant, white, and (at least in dress, consumption, and behavior) part of the developing middling classes—against the new demographics introduced by immigration and migration. He offered a vision of what people should be or, at the very least, what they could aspire to be.

By doing so, he had become a tastemaker—a responsibility he felt was charged with religious and moral obligation that he took on with evangelistic zeal. It was an endeavor that also made him lots of money, which he understood as God's blessing. In many ways, he had achieved what he had set out to do—to morally uplift the city and commerce or, more specifically, at least some of its inhabitants.

Protestants and Business

When Wanamaker opened his first store, Oak Hall, in 1861, department stores had not yet emerged on the urban landscape. As we have seen, many Protestants saw business as antithetical to religion, despite a long habit of blending religion and business. While Dwight L. Moody, the famous revivalist, had used business methods to enhance his revival tours, he, like many Protestants, adhered to a double standard. Moody and other Protestant religious leaders relied on business for financial underwriting for their projects and programs. Yet in the eyes of Protestant leaders, business—especially retail—remained problematic primarily due to its reputation of slack ethics. When Moody's friend Wanamaker turned away from full-time ministry to open a large store, he judged the decision with disdain. After Wanamaker's dynamic success with the opening of the Grand Depot annex to the Centennial Exhibition, Moody had urged him to leave his business behind to join Moody's ministry team. He feared that Wanamaker's triumphs in business would destroy his fiercely held religious commitments. At the same time, Moody feared losing the merchant's friendship. Wanamaker met many of Moody's pleas with silence, leading the revivalist to write several contrite letters asking for financial assistance for his struggling seminary in Northfield, Massachusetts.[4]

Wanamaker had accepted another point of view on business and religion, one whose development was fostered by the YMCA and other moral reform movements. For sixty-one years, Wanamaker mixed his business and religious commitments in the public space of his stores and brought his business acumen to his religious work in an effort to reform the urban world. He extended his reform work through his department stores. Wanamaker's efforts serve as a rich case study for understanding the development of relationships between religion, business, aesthetics, and commerce in the United States. Far from an anomaly, his innovative efforts are a part of a long line of Protestant efforts to blend religion and business, efforts that expanded in the twentieth century and continue today. Wanamaker exemplified a Protestant synthesis—making the old-time religion into something new.

Wanamaker saw business and religion as mutually supportive and beneficial. He took the money he earned from the YMCA to start his successful dry goods store. To make sense of his increasing wealth in light of his religious values, Wanamaker had also embraced and then promulgated what he called "practical religion," a version of Conwell's prosperity gospel. He came to understand his success as a sign of God's approval and his hard work. He took the money he made from his retail store to finance a myriad of religious organizations and endeavors.

Wanamaker and a generation of business leaders intentionally set out to resolve the tensions between business and religion and the trouble-some ethics of retail. Through what he called a "businessman's gospel," they tried to remake business into a Christian endeavor—one that followed the "Golden Rule" of the New Testament.[5] Wanamaker did so through the way he conducted business, advertised, trained his employees, and disseminated his business methods in an effort to evangelize others. Certainly, there were business leaders who used religion as a way to stave off criticism, as a method to induce employee loyalty, and a cheap ploy to make more money. Some business leaders gave money and support to religious concerns while pursuing a business agenda that appeared at odds with their religious values. But some sincerely attempted to bring together their religious and business lives for mutual benefit and support. Far from a declension narrative, a story that demonstrates the decline of American Protestantism and traces its diminishment to capitalism's co-opting of religion, this is a story of adaptation and expansion. As Robert S. Ogden described Wanamaker's approach, "Business is . . . not an end in itself, therein it is a means toward an end: a means for building up all virtues . . . making the life of the city a unity—stronger, more patriotic, nobler."[6] Wanamaker told friends, "my stores will be a pulpit for me."[7]

Material Practices of Moral Uplift

Protestants exercised extraordinary creativity in the nineteenth century in response to rapid changes in population, industry, and society in the United States and to a loss of cultural authority. They formulated a clever mix of strategies to address their concerns by crossing denominational and theological lines to work together, cobbling together a variety of methods, symbols, institutions, and organizations. These organizations joined Protestants from across the United States and Europe in a mutual collaboration of resources, time, and money. Leaders shared ideas through conferences, visits, and letter exchanges. The multiple reform movements cross-fertilized one another, informing the churches, civic institutions, and business. Through trial and error, they forged new institutions and movements like the YMCA, the Sunday school mission movement, the Salvation Army, settlement houses, and the women's Christian temperance movement, among dozens of others.

As we have seen, tapping into larger cultural forces that solidified in the nineteenth century, many moral reformers tied aesthetics to moral uplift and the cultivation of Protestant values. Spaces, places, artwork, music, and clothing had the power to shape people into moral citizens and to Christianize society as a type of aesthetic evangelism. The development of good taste and moral values needed beautiful and refined environments.[8] Cities needed beautiful buildings, gardens, and parks to usher in the desired changes to society. One's home and body needed to be dressed with tasteful and elegant goods, and Wanamaker and other Protestants like him were happy to provide the visual and material goods to build those environments.

Wanamaker exercised aesthetic evangelism in multiple ways. He used his building's architecture and design and his many programs to morally uplift the city and its inhabitants. Hiring Daniel Burnham, the visionary architect of Chicago's Columbian Exposition White City, was a concerted effort to affect Philadelphia through his building's design. He used his department store as an extension of his religious work at Bethany and especially the YMCA. Wanamaker's store and his art collection show how many Protestants navigated the changing urban world by imbuing the material world with spiritual and moralizing power. Wanamaker had a dual interest in promoting moral uplift through material aesthetics: these efforts both helped to align the city with Protestant values and increased profits. Wanamaker's Philadelphia building modeled this approach in its refined and luxurious appointments and the model homes and rooms it displayed. The shop windows gave glimpses to those standing on the street into a world, a life, a setting that was for purchase. For those for whom purchase was not possible, the store windows reached those looking in, bringing the carefully designed vision of the domestic world onto the city streets. Wanamaker drew the strands of moral uplift, good taste, and capitalism together.

Good taste was also equated with deportment; beautiful and well-kept spaces contributed to proper behavior. Behavior and dress became a shorthand way to distinguish visually an individual's location in society. Dress and manners enabled strangers in the city to identify those who shared a similar background, income, and home situation. The emerging middle-class aesthetics supported a new developing hierarchy.[9] Wanamaker's education and physical fitness courses offered his working-class employees a chance to move up in the ranks of society. Yet, as Bushman has pointedly noted, "Refinement created a standard for exclusion as well as a mode of association."[10] Wanamaker, other departments stores, and shoppers defined the boundaries.

As has become clear, the promises of Protestant refinement did not extend to everyone. African Americans were not afforded the same recognition for their acquisition of refined furnishings and manners. Black advancement was met by white people with open mockery through racist and demeaning caricatures in cartoons, minstrel entertainment shows, and advertisements marking African American efforts as foolhardy, among other indignities.[11] At the same time, the adoption of practices of refinement established class hierarchies within the African American community as well.

Ultimately, aesthetics and beautification centered on the socialization of the working class and the formation of a set of expectations for Protestants that mirrored the values of discipline, order, cleanliness, and purity. By exhibiting practices of good taste and refinement in his store's design and displays and through the bodies of his employees, Wanamaker lifted up consumerism and gave shopping a moral dimension. He was a part of a larger transformation in American material and visual culture. The aesthetics he promoted were developed and reinforced through print media, especially through the emergence of women's and shelter magazines; fashion and lifestyle magazines mutually reinforced an aesthetic ideal. Many Americans now had the opportunity to consume art and architecture on trips to Europe. And the aesthetics were further fueled by cultural critics and the great exhibitions, especially Chicago's White City. Wanamaker forwarded this idea through a domestic consumer aesthetic and through art displays that were both aesthetically beautiful and morally didactic. Middling class taste had a distinctively Protestant texture.

Protestants had readily adopted material practices for moral uplift. Good taste aligned with morality with a greater intensity. The sources for American taste and refinement were—unexpectedly—European aristocracy, Catholic art, and ecclesial architecture. Wanamaker's love of France was not happenstance. He followed the trend of other American elites, finding a model of living from Europe's elite by drawing on their architecture, clothing, and art scene for inspiration. Religion, on the other hand, turned to the Middle Ages with its knights and lords and ladies—an era depicted as a romantic, hegemonic Christian culture.

In one of the surprising reversals of the nineteenth century, Catholic art and medieval ecclesial architecture, once viewed with suspicion, were now appropriated by Protestants. What had been historically Catholic was now infused with Protestant meaning. Protestants and others organized and flocked to public religious festivals held in city centers and commercial buildings, piecing together new expressions of Christianity for the public square that were dramatic enough to compete with the emerging commercial cityscape. Artwork, especially Catholic paintings of biblical stories, was repurposed to play a didactic function. Catholic art and architecture became Protestant.

During this period, Protestants buttressed their churches with experiments in liturgy, architecture, and religious education, borrowing from Catholicism for many of these projects. They took to the streets, opening outreach centers for working-class immigrants and newly arrived men and women from rural America. Wanamaker took up the cause with his art galleries, history displays, and musical programs in the Grand Court, and his holiday decorations. His store functioned as an aesthetic showcase. Art galleries and displays in his lavishly decorated building had cultural power.

Wanamaker's was more than a place of employment and material consumption. It was an active site of evangelism. Generations of employees passed through the store's education programs, which were meant to cultivate a Protestant religious sensibility. Wanamaker cultivated morality through material practices that led to "formation" and moral uplift of his employees, such as summer camp, education programs in the store, and vocational training for black workers. In this process, he provided educational opportunities to all, including black workers and the women and girls who worked in his stores, but on an unequal level, thus replicating the expectations for behavior and participation for black workers and for white women workers. Here again, Wanamaker drew on existing trends, like muscular Christianity and Christian militarism, and then deployed them in new ways aimed at the moral formation of his employees. Wanamaker synthesized popular reform movements with employee programs to round out the edges in behavior, manners, and physical presentation. His goal was to develop in his shoppers and staff alike a moral character that was decidedly patriotic and Christian and, by those definitions, middle-class. These bold moves were done in service to an ideal rooted in an idea of moral superiority—a chance to remake the urban world into a Protestant one.

Commercial Christianity

In the world of department stores, Wanamaker's was not entirely unique, though he liked to position his store that way. Wanamaker's store shared many of the same characteristics of European and American department stores. Holiday decorations and celebrations, for instance, abounded in the stores up and down Market Street in Philadelphia and in other American cities. However, Wanamaker also offered new ways of being religious in addition to going to church and in some cases, instead of attending. The content of Wanamaker's holiday displays had a civilizing purpose about which he and his staff informed customers at every turn. Inside his stores, he had crafted a multisensory world that was climate-controlled while visually and aurally astounding. During the holiday season and in particular parts of the store, Wanamaker's team created utopian spaces much like the exhibition halls of the world's fairs.

Bridging the divide between home and commercial Christianity was architecture's Gothic Revival movement. By bringing the Gothic Revival inside the store, Wanamaker borrowed an architectural design that had a pan-Protestant cultural power. Even when the Grand Court was not dressed as a cathedral, the decorations were rich in intricate symbolism still recalling the cathedral form's stained-glass windows, stone, and wood carvings. Bringing together symbols that operated on religious and patriotic levels, Wanamaker crafted a new patriotic, commercial Christianity using the Great Organ, the eagle statue, hymns, and flags. He connected the dream world of the great exhibitions to his store by naming his atrium the Grand Court of Honor. By designing a space that echoed both Gothic cathedrals and the world's fairs, Wanamaker experimented with crafting a civil religion, tying together both patriotic and religious themes for the purpose of cultivating a particular and public Protestant middle-class ethos.

Wanamaker deployed a symbolic lexicon in his holiday displays that was recognizable to the people visiting his store. Weaving a variety of symbols together, Wanamaker's presented a nostalgic version of Christianity that linked a romantic "ancient" Christianity with patriotism and consumption. Wanamaker dressed his store during the holidays in an emerging pan-Christian imagery. Stained-glass windows, paintings of the Nativity complete with a beam of light focused on the manger, and angels watching graced the Grand Court's massive space. At holiday time, Wanamaker's sought to truly offer one-stop shopping—the ability to purchase gifts and train one's religious sensibilities. He was teaching his customers new ways of being religious.

At other times of the year, Wanamaker's presented musical concerts and educational lectures in a polite, refined, and beautiful space, helping to develop and curate the American canon of music. Attractive clothes, housewares, musical instruments, toys, and anything a person imagined was offered for sale at Wanamaker's. Wanamaker offered lessons in lifestyle—an upwardly mobile middle- and upper-middle-class lifestyle imbued with the values of Protestant Christianity. Wanamaker's was a place to learn how to live.

The popularity of his Christmas cathedrals and Easter arrangements during his lifetime, and the Munkácsy paintings during Lent in the

Grand Court after his death, points to the power of the store displays to meet the needs of shoppers. Christmas and Easter obscured the boundaries of shop and religious space. Tour guides invited prayer, and letters from shoppers attest to religious experiences they had at the store. Wanamaker understood his blending of religion and commerce as creating symbiosis rather than conflict. He approached the rapidly changing urban milieu with a set of strategies intended to promote Christian morality and taste.[12] His business was as important as the church he founded and the YMCA in his moral reform work. He used his store in multiple ways to improve the moral and aesthetic ambiance of the city.

Wanamaker ushered in a new way to relate to Christianity in the public sphere; Christian practice was no longer sequestered to church and home. The YMCA, Salvation Army, and women's temperance movement had brought religion out into the streets into the center of the city. Wanamaker and his store's holiday celebrations and art galleries invited the public to experience Christianity in the commercial and urban world. Wanamaker, his son, and his employees designed an electrifying spectacle of religion in public space, and people responded. He invited public expression of private religious beliefs. Wanamaker acted as a mediator of history, art, religion, and taste.

Wanamaker was not so much an innovator as an early and eager adopter of a variety of methods, approaches, and trends. His innovation came through his stitching together of multiple approaches and his deployment of them. Middling class aesthetics centered primarily on socialization. Through his education programs, summer camp, and employee training, Wanamaker attempted to mold his employees—their bodies, minds, and dress—into models of his Protestant Christian aesthetic vision. That vision reflected assumptions about race, class, gender, and ethnicity that were rooted in a muscular Christianity and white middle-class identity. Wanamaker tied aesthetics to moral uplift and the cultivation of Protestant values and character.

Though never said explicitly, many of these projects by Protestant Christians were about defining whiteness in a time when it felt threatened. While many white Protestants supported African American education and religious organizations, racial hierarchies and racism remained. Minstrel shows thrived as a popular form of entertainment and served as a way for white workers to associate themselves with other more economically secure and upwardly mobile whites. African Americans were actively kept out of jobs, and black workers were permitted to advance only in supporting roles to the wider culture, or for their "entertainment value."

Neither the division between commercial and religious nor a separation between "profane" and "sacred" existed for Wanamaker. The Grand Court served as both his stage and his pulpit, while other spaces in the store served didactic purposes. For Wanamaker, his store was a way to provide the benefits of the YMCA and church to a wider audience. Wanamaker was part of a generation of business leaders who actively set out to resolve the tensions between business and religion. Business procedures, architecture, educational programs, art, and aesthetics were more than just practices—they worked together to create a new kind of space, brick by brick, stone by stone. His store was not in competition with the church, and the church was not a project to assuage guilt. Wanamaker's store, through its business practices and then its architecture, served as an extension of his moral reform efforts. The building offered an all-encompassing opportunity: here shoppers could spend the entire day in a morally upright and wholesome space. He offered material expression to matters of the spirit. Shopping, whether it was for everyday necessities or celebration of a religious holiday, became a moral endeavor.

* * *

In 1953 a group of business, civic, media, and education leaders honored John Wanamaker's contributions to American retail at a summer black-tie dinner party on the rooftop of Chicago's Merchandise Mart, an immense Art Deco building on the north bank of the Chicago River. Joseph Kennedy, a successful businessman, former ambassador to Great Britain, and owner of the Mart, threw the party to draw attention to his hopes for American commerce, and to attract tenants to the Mart by honoring inspirational merchants of the past with the dedication of the Merchants of America Hall of Fame.[13] Earlier that year, Kennedy's staff had solicited leading retailers for names of deceased merchants who deserved the honor of being inducted into the hall of fame. Forty-one names were submitted, and his staff whittled the list down to a slate of ten merchants. The ballot was sent to leading newspaper editors of business and finance, writers, university marketing professors, and other leaders for a vote.[14] Four inductees were announced at the dinner: George Huntington Hartford, the founder of the A&P grocery store chain; Frank Winfield Woolworth, the creator of the dime store chain Woolworth's; and the department store moguls Marshall Field and John Wanamaker. To commemorate the inductees, Kennedy had commissioned a bronze sculpture of each merchant's head, four times life-size, by leading artists. He envisioned the hall of fame as an enduring yearly event to both celebrate and encourage American retail and merchandising.[15]

In the following year, Kennedy unveiled the sculptures of the first four hall of fame members at a ceremony where two more merchants were inducted into the hall of fame: Edward Albert Filene, the founder of Filene's department store, and Julius Rosenwald, of Sears, Roebuck and Company. The hall of fame lost some of its national focus in 1955 with the final two inductees, General Robert E. Wood, also from Sears and still living at the time of the ceremony, and—a late addition in 1972— Aaron Montgomery Ward, the founder of the dry goods mail-order business and chain of stores. Kennedy placed the hall of fame bronzes in a prominent public spot, along the bank of the Chicago River. The eight bronze heads were placed on slim stone plinths facing the south entrance of the Mart.

Five years later, in 1958, the great-grandson and namesake of John Wanamaker carried the optimism demonstrated five years before at the Merchants Hall of Fame in an article he wrote describing the Christmas traditions of the Wanamaker department store for the *Christian Monitor*.[16] He called his family's store one of the "historic shrines" of Philadelphia, in the same league as the Liberty Bell. He posed the question, "Why do visitors want to include Wanamaker's on their tour?" Because it was "a beautiful store," he argued, "one of the largest in the world" and "one that houses great and famous works of art" and offers "an artistic architectural beauty." He boasted that "the Grand Court is a sight not quickly forgotten." It was no less than "the crossroads of the city itself," with the Wanamaker eagle serving as a "landmark," "a meeting place of thousands," and, he proudly noted, "a part of the parlance of the city." The physical dominance of the Wanamaker department store continued.

Turning to the Christmas rituals of the store, Wanamaker described the great "Wanamaker Cathedral" that stood every year at one end of the

Grand Court. As it had been in his great-grandfather's day, it remained a "masterpiece of workmanship" depicting the great cathedrals of Europe. On the other side of the court, "gargantuan figures magnificently robed" told "the story of Christ Jesus," while perched on the surrounding ledges were "other romantic displays of the Christmas customs in many lands." Seemingly little had changed inside the store in the thirty-six years since John Wanamaker's death. His namesake store, under the guiding hand of his great-grandson, appeared to thrive as it carried on the traditions of its now long dead founder. But outside Wanamaker's, the decline of the great American department store had already begun. Retail was changing.

At the time of Wanamaker's induction to what is now called the Merchandise Mart Hall of Fame, American retailers and merchandisers harbored hope for ongoing expansion and prosperity of production and merchandising businesses in the postwar economy. However, changes that had started in the late 1920s gained momentum in the 1950s, altering the landscape of American retail. Today, only one of the stores honored in the hall of fame still exists.

Much of the magic of America's great urban department stores began to fade with increased competition and the move of urban populations to the suburbs. A proliferation of stores and brands lessened the dominance of the older stores locally and nationwide. City center department stores lost their prominence as people moved further from downtown shopping districts. Although department stores followed their shoppers by anchoring new suburban malls sprouting up across the country, the tremendous cultural power of the centrally located department store was diluted across dozens and hundreds of branches, making it impossible to hold grand events on the scale of the big urban flagship stores. Suburban stores were also much smaller than the large multifloor downtown buildings, with fewer departments, leaving little room for "wasted" floor space for an art gallery, a fancy tea room, or an educational display.

Department stores had once been the leading tastemakers of their day and fostered the growth of magazines and newspaper advertisements that extended their reach into people's homes. The large department stores with only one or two locations exercised a strong curatorial power over what goods they brought into their stores and the cities they served. Over time, print culture and stores both democratized access to fashion and material goods and deepened the furrows between classes and taste. From small towns to metropolises, department stores' fashion shows, sales, and advertisements guided American taste in home, clothing, and music and shaped American behavior—how they used rooms in the home, how they entertained, and what they wore for work in the home and at the office. They defined a sense of Americanness. As they expanded into the suburbs, taste became localized, with more store buyers making the purchasing decisions for store stock that better fit the needs of the store's location. Taste lost some, although not all, of its association with morality. The interpretation of what constitutes proper and improper dress broadened.

Yet the lifespan of the suburban mall proved shorter than the city center department store with the advent of Internet shopping. The retail market moved from city to suburbs to online. In a sense, Internet retailers are the department stores of today, with their myriad goods all found in one place. The dominance and authority of department stores as the tastemakers have been replaced by a crowded field of retailers and social media influencers that the shopper self-curates by deciding who to follow and that is also customized to the viewer through Internet history tracking.

The role of religion in department stores changed with the passing of time and the founders. Santa Claus and gingerbread men, Easter bunnies and eggs came to define the Christmas and Easter holidays instead of the baby Jesus and the cross. Other stores, recognizing religious worlds outside Christianity, brought new holidays into the pantheon of celebrations, but often in haphazard ways that attempted to correlate other religions' holy days as merely different versions of Christian ones. An exception was Wanamaker's. The flagship store kept the explicitly Christian displays into the 1960s while at the same time encorporating nonreligious symbols. Despite these changes, a fusion of Christianity and consumerism was complete.

The tensions between religion and commerce changed and moved from the store into the churches, with new church architecture sometimes holding more in common with an outlet of a mall than the church edifices of the late nineteenth and twentieth centuries. "Church shopping" became common language for people looking for a religious home, and many megachurches resemble malls with their open spaces, coffee shops, restaurants, and food courts. Some churches have started businesses to underwrite their religious institutions. A variety of church services cater to the different tastes of churchgoers—from Sunday night jazz, to praise rock band Sunday mornings, and dozens of small groups bringing together people with shared interests or concerns. Religion and commerce remain intertwined.

Wanamaker's department store began with the Moody revival, was informed by it, and in a sense, tried to ensure that the revival never ended. Or as Ruskin put it in his essay "Traffic," "Good taste is morality" and "taste is not only a part and an index of morality; it is the ONLY morality."[17]

Most of the great names in American department stores have disappeared, their enormous buildings divided into offices or destroyed by the wrecking ball to make way for new development. Those that remain, with a few exceptions, no longer carry the names of their founders. But memories of the magical worlds they built abide.

ACKNOWLEDGMENTS

Every book has a genealogy—a record of those who provided encouragement and support that helped usher the text into being. It largely began with this group of people: Janet Nobles, Anna Coffman, William A. Young, Christopher Hauer, Hal Oakley, Amy-Jill Levine, Jack Fitzmier, Claudia Shook, John Langton, David Collins, Ruppert Lovely, Marty Atherton, Shannon Smythe, Brittany Wilson, Anna Kate Shurely, Kara Lyons Pardue, Anthony Petro, Emily Mace, Ben Zeller, Ken Reynhout, Ryan Harper, Jason Bruner, Kaley Carpenter, Aaron Sizer, Josh Ziefel, Sloane Franklin, Travis McMaken, David Congden, Matt Bruce, and Carmen Maier.

Inspiration and guidance came from Leigh Eric Schmidt through his writing on consumerism and religion. Yolanda Pierce (who is wonderful and modeled good teaching and mentoring) and James Deming at Princeton Theological assisted me along the way. James Moorhead, my advisor, brought amazing insight to every conversation (and I liked to think he brought along the spirit of Sydney Ahlstrom). New colleagues appeared and offered friendship and feedback, including April Armstrong, Caleb Maskell, James Young, Vaughn Booker, Beth Stroud, and Leslie Ribovich. Conversations and shared laughter with Rachel Gross and Rachel Lindsey in the basement of 1879 Hall and beyond will always be cherished. They believed in me from the beginning.

I learned a lot about writing and scholarship from Elaine Pagels. For four years, I moonlighted as her research assistant and preceptor while she wrote her book *Revelations*. She demonstrated the importance of tenacity and dedication in writing and excellence in teaching.

DOPEsters Judith Weisenfeld, Kathryn Gin Lum, and Jessica Delgado have seen this project through all its stages—it works! Without them, I would not have finished this book. They each deserve a bottle of Pappy Van Winkle. Please note: Annie Blazer is an instigator—for which we are thankful. I am forever grateful for my editor at New York University

Press, Jennifer Hammer, her encouragement, willingness to read messy chapter drafts, and her ability to pry pages out of my hands.

I have deep gratitude for AnneMarie Luijendijk (and her family) for her friendship and teaching. I carry with me appreciation for my "go to" man Lance Jenott, John Gager for his unwavering support, and the rest of the fabulous Princeton contingent: Jeff Guest, Lorraine Fuhrman, Mary Kay Bodner, Kerry Smith, and Pat Bogdziewicz.

The American Religion Workshop at Princeton University heard early drafts of each chapter; many of the participants are thanked above. I want to also sing the praises of Michael Robertson, Amy Kittelstrom, Marie Griffith, Wallace Best, Katie Lofton, Kathi Kern, Lauren Winner, Martha Finch, Kathleen Holecher, Lindsay Reckson, Bri Hopper, and Matt Hedstrom. Research trips are better when Jenny Wiley Legath and her family are involved.

Libraries and librarians were stalwart partners in writing this book, including Kate Skrebutenas, Steve Crocco, and Julie Dawson at Princeton Theological Seminary, and Kaitlyn Pettengill and the team at the Historical Society of Pennsylvania.

I am particularly grateful to the Panel on Theological Education of the Unitarian Universalist Association for their generous fellowship, which made early research and writing of this book possible, and for mentoring by John Buehrens.

The following individuals provided encouragement and inspiration in numerous ways: Sylvester Johnson and his Northwestern American Religion Workshop (especially Matthew Smith and Jennifer Callaghan). Over the years I presented papers on Wanamaker and his store at the American Academy of Religion, the American Society of Church History, the Columbia University Religion Graduate Students' Conference, and the Unitarian Universalist Scholarship Conference— meetings where I received invaluable feedback and questions. Thanks to Karen Spielman for sharing letters John Wanamaker wrote to her grandfather. I want to thank eagle-eyed Jeremy Rehwaldt, David Morgan, Sally Promey, Paul Harvey (Sooner), Anthea Butler, Gary Dorrien, Kate Bowler, Elizabeth Jemison, Ed Blum, Richard Fenn, Claudia Espinel, Leslie Takahashi, Arvid Straube, John Tolley, Susan Stenovec (and family), Darrick Jackson, Larry Peers, Emily Clark, Cara Burnidge, John Corrigan, Christopher Cantwell, Isaac Weiner, Amy DeRogatis, Heather

Rachelle White, Anthony Pinn, Kate Carté Engel, Elesha Coffman, Rachel Wheeler, Jessica Parr, Tisa Wenger, Steve Zuckerman, Galen Gingenrich, Bruce Mickey, Ted Lang, Daniel Budd, Earl and Marilyn Holt, Brent Smith, Burton Carley, Stephanie Mitchem, Chip Hardwick, the Reverend Yukitaka Yamamoto, the Tsubaki Grand Shrine in Japan, and the Reverend Tetsuji Ochiai, Kyohei Mikawa, Rissho Kosei-kai of Japan, and Amy, David, Zane, and Cullen Luper. Thanks to John Tolley and Leslie Takahashi.

Dorcy Erlandson and the Reverend Dr. Scott Herr deserve special thanks for arranging a visit to the Tiffany stained-glass windows that Rodman Wanamaker donated to the American Church in Paris.

The friendship and sound advice of Heather Nicholson has made the last eighteen months of the book and my life far brighter. David Lazar has been a dear companion through many Chicago seasons. Laurel Hallman has been a true friend and guide. Thanks to Connie Simon for answering the call for help and going to the archive when I needed it most. Thanks to Susan and Tom Stenovec for sharing Chautauqua. Monsieur Pouki slept through most of the writing of the book, but nevertheless provided support by sleeping on my notes. I treasure my French family's interest in this project and their demand that I see *les passages* of Paris during my last visit: Jean-Yves and Agnès Chabrol, Matthieu Chabrol, Agnès Lahaye, and dear Alexandre Lahaye, who sees the world in color and movement. I am grateful for Frédéric Lahaye's, love and support—and all those meals he cooked and those champagne corks he popped.

Special thanks to all of my colleagues at Meadville Lombard Theological School, from the staff to the board of trustees, and especially, above all, my students, who are making a difference in the world. My colleagues made the work endurable and possible: Mark Hicks, Mike Hogue, Sharon Welch, and Lee Barker.

In closing, I bow in gratitude to my parents, Phil and Linda, and especially my son Kirk, who steadfastly and faithfully saw me through this project. He grew up with the book; the book grew up with him.

NOTES

INTRODUCTION

1 "Moody and Sankey: The Beginning of the Revival," *Philadelphia Times*, November 22, 1875.

2 Ibid.

3 Evensen, "It's Harder Getting into the Depot Than Heaven."

4 Bell, *Crusade in the City*, 236.

5 Ibid.

6 "Moody and Sankey."

7 Ibid.

8 Dwight L. Moody to John Wanamaker, November 8, 1877, Letters and Correspondence 1860–1877, Box 1, Folder 2, Wanamaker Papers, Historical Society of Pennsylvania (hereafter referred to as WP).

9 Ibid.

10 Gloege, *Guaranteed Pure*, 45.

11 Moody to Wanamaker, November 8, 1877.

12 This was true of not only white urban men but also African American women and men. See Weisenfeld, *African American Women and Christian Activism*.

13 Kilde, *When Church Became Theatre*; Boyer, *Urban Masses and Moral Order*.

14 "Many Tributes Paid to Wanamaker Here," *New York Times*, December 13, 1922.

15 Corrigan, *Business of the Heart*, 79.

16 Ibid.

17 Ibid., 80.

18 William Thomas Stead, *If Christ Came to Chicago! A Plea for the Union of All Who Love in the Service of All Who Suffer* (Chicago: Laird & Lee, 1894), 75. See also Smith, *The Search for Social Salvation*, 73, 78.

19 Stead, *If Christ Came to Chicago!*, 110. For a history of Protestants and money, see Hudnut-Beumler, *In Pursuit of the Almighty's Dollar*.

20 See Marchand, *Creating the Corporate Soul*, 7–8.

21 Ibid., 7–9.

22 See Leach, *Land of Desire*; Schmidt, *Consumer Rites*; and Moore, *Selling God*.

23 Leach, *Land of Desire*, 34–35.

24 Ibid., 213.

25 Ibid., 34–35.

26 Ibid.

27 See ibid.; Moore, *Selling God*; Engel, *Religion and Profit*; and Callahan, Lofton, and Seales, "Allegories of Progress."

28 Noll, *God and Mammon*, 3.

29 Valeri, *Heavenly Merchandize*; Valeri, "Weber and Eighteenth-Century Religious Developments"; Porterfield, Grem, and Corrigan, *The Business Turn in American Religious History*.

30 The following paragraphs are grounded in the work of Robert Orsi, "Introduction: Crossing the City Line," in *Gods of the City*; Boyer, *Urban Masses and Moral Order*, 8; and Wiebe, *Search for Order*.

31 Marchand, *Creating the Corporate Soul*, 10.

32 Wiebe, *Search for Order*, 12.

33 Ibid.

34 See Trachtenberg, *Incorporation of America*, 39, 72, 109, passim. Trachtenberg traces the development of capitalism in nineteenth-century America and its effects on cities, people, and culture.

35 Orsi, *Gods of the City*, 15–16.

36 Ibid., 16.

37 Wiebe, *Search for Order*, 14.

38 Ibid.

39 Ibid., 12.

40 Winston, *Red-Hot and Righteous*, 47.

41 Boyer, *Urban Masses and Moral Order*, 124–25.

42 Ibid., 69, 71.

43 Ibid., 126–27. See Carter, *Union Made*, for analysis of labor and religion in Chicago.

44 Moore, *Selling God*, 30, 23–35.

45 Orsi, *Gods of the City*, 18.

46 Boyer, *Urban Masses and Moral Order*, 122.

47 Ibid., 138.

48 Anderson, *Imagined Communities*.

49 I follow David Morgan's work on "moral influence" here rather than Wiebe's concept of "social control." See Morgan, *Protestants and Pictures*. See also Robert Wiebe's earlier interpretation in *The Search for Order*.

50 McDannell, *Christian Home in Victorian Times*, 48.

51 Bushman, *Refinement of America*, 331.

52 McDannell, *Christian Home in Victorian Times*, xiii.

53 Orsi, *Gods of the City*, 30; and Bushman, *Refinement of America*, xiv.

54 Morgan, *Protestants and Pictures*; and Kilde, *When Church Became Theatre*.

55 Anderson, *Imagined Communities*, 6; Wiebe, *Search for Order*, 35; and Orsi, *Gods of the City*, 29–30.

56 Anderson, *Imagined Communities*, 6, 33–42, 44–45.

57 On church architecture, see Kilde, *When Church Became Theatre*, 67–68.

58 Bushman, *Refinement of America*, xiii.

59 Ibid., xiii. Bushman argues that the refinement of America began in the 1690s but was not embraced by merchants until later.

60 Bourdieu, *Outline of a Theory of Practice*.

61 Bushman, *Refinement of America*, xvii.

62 Following ibid. Also see Campbell, *The Romantic Ethic and the Spirit of Modern Consumerism*.

63 Paula Lupkin in her discussion of YMCA buildings calls it "moral evangelism," and Paul Boyer in his study of City Beautiful movements termed it "positive environmentalism." Both terms, while apt, focus on buildings and miss the other material ways Protestants sought to morally affect urban spaces and their inhabitants.

64 The "middle class" was an evolving, many-layered category throughout the nineteenth and early twentieth centuries, and it continues to be contested by scholars. My working definition for this study encompasses more than economic and occupational levels. The middle class, as I am using it here, included "a common awareness and acceptance of similar attitudes and beliefs, linked to a common style of life, among the members of the class" who were in middling social and economic standing in American society. Blumin, *Emergence of the Middle Class*, 10, 12–13. See also Hepp, *Middle-Class City*, 15–16; and Wiebe, *Search for Order*.

65 Marshall Field's slogan was "Give the Ladies What They Want." See Appel and Hodges, *Golden Book of Wanamaker Stores*, 238.

CHAPTER 1. RETAIL REFORM

1 Conwell's congregation was intimately involved in the establishment of the university and hospital. They provided the fundraising and support for these institutions in their early days.

2 *Philadelphia Record*, May 22, 1914.

3 Conwell, *Acres of Diamonds*, 16. For more on the prosperity gospel then and now, see Bowler, *Blessed*; Walton, *Watch This!*; and Rzeznik, *Church and Estate*, 185–87.

4 "Jam Academy to Hear Him: Receives Tokens and Promise of $50,000 after Repeating Famous Address," *Philadelphia Record*, May 22, 1914.

5 Versions of Conwell's "Acres of Diamonds" uses A. T. Stewart, the creator of one of the first great department stores in the United States in the early nineteenth century, as one of many examples. Conwell's childhood involved retail: his father owned and ran a country store.

6 Alger published his first story, *Ragged Dick*, in 1867 and helped popularize the dime novel for youth. His stories focused on impoverished boys living in the urban milieu who, with moral fortitude and hard work, rise above their humble beginnings to achieve great success. See Lears, *No Place of Grace*, 18.

7 See Marchand, *Creating the Corporate Soul*. For the Golden Jubilee celebration, a two-volume book was compiled and entitled *Golden Book of Wanamaker Stores*. See Appel and Hodges, *Golden Book of Wanamaker Stores*, passim.

8 This narrative is further perpetuated and emphasized by Wanamaker biographers.

9   One of a series of economic panics and depressions of the nineteenth century, the Panic of 1837 was the beginning of a five-year depression following the failure of British and American banks, property speculation, unsecured printed currency, and the policies of President Andrew Jackson. See McGrane, *Panic of 1837*, 106–26; and North, *Economic Growth of the United States*.

10 The 1850 census lists Nelson "Wunnemacker" and wife and children. It notes his occupation as a brickmaker and indicates that the family is living in the Grays Ferry area of Philadelphia. The 1860 census lists Nelson as a brickmaker but living in Chambersburg, Pennsylvania. Nelson died at the age of fifty.

11 His mother's maiden name was mistakenly recorded as Deshong in Appel, *Business Biography*, 9.

12 The inn had been the historic Grays Inn and Tavern. The family named it Sans Souci, but it became known by the family name.

13 See Clendenin, *Building Industrial Philadelphia*.

14 The Naval Home was established in 1826 with the purchase of twenty-five acres of land in Grays Ferry. A hospital and school for seamen were built. Later, the institution moved to Annapolis and became the U.S. Naval Academy. Wanamaker recalled that the land for the home was given or purchased from his mother's family. Grays Ferry was consolidated with the city of Philadelphia in 1854. See Gibbons, *John Wanamaker*, vol. 1, 8; Ershkowitz, *John Wanamaker*, 14; and Philadelphia History Museum, "Neighborhood Tours, A Walk through Grays Ferry," www.philadelphiahistory.org (accessed March 2, 2012).

15 Wiebe, *Search for Order*, 4.

16 Gibbons, *John Wanamaker*, vol. 1, 7.

17 Ershkowitz, *John Wanamaker*, 21.

18 Wanamaker never went to college, and his early education was limited. He was largely self-taught with the help of Sunday school and his work in retail. See Conwell, *Romantic Rise of a Great American*, 18.

19 Marianne Brown, *Sunday-School Movements in America*, 173–74. John Neff served as the first Sunday school superintendent of the school and was one of its organizers. Later, he started another Sunday school mission that became Hope Presbyterian Church. The name Landreth came from the old schoolhouse building the Sunday school used.

20 Ershkowitz, *John Wanamaker*, 22.

21 Gibbons, *John Wanamaker*, vol. 1, 13.

22 Ershkowitz, *John Wanamaker*, 22–23. In chapter 5, the relationship of Wanamaker and race is briefly explored. As a boy, Wanamaker recalls that besides the Bible, a dictionary, and a copy of *Pilgrim's Progress*, the first book he read was *Robinson Crusoe*. He noted that "it was given to me by a colored man" and became his favorite book. Later, it was the text he most often gifted to young boys he knew through his Sunday school and his department store. See Appel, *Business Biography*, 15–16. John Sr. also would house his black workers to protect them from white thugs.

23 Appel, *Business Biography*, 9.

24 Gibbons, *John Wanamaker*, vol. 1, 18; Appel, *Business Biography*, 20; Conwell, *Romantic Rise of a Great American*, 17. It was in Indiana that Wanamaker first met Native Americans, and there he developed a fascination that lasted all his life. Later, he would sponsor his son Rodman's three "expeditions" (1908–1913) with the photographer Joseph K. Dixon to photograph the "vanishing race." They later published a book by the same title as well as two films: *Hiawatha* and *Reenactment of Battle of Little Big Horn*.

25 Gibbons, *John Wanamaker*, vol. 1, 21; Ershkowitz, *John Wanamaker*, 16.

26 Hepp, *Middle-Class City*, passim.

27 Boyer, *Urban Masses and Moral Order*, 123.

28 Rzeznik, *Church and Estate*, 4.

29 Ibid.

30 Ibid.

31 Ibid., 14.

32 Hepp, *Middle-Class City*, 25–31.

33 McDannell, *Christian Home in Victorian Times*, 9.

34 Rev. E. Morris Fergusson, "The First Sunday-School Days of a Cabinet Officer," *Sunday School Times* 31 (1889): 324.

35 Ershkowitz, *John Wanamaker*, 24. The booksellers were Troutman and Hayes.

36 Iarocci, *Urban Department Store in America*, 73.

37 Gibbons, *John Wanamaker*, vol. 1, 11–23.

38 Conwell, *Romantic Rise of a Great American*, 23.

39 Gibbons, *John Wanamaker*, vol. 1, 27.

40 Appel, *Business Biography*, 29.

41 Ibid.

42 Wanamaker remarked that his mother "was very anxious to have me take up" ministry. Gibbons, *John Wanamaker*, vol. 1, 29.

43 Appel, *Business Biography*, 10.

44 GroJLart, "Chambers-Wylie, Limestone Legacy on Broad Street," Hidden City Philadelphia, June 16, 2014, hiddencityphila.org.

45 Gibbons, *John Wanamaker*, vol. 1, 32; Ershkowitz, *John Wanamaker*, 26. Slapped with a charge of "unorthodoxy" by his local presbytery, Chambers was forced to seek ordination from the Congregationalists in New Haven. Returning to Philadelphia, he was called by the Ninth Presbyterian Church. The slighted Philadelphia Presbytery sued, ultimately winning the rights to the church property. Chambers's followers quickly secured a new lot on Broad and Sansom Streets to establish the new First Independent Church for their minister. The congregation grew quickly, and by 1860 it was one of the largest religious organizations in Philadelphia, with a membership of twelve hundred.

46 Conwell, *Romantic Rise of a Great American*, 31.

47 Wasson, *History of the Bethany Presbyterian Church*, 3; and Gibbons, *John Wanamaker*, vol. 1, 33–34. Wanamaker recorded another version of Chambers's teach-

ings in "his own hand" as "1. Christ demands full surrender; 2. Every follower of Christ is His messenger of good tidings; 3. Sunday is the Lord's Day; it belongs to Him; 4. Alcohol is Satan's most powerful ally; 5. No man is beyond redemption." See Appel, *Business Biography*, 24.

48 First Independent Church later rejoined the Presbyterians in 1897 through a merger with Wylie Memorial Presbyterian Church, together forming the Chambers-Wylie Memorial Presbyterian Church. Another merger was proposed in 1948 between the First, Second, and Chambers-Wylie Memorial Presbyterian Churches. In the end, First and Second united, while Chambers-Wylie left the merger process. In 2000 Wylie-Chambers dissolved. See "Philadelphia, Chambers-Wylie Memorial Presbyterian Church," Presbyterian Historical Society, www.history.pcusa.org.

49 Appel, *Business Biography*, 23.

50 Ibid.

51 Ibid. Later, when he started his own men's store, Wanamaker hired Walton to work for him as the lead hatter for the store.

52 John Wanamaker to S. A. Keen of YMCA Columbus, Ohio, December 14, 1906, John Wanamaker Letter Book, WP. A slightly different version is in Gibbons, *John Wanamaker*, vol. 1, 33; and Conwell, *Romantic Rise of a Great American*, 30.

53 Wasson, *History of the Bethany Presbyterian Church*, 3; and Gibbons, *John Wanamaker*, vol. 1, 3.

54 Ferry, *History of the Department Store*, 25. For references to Wanamaker's health, see Appel, *Business Biography*, 14; and Ershkowitz, *John Wanamaker*, 19.

55 Hopkins, *History of the YMCA*, 36.

56 Ibid.

57 Long, *Revival of 1857–58*, 13.

58 Corrigan, *Business of the Heart*, 17.

59 Ibid., 80, and passim.

60 Long, *Revival of 1857–58*, 13.

61 Ibid.

62 Corrigan, *Business of the Heart*, 18.

63 Gibbons, *John Wanamaker*, vol. 1, 34–35. See also Bell, *Crusade in the City*, 183.

64 Long, *Revival of 1857–58*, 59–60. Long and Bell both cover the YMCA's involvement in the Businessmen's Revival in Philadelphia. In many ways, the event and the organization found mutual strength and support in each other.

65 Ibid., 5.

66 Lupkin, *Manhood Factories*, 2.

67 Hopkins, *History of the YMCA*, 5–6.

68 Ibid., 15.

69 Ibid., 36.

70 Ibid., 21–23.

71 Ibid., 15.

72 Ibid.

73 Francis, "Religious Revival of 1858," 60. The first North American branches of the YMCA were founded in Montreal and Boston in 1851. See the introduction to Hopkins, *History of the YMCA*, for a more detailed picture of the founding of the YMCA and its spread to the United States.

74 Francis, "Religious Revival of 1858," 60.

75 Ibid.; Hopkins, *History of the YMCA*, 46.

76 Conwell, *Romantic Rise of a Great American*, 26.

77 Ibid., 82.

78 Hopkins, *History of the YMCA*, 44.

79 Quoted in Glass, "Liberal Means to Conservative Ends," 185, from the Philadelphia YMCA Constitution.

80 Ibid.

81 Francis, "Religious Revival of 1858," 63.

82 Ibid., 61.

83 Appel, *Business Biography*, 32.

84 Hopkins, *History of the YMCA*, 44.

85 Gibbons, *John Wanamaker*, vol. 1, 43.

86 Bell, *Crusade in the City*, 185.

87 Gibbons, *John Wanamaker*, vol. 1, 34–35. The Revival of 1858 is often listed as the Revival of 1857 since it began in November of that year. But the main body of meetings occurred in the first six months of 1858. See Bell, *Crusade in the City*, 183, 187.

88 Bell, *Crusade in the City*, 187.

89 Ibid.

90 Conwell, *Romantic Rise of a Great American*, 33; Rice, *A History of the American Sunday-School Union*, 28.

91 Rice, *History of the American Sunday-School Union*.

92 Appel, *Business Biography*, 34.

93 Wasson, *History of the Bethany Presbyterian Church*, 3.

94 Gibbons, *John Wanamaker*, vol. 1, 52.

95 Ibid., 53.

96 Wasson, *History of the Bethany Presbyterian Church*, 3.

97 Ibid.

98 Another version of the story claims that news of the attacks spread, and the firemen responded to the crisis on their own.

99 Wasson, *History of the Bethany Presbyterian Church*, 3.

100 Ibid.

101 *Encyclopedia of Contemporary Biography of Pennsylvania*, vol. 3 (New York: Atlantic Publishing & Engraving, 1898), 214.

102 Appel, *Business Biography*, 35.

103 Luke 24:49–52 (KJV): "And, behold, I send the promise of my Father upon you: but tarry ye in the city of Jerusalem, until ye be imbued with power from on high.

And he led them out as far as to Bethany, and he lifted up his hands, and blessed them. And it came to pass, while he blessed them, he was parted from them, and carried up into heaven. And they worshipped him, and returned to Jerusalem with great joy: And were continually in the temple, praising and blessing God."

104 Wasson, *History of the Bethany Presbyterian Church*, 3.

105 Wanamaker also helped found a total of four Presbyterian congregations in the Philadelphia area, including Bethany Presbyterian Church in 1858, John Chambers Memorial Presbyterian Church in 1897, and the Bethany Temple Presbyterian Church in 1906. John Chambers Memorial Church was built as an offering of thanks to God when the main portion of Wanamaker's store was spared from a fire that consumed several businesses on Market Street in 1897. Bethany Presbyterian is now Bethany Collegiate Church and moved to Havertown, Pennsylvania, in 1948; the congregation named the bell tower for their new building the John Wanamaker Memorial Tower. His original pew from Bethany is also at the church with a plaque identifying it. See Zulker, *John Wanamaker*, 80–88.

106 Ibid., 187–88.

107 Wasson, *History of the Bethany Presbyterian Church*, 3.

108 John Wanamaker quoted in *Encyclopedia of Contemporary Biography of Pennsylvania*, vol. 3, 215; and Appel, *Business Biography*, 35.

109 Kilde, *When Church Became Theatre*, 57. For additional history on the Gothic Revival movement in church architecture, see Williams, *Religion, Art, and Money*; and Lears, *No Place of Grace*. For additional discussion of nineteenth-century urban church architecture in Philadelphia, see Rzeznik, *Church and Estate*, 75–107; for New York City, see Bowman, *The Urban Pulpit*, 53–84.

110 Kilde, *When Church Became Theatre*, 58.

111 Ibid., 45.

112 Appel, *Business Biography*, 38; and Kilde, *When Church Became Theatre*, 177–79.

113 Kilde, *When Church Became Theatre*, 46, 47.

114 Ibid.

115 Ibid., 170, 177; and Wagner, *My Impressions of America*, 84.

116 Wagner, *My Impressions of America*, 85.

117 International Sunday School Convention, 1896 speech, Box 20B, Folder 9, WP.

118 Kilde, *When Church Became Theatre*, 111.

119 Ibid.

120 Glass, "Liberal Means to Conservative Ends," 183.

121 Pierson's father, Stephen Pierson, worked for the famous silk importer and abolitionist Arthur Tappan.

122 The three men also shared a premillennial theology. Pierson was the first editor of the premillennialist Scofield Reference Bible.

123 Robert, *Occupy until I Come*, 48.

124 Arthur T. Pierson in London, June 1867 to JW, Box 1A, Folder 6, WP.

125 Robert, *Occupy until I Come*, 73.

126 Smith, *Search for Social Salvation*, 46.

127 Ibid., 48.

128 Ibid., 190.

129 Robert, *Occupy until I Come*, 72.

130 Dorrien, *Social Ethics in the Making*, 76.

131 Robert, *Occupy until I Come*, 72–73.

132 Ibid., 90.

133 Ibid., 91.

134 Ibid., 94.

135 Ibid.

136 "Our History," Fort Street Presbyterian Church (Detroit, Michigan), fortstreet.org (accessed August 25, 2017).

137 Robert, *Occupy until I Come*, 119–20.

138 Ibid.

139 See Smith, *Search for Social Salvation*, 5. Gary Smith follows White and Hopkins, *Social Gospel*. Smith's chapter "Social Christianity, Businessmen, and the Golden Rule" paints a detailed portrait of Wanamaker as a businessman concerned with moral and religious principles in business operations. He does so without a focus on what went on inside the Wanamaker store and without in-depth knowledge of Bethany's programs. See Smith, *Search for Social Salvation*, 9. Smith references Ken Fones-Wolf for this tidbit; see Fones-Wolf, *Trade Union Gospel*. Smith noted that in Philadelphia, liberal and evangelical supporters of social Christianity mingled until around 1910.

140 Smith, *Search for Social Salvation*, 7–8.

141 Quoted in ibid., 25–26.

142 Glass, "Liberal Means to Conservative Ends," 183.

143 Ibid.

144 Alice Graham McCollin, "Unknown Wives of Well-Known Men: XIII.—Mrs. John Wanamaker," *Ladies' Home Journal* 9, no. 2 (1892).

145 Putney, *Muscular Christianity*, 84–86. Also known as The Brotherhood of Andrew and Phillip.

146 Glass, "Liberal Means to Conservative Ends," 186–87.

147 Robert, *Occupy until I Come*, 123.

148 Glass, "Liberal Means to Conservative Ends," 188.

149 Wagner, *My Impressions of America*, 84.

150 Ibid. Charles Wagner, a French Lutheran pastor and leader of a popular "simplicity" movement, visited Wanamaker and Bethany. He recorded his trip to the United States, including a visit to Wanamaker's church, in a book titled *My Impressions of America*.

151 See William Zulker's website on John Wanamaker, "Wanamaker Introduction," williamzulker.com. In addition to publishing a biography, Zulker also published three online papers on Wanamaker. Zulker was a minister at Bethany Temple and retired early to work on a book on Wanamaker. He was one of the first to work with the Wanamaker papers, which were uncatalogued at the time, and he created the first finding aid for the Historical Society of Pennsylvania.

152 Appel, *Business Biography*, 41.

153 Ibid., 40.

154 Ershkowitz, *John Wanamaker*, 29.

155 Gibbons Drawer 1, Appendix A, WP.

156 Appel, *Business Biography*, 39. Certificate of Exemption for "A Drafted Person on Account of Disability" for the State of Pennsylvania, September 26, 1863, Box 1, Folder 2, Correspondence 1860–65, WP. See Gibbons, *John Wanamaker*, vol. 1, 78–79.

157 Appel, *Business Biography*, 40.

158 Wanamaker had gained some additional retail experience since working for Tower Hall when his younger brother William started a dried-meat shop on Market Street, west of today's city hall. John ran the books for his brother and provided additional income to support their parents. See Appel, *Business Biography*, 61.

159 Ibid., 45.

160 Ershkowitz, *John Wanamaker*, 39.

161 Ibid., 152.

162 Appel, *Business Biography*, 46.

163 Whitaker, *World of Department Stores*, 152; and also Appel, *Business Biography*, 46–47.

164 Whitaker, *World of Department Stores*, 152.

165 Although Wanamaker did not use or like the term "department store," his customers and other businessmen called it a department store. Why Wanamaker rejected the label is not certain. I will be using "department store" throughout the book to describe Wanamaker's stores.

166 Appel, *Business Biography*, 51.

167 "Oak Hall—growth of—(1868–1871)," Gibbons Drawer 1, Appendix A, WP.

168 Gibbons, *John Wanamaker*, vol. 1, 112.

169 Ibid., 111–12.

170 Ershkowitz, *John Wanamaker*, 39. Forty-five tenants had previously occupied the same space.

171 See Stephanie Grauman Wolf, "Centennial Exhibition (1876)," *Encyclopedia of Greater Philadelphia*, 2013, philadelphiaencyclopedia.org.

172 Greenhalgh, *Ephemeral Vistas*, 3.

173 Bowlby, *Just Looking*, 1.

174 Harris, *Cultural Excursions*, 31.

175 Levenstein, *Seductive Journey*, Kindle location 123/5247.

176 Quoted in Buck-Morss, *Dialectics of Seeing*, 88.

177 Benjamin, *Arcades Project*, 17.

178 Ibid., 3, 16–17.

179 Ibid., 18.

180 Greenhalgh, *Ephemeral Vistas*, 1.

181 Ibid.

182 Harris, *Cultural Excursions*, 63.

183 Ibid.

184 Gibbons, *John Wanamaker*, vol. 1, 153.

185 Ibid., 30.

186 Appel, *Business Biography*, 75.

187 Gibbons, *John Wanamaker*, vol. 1, 131. European stores contained a wider variety of merchandise in one store than a typical American dry goods store in this period. Le Bon Marché and other department stores were in full swing by the time of Wanamaker's visit.

188 Appel, *Business Biography*, 77.

189 Evensen, *God's Man for the Gilded Age*, 82.

190 Hutton would also design Bethany Presbyterian's second building at Twenty-Second and Bainbridge. See Evensen, *God's Man for the Gilded Age*, for details on the Moody revival.

191 "Moody and Sankey."

192 Rydell, *All the World's a Fair*, 7–8.

193 Ibid., 11.

194 Ibid., 15–16.

195 Ibid., 11.

196 Greenhalgh, *Ephemeral Vistas*, 1.

197 Ibid.

198 Appel, *Business Biography*, 70.

199 Appel and Hodges, *Golden Book of Wanamaker Stores*, 43. An earlier exhibition was held in New York City in 1853 with an "American Crystal Palace" as the focus. It was not a success, in part because of its location—the current site of the New York Public Library.

200 Appel, *Business Biography*, 107.

201 Ferry, *History of the Department Store*, 105.

202 Iarocci, *Urban Department Store in America*, 85.

203 Gibbons Drawer 1, Appendix A, annals, p. 8, WP.

204 For a detailed discussion of Wanamaker's floor plan, see Iarocci, *Urban Department Store in America*, 84.

205 Appel and Hodges, *Golden Book of Wanamaker Stores*, 43.

206 J. W. Forney in Forney's Progress, 1877; Drawer 1, Appendix A, WP.

207 Ibid.

208 Gibbons, *John Wanamaker*, vol. 1, 235.

209 Iarocci, *Urban Department Store in America*, 91.

210 Drawer 1, Appendix A, WP.

211 Gibbons, *John Wanamaker*, vol. 1, 215–17.

212 Ferry, *History of the Department Store*, 106.

213 Fischer, "'Holy John' Wanamaker," 455.

214 Ibid., 458.

215 See ibid., 454.

216 Ibid., 455.

217 Ibid., 461.
218 Ibid., 464–66.
219 Ibid., 469.
220 Undated clipping, Box 128, Folder 14, WP.
221 Fischer, "'Holy John' Wanamaker," 472–73.
222 Grant Hamilton, "Another 'Stuffed Prophet,'" *Judge*, June 12, 1897.
223 Rodman Wanamaker Scrapbook, Box 241, WP.
224 Quoted in Conwell, *Romantic Rise of a Great American*, 11–12.
225 Gibbons, *John Wanamaker*, vol. 1, 51.
226 "Egyptian Hall, The New Wanamaker Auditorium," *Anniversary Herald*, April 21, 1908, Box 75, Folder 6, WP.
227 Ibid.

CHAPTER 2. MORAL ARCHITECTURE

1 Peter Brown, *Rise of Western Christendom*, 29. Special thanks to Sloane Franklin for drawing my attention to this quote.
2 Zola, *Ladies' Paradise*, 216–17, 233.
3 Émile Zola coined this phrase, "cathédrale du commerce moderne," in *Au bonheur des dames (Ladies' Paradise)*. See Bowlby, *Just Looking*, 71, 216–17, 233.
4 Zola, *Ladies' Paradise*, 427.
5 Ibid.
6 The department store lacks a clear point of origin, although many stores lay claim to the title. However, the list of the leaders of this movement inevitably includes Aristide Boucicaut of Le Bon Marché in Paris, A. T. Stewart of the Marble Palace in New York City, and John Wanamaker. See Iarocci, "Spaces of Desire."
7 Pevsner, *History of Building Types*, 257.
8 Leach, *Land of Desire*; Iarocci, *Urban Department Store in America*, 15.
9 McKendrick, Brewer, and Plumb, *Birth of Consumer Society*, 19.
10 Plumb, "The Commercialization of Leisure in Eighteenth-Century England," in McKendrick, Brewer, and Plumb, *Birth of Consumer Society*, 284.
11 Whitaker, *World of Department Stores*, 7.
12 Miller, *Bon Marché*, 25.
13 Pevsner, *History of Building Types*, 261–63.
14 See Walter Benjamin's unfinished book, *The Arcades Project*.
15 Ibid., 37.
16 Ibid.
17 Brian Nelson, introduction to Zola, *Ladies' Paradise*, xi–xii. *Flânerie* is another term developed in late nineteenth-century Paris to describe the phenomenon of men and women leisurely strolling, sometimes loitering to look at merchandise through store windows.
18 Benjamin, *The Arcades Project*, 17.

19 Pevsner, *History of Building Types*, 262. Paris had over three hundred arcades in the early nineteenth century. Only about thirty remain. The United States had several arcades. One of the best examples, the Cleveland Arcade, is well-preserved and still in use as a shopping venue and hotel in Cleveland, Ohio.

20 Harris, *Cultural Excursions*, 114.

21 Ibid.

22 Bowlby, *Just Looking*, 3.

23 Herbert Muschamp, "The Passages of Paris and of Benjamin's Mind," *New York Times*, January 16, 2000.

24 Miller, *Bon Marché*, 20.

25 Ibid., 39.

26 Pevsner, *History of Building Types*, 267.

27 Whitaker, *World of Department Stores*, 184.

28 Louisa Iarocci provides a detailed survey of urban department store architecture, development, and design in *Urban Department Store*.

29 Whitaker, *World of Department Stores*, 32–38.

30 Miller, *Bon Marché*, 3.

31 Hepp, *Middle-Class City*, 27.

32 Pevsner, *History of Building Types*, 270; Ershkowitz, *John Wanamaker*, 135.

33 Hendrickson, *Grand Emporiums*, 34.

34 Iarocci, *Urban Department Store*, 70.

35 Hendrickson, *Grand Emporiums*, 35.

36 Ibid.

37 Ibid.

38 Ibid., 37.

39 Whitaker, *World of Department Stores*, 67; and Nadine Brozen, "Panel Gives Ladies' Mile Historic District Status," *New York Times*, May 3, 1989.

40 Hendrickson, *Grand Emporiums*, 40.

41 Iarocci, *Urban Department Store*, 75.

42 Wanamaker's purchase of Stewart's store was an emotional one. He had long admired Stewart and in some sense felt that by purchasing Stewart's he inherited his legacy. But the emotional tie clouded his judgment. As New York City's shopping shifted toward Herald Square and Pennsylvania Station, Wanamaker refused to relocate the store, maintaining an allegiance to the original site. Macy's started in 1858 and became a full-fledged department store in 1877. Bloomingdale's was founded in 1872. Gimbels started in Milwaukee in 1887, opening branches in Philadelphia in 1894 and in New York City, directly across the street from Macy's, in 1910. By the 1890s, department stores appeared across the United States. See Whitaker, *World of Department Stores*, 270.

43 John Wanamaker, "Address by Mr. John Wanamaker to his Employees delivered Tuesday Evening November 17th, 1885," Box 20B, Folder 5, WP.

44 Quoted by Gibbons in Drawer 1, Appendix A, WP, clipping from the *Philadelphia Store News*, September 1883.

45 The five major Philadelphia department stores on Market Street that competed with Wanamaker's were Strawbridge and Clothier, Lit Brothers, Gimbels, and N. Snellenburg and Co. See Arrigale and Keels, *Images of America*.

46 Ibid.

47 Ibid.

48 Schaffer, *Daniel H. Burnham*, 70.

49 For Wanamaker's Chicago visit, see Gibbons, *John Wanamaker*, vol. 2, 194. By 1893, Marshall Field had already constructed a couple of store buildings after fire destroyed two of his buildings, in 1871 and in 1877. The year before the fair, Field broke ground on the first section of a multisection building project that would eventually create one large store. The sections (built in 1902, 1906, 1907, and 1914) matched architecturally on the outside and were joined on the inside. Geoffrey Johnson, "The Annotated: Marshall Fields," *Chicago Magazine*, June 6, 2007, www. chicagomag.com.

50 Iarocci, *Urban Department Store*, 109–11.

51 Gibbons, *John Wanamaker*, vol. 1, 145.

52 Ershkowitz, *John Wanamaker*, 137.

53 Boyer, *Urban Masses and Moral Order*, 162–87; Harris, *Artist in American Society*, 188–216; Bushman, *Refinement of America*, passim.

54 Boyer, *Urban Masses and Moral Order*, 224–25; Harris, *Artist in American Society*, 303; Williams, "Gospel of Wealth," 173.

55 Morgan, *Protestants and Pictures*, 316.

56 Harris, *Artist in American Society*, 303.

57 Boyer, *Urban Masses and Moral Order*, 222, 238.

58 Ibid., 252, 262.

59 Lupkin, *Manhood Factories*, 12.

60 Glass, "Liberal Means to Conservative Ends," 185.

61 Ibid., 190.

62 Lupkin, *Manhood Factories*, 3.

63 Ibid., 25.

64 Ibid., 22, 35.

65 Ibid.

66 Ibid., 81.

67 Gibbons, *John Wanamaker*, vol. 2, 351–52. Other sources indicate he gave a substantial amount of money to these international projects.

68 Lupkin, *Manhood Factories*, xxi.

69 JW to R. M. Luther, December 31, 1896, Letterbook, WP.

70 Address by Mr. John Wanamaker to his Employees delivered Tuesday Evening November, 17th, 1885," Box 20B, Folder 5, WP.

71 Ibid.

72 Valeri, *Heavenly Merchandize*; Schmidt, *Consumer Rites*. Also see Moore, *Selling God*; and Giggie and Winston, *Faith in the Market*.

73 Smith, *Search for Social Salvation*, 245.

74 For one version of the story, see Appel, *Business Biography*, 55.

75 "Oak Hall," Gibbons Drawer 1, WP.

76 Ershkowitz, *John Wanamaker*, 36–37, 41–42. A. T. Stewart and Arthur Tappan both laid claim to inventing the money-back guarantee, and scholars disagree about who first fully expressed the concept. European department stores also made changes to retail practices and did so earlier than their American counterparts. Although several store publications and biographers perpetuate the myth that Wanamaker invented many of the "firsts" of modern retail, he certainly contributed to a metamorphosis in retail practice.

77 "The Evolution of the Modern Store and How It Has Been Advanced by the Wanamaker System" (1899), Box 75, Folder 7, WP.

78 Ibid.

79 "Oak Hall (1861) Founder's Aim," Gibbons Drawer 1, WP.

80 See Boyer, *Urban Masses and Moral Order*, 252–76.

81 Whitaker, *World of Department Stores*, 114.

82 Gibbons, *John Wanamaker*, vol. 2, 205.

83 Boyer, *Urban Masses and Moral Order*, 264.

84 Gibbons typed notes, Drawer 1, Appendix A, WP.

85 Prior to hiring Burnham for the flagship store project, Wanamaker had hired him to help build a large multistory addition to Stewart's original Marble Palace in New York City and a sky bridge (he grandly called it the Bridge of Progress) between the two buildings.

86 Hines, *Burnham from Chicago*, 288. Burnham's firm also designed an addition to the Land Title Building five years later.

87 Ibid., 291. Burnham's firm designed the following buildings: Field Warehouse, 1900; Marshall Field's Company Store, 1902; Marshall Field's Company Store Power Plant, 1902; Gimbel Brothers Store addition, Milwaukee, 1903; Wanamaker's Department Store, New York, 1903; Wanamaker's Department Store, Philadelphia, 1902; McCreery Store, Pittsburgh (building built for another store, then purchased by McCreery), 1903; Marshall Field's Company Store, 1905; Marshall Field's Company Store (riverside) Warehouse, 1905; Selfridges Department Store, London, 1906; Alms and Doepke Department Store addition, Cincinnati, 1908; Gimbel Brothers Department Store, New York, 1909; Filene's Department Store, 1912; May Department Store, Cleveland, 1912; Steven and Brothers Department Store, Chicago, 1912.

88 Whitaker, *World of Department Stores*, 112.

89 Other than Burnham's famous department store designs, few American department store buildings receive merit for their exterior or interior design. The lone exception is Louis Sullivan's spectacular wrought-iron design of the entry of

Schlesinger and Mayer (later Carson Pirie Scott) in Chicago, completed in 1903. See ibid., 114.

90 Schaffer, *Daniel H. Burnham*, 72.

91 Boyer, *Urban Masses and Moral Order*, 252.

92 Schaffer, *Daniel H. Burnham*, 166.

93 Ershkowitz, *John Wanamaker*, 139.

94 Ibid., 138.

95 See Hines, *Burnham of Chicago*, 303.

96 Burnham, on a larger scale, copied major exterior elements of his Wanamaker design in the Henry W. Oliver Building (1907–1910). See Schaffer, *Daniel H. Burnham*, 152, and the images on 154–55.

97 Kirshenblatt-Gimblett, *Destination Culture*, 265.

98 Hines, *Burnham of Chicago*, 281.

99 Schaffer, *Daniel H. Burnham*, 170.

100 Hines, *Burnham of Chicago*, 303. Although the building design was a success, frustration characterized Burnham and Wanamaker's relationship, as the merchant made multiple changes and constantly meddled.

101 Store Program, Box 75, Folder 7, WP. The Wanamaker radio station call letters were WOO. The store operated the station from 1922 to 1928. Other department stores experimented with radio during this period. Wanamaker's was one of the early operators.

102 See Hepp, *Middle-Class City*, 148.

103 *Bulletin*, December 19, 1906, Drawer 1, Appendix A, WP.

104 Ershkowitz, *John Wanamaker*, 137.

105 Benson, *Counter Cultures*, 39.

106 Appel and Hodges, *Golden Book of Wanamaker Stores*, 93.

107 Gibbons typed notes, Drawer 1, Appendix A, WP.

108 Appel and Hodges, *Golden Book of Wanamaker Stores*, 246. Capital letters are in the original.

109 "History," Philadelphia City Hall Virtual Tour, www.phila.gov.

110 Whitaker, *World of Department Stores*, 101.

111 Ibid., 64.

112 Unpublished biography by Robins, 209, Box 24, Folder 51, WP.

113 Appel and Hodges, *Golden Book of Wanamaker Stores*, 129.

114 Ibid., 130.

115 Ibid.

116 Ibid.

117 Bowman, *Urban Pulpit*, 24.

118 Boyer, *Urban Masses and Moral Order*, 221.

119 Lupkin, *Manhood Factories*, 5.

120 Appel and Hodges, *Golden Book of Wanamaker Stores*, 143.

121 Ibid., 104.

122 Ibid., 246–47.

CHAPTER 3. CHRISTIAN CADETS

1 Staff Correspondent, "The President at Wanamaker's," *Baltimore American*, December 31, 1911.

2 See Griffith, *God's Daughters*, for an overview history of Protestants and embodied religion. For additional critical framework, see Finch, *Dissenting Bodies*; and Klassen, *Spirits of Protestantism*.

3 Wanamaker faced the challenge in two cities, with his acquisition of the old Stewart's store in New York City and with the building addition he made in 1902.

4 Gibbons, *John Wanamaker*, vol. 2, 260.

5 Ibid., 261.

6 Ibid., 263.

7 Ibid., 264.

8 Ibid.

9 Conwell, *Romantic Rise of a Great American*, 86.

10 Quoted in Gibbons, *John Wanamaker*, vol. 2, 262.

11 Benson, "Cinderella of Occupations," 3.

12 Gibbons, *John Wanamaker*, vol. 2, 275.

13 Ibid., 264.

14 Benson, *Counter Cultures*; and Benson, "Cinderella of Occupations," 6, 22.

15 Nasaw, *Children of the City*, 43–44.

16 Brewer, "Child Labor in the Department Store," 167.

17 Benson, *Counter Cultures*, 130; and Benson, "Cinderella of Occupations," 8.

18 Bjelopera, *City of Clerks*, location 1121.

19 Benson, *Counter Cultures*, 5.

20 Du Bois, *The Philadelphia Negro*; and Bjelopera, *City of Clerks*, location 535. The city of Philadelphia employed black clerks in the main post office, and Wanamaker had hired African American postal clerks and postmasters.

21 Benson, *Counter Cultures*, 209.

22 Cooper, "The Limits of Persuasion."

23 Bjelopera, *City of Clerks*, location 509.

24 Ibid., location 548.

25 This section relies on Cooper, "Limits of Persuasion."

26 Ibid., 99.

27 Benson, "Cinderella of Occupations," 1–25, passim; and Wanamaker, "John Wanamaker Commercial Institute," 152.

28 Wanamaker, "John Wanamaker Commercial Institute," 151–54.

29 Ibid.

30 *JWCI Yearbook*, 1917, WP. In April 1916 Wanamaker changed the name of the JWCI to the American University of Trade and Applied Commerce. "Dedicate New University," *New York Times*, April 9, 1916.

31 Gibbons, *John Wanamaker*, vol. 2, 284.

32 Bowler, *Blessed*, 31–32.

33 See Marchand, *Creating the Corporate Soul*, 14.

34 Benson, *Counter Cultures*, 128.

35 See Marchand, *Creating the Corporate Soul*, 14; and Boyer, *Urban Masses and Moral Order*, 126–27.

36 Appel and Hodges, *Golden Book of Wanamaker Stores*, 230.

37 Wanamaker, "John Wanamaker Commercial Institute," 153.

38 John Wanamaker, "Speech to the Cadets," Folder JWCI Box, WP.

39 Hepp, *Middle-Class City*, 79, 164–65.

40 Hampton University, "History," www.hamptonu.edu.

41 Kendi, *Stamped from the Beginning*, 243–44. The divide between black liberal arts and vocational schools led to the development of a divide between light-skinned and dark-skinned blacks, with the majority of darker-skinned African Americans barred from admission to liberal arts schools and steered into vocational training.

42 Lester Sullivan, "American Missionary Association," Amistad Research Center, University of Illinois at Urbana-Champaign, amistadresearchcenter.tulane.edu.

43 Ibid.

44 The relationship between Armstrong and Washington was extremely close and involved a high level of mutual admiration. At the end of Armstrong's life, when he was partly paralyzed, Washington cared for him in his own home. See Booker T. Washington, *Up from Slavery: An Autobiography*, chap. 3, "The Struggle for an Education," available at xroads.virginia.edu; and Hampton University, "Samuel Chapman Armstrong," www.hamptonu.edu.

45 Kendi, *Stamped from the Beginning*, 277.

46 Ibid.

47 William H. Doris, "Negro Business Men Finish with a Banquet: John Wanamaker Gave Them Advice in the Day Session," *New York Times*, August 19, 1905.

48 Robert Jefferson Norrell, *Up from History: The Life of Booker T. Washington* (Cambridge: Harvard University Press, 2009), 7.

49 *JWCI Yearbook*, 1917.

50 Wanamaker, "John Wanamaker Commercial Institute," 152.

51 Brewer, "Child Labor in the Department Store," 169.

52 Ibid.

53 Ibid.

54 Ibid., 167.

55 Ibid., 169.

56 Ibid., 168.

57 JWCI, "Monthly Record," Box 34b, Folder 4, WP.

58 Brewer, "Child Labor in the Department Store," 168.

59 Ibid.

60 Ibid.

61 Other "character builder" groups embraced the Y's fourfold mission as well. In 1895 the YMCA adopted the simplified triangle of mind, body, and spirit that persists today. See Putney, *Muscular Christianity*, 29.

62 *The Rule of Four: How Boys and Girls Can Develop into Full-Rounded Men and Women*, Wanamaker Stores Booklet, author's collection.

63 *JWCI Yearbook*, 1917.

64 "History of the YMCA Logo," Greater Green Bay YMCA, www.greenbayymca. org.

65 "A Message to Garcia" first appeared in Hubbard's monthly self-published magazine *The Philistine: A Periodical of Protest* (1895–1915). The story became a national bestseller and a favorite of the American military. Hubbard's magazine had a circulation of two hundred thousand. He had named it the "Philistine" in a sarcastic nod to the use of the term by the upper class to describe someone as uncultured and uneducated.

66 MacLeod, *Building Character in the American Boy*, 85–86.

67 *The Wanamaker Primer on Abraham Lincoln: Strength, Mind, Heart, Will, the Full-Rounded Man, the Typical American Example of the Rule of Four* (Philadelphia: Times Printing House, 1919), 141.

68 Winston, *Red-Hot and Righteous*, 83.

69 MacLeod, *Building Character in the American Boy*, 87. "Onward Christian Soldiers" was adopted by Theodore Roosevelt's 1912 Bull Moose campaign. Putney, *Muscular Christianity*, 35.

70 See MacLeod, *Building Character in the American Boy*, 45.

71 Ibid., 29.

72 "John Wanamaker Commercial Institute Manual of Commands," 153, Box 34b, Folder 3, JWCI Box, WP.

73 Ibid., 7.

74 Ibid.

75 Brewer, "Child Labor in the Department Store," 170.

76 Ibid., 171; and "John Wanamaker Commercial Institute Manual of Commands," 153.

77 "John Wanamaker Commercial Institute Manual of Commands."

78 Ibid.

79 Winston, *Red-Hot and Righteous*, 87.

80 Ibid.

81 "John Wanamaker Commercial Institute Manual of Commands," 153.

82 Ibid.

83 Ibid.

84 *JWCI Yearbook*, 1917.

85 Putney, *Muscular Christianity*, 26–30, passim.

86 Lears, *No Place of Grace*, 12–15.

87 See Anne Braude, "Women's History Is American Religious History," in Tweed, *Retelling U.S. Religious History*.

88 Putney, *Muscular Christianity*, 1. The term "muscular Christianity" first appeared in the 1850s.

89 McDannell, *Christian Home in Victorian Times*, 116.

90 Higginson, "Saints and Their Bodies."
91 Ibid.; and Putney, *Muscular Christianity*, 2.
92 Higginson, "Saints and Their Bodies." Clifford Putney traces the emergence of muscular Christianity to England in the 1850s and 1860s through a series of novels and publications. Its leap to the United States was at first hindered by Protestantism's negative view of physical exercise and exertion, yet it found fertile soil in theologically liberal circles. Later, muscular Christianity secured acceptance in theologically conservative groups as attitudes about bodies and physical exercise changed.
93 MacLeod, *Building Character in the American Boy*, xii.
94 Finch, *Dissenting Bodies*, 3.
95 *Wanamaker Primer on Abraham Lincoln*, 98, 99. See also *The Wanamaker Primer on the North American Indian: Hiawatha Produced in Life* (1909).
96 Gibbons, *John Wanamaker*, vol. 2, 278.
97 Putney, *Muscular Christianity*, 67, 149, and passim.
98 Van Slyck, *A Manufactured Wilderness*, 4.
99 Ibid., 15.
100 *JWCI Yearbook*, 1917; Appel and Hodges, *Golden Book of Wanamaker Stores*, 233. Here in the fresh ocean air, using a combination of "education and recreation," John Wanamaker started the camp "to develop in a boy manliness, loyalty, uprightness, obedience, self-reliance and courtesy."
101 Brewer, "Child Labor in the Department Store," 169.
102 Historic American Buildings Survey, Wanamaker Hall, HABS No. NJ-1144, available at cdn.loc.gov. In 1907 the Philadelphian Club, Princeton University's YMCA branch, founded a camp in nearby Bay Head for poor inner-city boys. Selden, *Princeton Summer Camp*, 22.
103 The official name of the camp found on postcards and other documents was the John Wanamaker Commercial Institute Camp.
104 Ibid.
105 "Island Heights Borough," Living Places, Gombach Group, www.livingplaces.com.
106 Van Slyck, *Manufactured Wilderness*, 7.
107 Appel and Hodges, *Golden Book of Wanamaker Stores*, 234.
108 Van Slyck, *Manufactured Wilderness*, 16.
109 *1915 JWCI Yearbook*, Box 34B, Folder 3, WP.
110 Messenger, *Holy Leisure*, 59.
111 Ibid., 90.
112 Ibid., 93.
113 Appel and Hodges, *Golden Book of Wanamaker Stores*, 234.
114 Jacqueline Urgo, "Future in Doubt for Place of the Past," *Philadelphia Inquirer*, July 22, 1996.
115 Ibid.
116 Appel and Hodges, *Golden Book of Wanamaker Stores*, 103.
117 Ibid.

118 Ibid., 233.

119 "Wanamaker Gift to Clerks: Athletic Field on Philadelphia Store Roof Dedicated," *New York Times*, July 12, 1915; and Appel and Hodges, *Golden Book of Wanamaker Stores*, 228.

120 See Gibbons, *John Wanamaker*, vol. 1, 50.

121 See ibid., 276; and Dave Hackenberg, "The Wanamaker Trophy: A Tradition with Tales to Tell," PGA/Turner Sports Interactive, www.pga.com.

122 John Wanamaker Store, *A Friendly Guide-Book to the Wanamaker Store*, 24. The guidebook was first published in 1913.

123 Golf News Net, "Wanamaker Trophy Facts," July 25, 2016, thegolfnewsnet.com.

124 Gibbons, *John Wanamaker*, vol. 2, 275.

125 Marchand, *Creating the Corporate Soul*, 105–7.

126 Special thanks to Karen Spielman and Kate Carté Engel for sharing family memories and correspondence between family members and John Wanamaker.

127 Conwell, *Romantic Rise of a Great American*, 95–99; Gibbons, *John Wanamaker*, vol. 2, 267–69. His biographies and personal papers are replete with stories of the employees' regard for Wanamaker. Negative stories must exist, but they are not extant in his personal papers.

128 Gibbons, *John Wanamaker*, vol. 2, 259–60.

129 Ibid., 265.

130 Wagner, *My Impressions of America*, 139.

131 Allan Greenville, "Man Unprompted after 56 Years Shows Need for Permanent FEPC," *Chicago Defender*, national edition, March 22, 1947.

132 See Cooper, "Limits of Persuasion"; and Bloom, Fletcher, and Perry, *Negro Employment in Retail Trade*.

133 Conwell, *Romantic Rise of a Great American*, 91–92.

134 Ibid., 79, 164–65.

135 For more on the popularity of minstrel groups in Philadelphia department stores, see Bjelopera, "White Collars and Blackface." Wanamaker's *JWCI Yearbook* includes a photograph of two large employee minstrel groups posing in full regalia. There is no mention of the employee minstrel groups in broadly circulated store publications.

136 Bjelopera, "White Collars and Blackface," 478.

137 Ibid., 480.

138 John Wanamaker quoted in the *Meadowbrook Yearbook*, 1917, JWCI Box, WP.

CHAPTER 4. SERMONS ON CANVAS

1 There were two Lindenhursts. Wanamaker purchased the land in 1868. The first house was built between 1880 and 1884. An adjacent art gallery, connected to the main house by a covered passageway, housed a large portion of Wanamaker's art collection that did not fit in the house or was not on display at his stores. The second house was constructed after the 1907 fire. Fire safety was long a passion of Wanamaker's. The home of Thomas, his oldest son, burned to the ground in 1901

and also consumed a massive art collection. See "Flames Pursue the Wanamaker Paintings," *Pittsburgh Dispatch*, August 11, 1907, 8 (found in Box 49A, Folder 12, WP); and Gibbons, *John Wanamaker*, vol. 2, 139.

2 "Thomas B. Wanamaker's Country Home Burned," *New York Times*, May 19, 1901.

3 "Three Fires Destroy $3,000,000 Worth of Art," *Brooklyn Daily Eagle*, August 11, 1907.

4 Ibid.

5 "Looters at Burning Wanamaker Home," *New York Times*, February 9, 1907.

6 Ibid.

7 Ibid.

8 Ibid.

9 Ibid.

10 Ibid. *Bucheron* more accurately translates as "lumberjack."

11 Ibid.

12 "Wanamaker Planned Book on Luther," *New York Times*, February 10, 1907.

13 Gibbons, *John Wanamaker*, vol. 2, 140.

14 "Wanamaker Planned Book on Luther." One of the great losses for Wanamaker was his research for a book he planned to write on Martin Luther. Luther is an interesting subject choice, given that Wanamaker was a Presbyterian and teetotaler. See also Promey, "Public Display of Religion," 31 and passim.

15 Gibbons, *John Wanamaker*, vol. 2, 74.

16 Ruskin quotes can be found in Appel and Hodges, *Golden Book of Wanamaker Stores* as well other store materials, for example, Wanamaker's Anniversary Book (1906), Box 20B, Folder 13, WP.

17 Weinberg, "Americans in Paris."

18 Ibid. Also see David McCullough, *The Greater Journey: Americans in Paris at Home and Abroad* (New York: Simon and Schuster, 2011).

19 Weinberg, "Americans in Paris."

20 For example, Wanamaker's supported Frieseke's early career in a variety of ways that included employing him as the artistic director of the department store's catalog and as an art advisor to Thomas's newspaper, the *North American*. They also commissioned him to paint a mural for the New York store's elevator lobby.

21 Appel and Hodges, *Golden Book of Wanamaker Stores*, 252.

22 Gibbons, *John Wanamaker*, vol. 2, 80.

23 Kirshenblatt-Gimblett, *Destination Culture*, 271.

24 *Philadelphia Times* article; and Appraiser assessment of Rodman's collections, Box 49A, WP.

25 Appel and Hodges, *Golden Book of Wanamaker Stores*, 197.

26 "Minnie" Wanamaker, John Wanamaker's daughter, married Major Barclay Warburton and also spent time in France, especially at Biarritz, where they had property. It was through Warburton's connections that Minnie and Barclay Warburton came into contact with the tsar of Russia and his family before World War I. See Megan Evans, "Of Wanamakers and Romanovs: A History Mystery from

the Archives," November 11, 2015, Historical Society of Pennsylvania, https://hsp.org.

27 Gibbons, *John Wanamaker*, vol. 2, 81.

28 Ibid., 79. Brožík's dealer was the same as Munkácsy's.

29 Quoted in Ibid.

30 Quoted in ibid. I have not been able to locate the diaries Gibbons cites at HSP.

31 When the paintings were sold in the 1980s, some of the artwork that was recorded in store catalogs as original works by famous artists turned out to be copies. Lita Solis-Cohen, "Sotheby's to Auction Wanamakers' 19th-Century Art," *Philadelphia Inquirer*, February 22, 1988.

32 Morgan, *Protestants and Pictures*, 19.

33 Ibid.

34 Ibid.

35 Harris, *Artist in American Society*, 300.

36 For a wonderful history of wealthy Americans, especially Episcopalians and their art collections, see Williams, *Religion, Art, and Money*. Regular steam-packet service began in 1816 between New York and Liverpool, opening a path for Americans to visit Europe with more ease. See Lears, *No Place of Grace*, 185–86. See also Williams, "Gospel of Wealth."

37 Levenstein, *Seductive Journey*, Kindle location 844/5247.

38 See Franchot, *Roads to Rome*; Davis, "Catholic Envy"; and Lears, *No Place of Grace*.

39 Again, see Franchot, *Roads to Rome*; Davis, "Catholic Envy"; and Lears, *No Place of Grace*.

40 Lears, *No Place of Grace*, 184.

41 Williams, *Religion, Art and Money*, Kindle location 499/6524.

42 Stein, *John Ruskin and Aesthetic Thought*, 41.

43 Lears, *No Place of Grace*, 150.

44 Stein, *John Ruskin and Aesthetic Thought*, 76–77.

45 Harris, *Artist in American Society*, 303.

46 Morowitz, "Passion for Business," 193.

47 Ibid.

48 Morgan, *Protestants and Pictures*, 270–71.

49 Ibid., 309.

50 Quoted in ibid.

51 Ibid., 290–91.

52 Tomkins, *Merchants and Masterpieces*, 22.

53 Harris, *Artist in American Society*, 300.

54 Ibid.

55 Morgan, *Protestants and Pictures*, 336.

56 See ibid., 244–56; and Bethany Sunday Record Books, Presbyterian Historical Society.

57 Wanamaker purchased the financially struggling *Sunday School Times* in 1871 and made it profitable. Wanamaker favored lesson plans in his own Sunday

school work. The *Sunday School Times* used sketches and encouraged the use of a blackboard for lessons. An in-depth study of the publication may also reveal new information on Wanamaker's perspective. See Morgan, *Protestants and Pictures*, xiii, 240, 242, 245, and so on. Wanamaker revamped the *Sunday School Times* with the help of Congregationalist minister and educator Henry Clay Trumbull.

58 Appel and Hodges, *Golden Book of Wanamaker Stores*, 245.

59 Gibbons, *John Wanamaker*, vol. 2, 74.

60 Lears, *No Place of Grace*, 195; and Campbell, *Romantic Ethic and the Spirit of Modern Consumerism*.

61 Gibbons, *John Wanamaker*, vol. 2, 73.

62 Ibid., 74.

63 *Art Journal*, vol. 54, 245.

64 John Preston Beecher, "The Salons of 1892," *Collector* 3, no. 15 (June 1, 1892): 23.

65 Appel's biography differs from Gibbons's and claims that Rodman purchased the painting for his father.

66 *Wanamaker Herald*, March 1905, Box 75, Folder 3, WP.

67 Ibid.

68 Gibbons, *John Wanamaker*, vol. 2, 77.

69 "The Price of Human Glory," *New York Times*, October 20, 1912.

70 Store newspaper clipping, Box 49, Folder 6, WP.

71 Store correspondence, Box 49, Folder 6, WP.

72 Ibid.

73 Harris, *Cultural Excursions*, 17. The founding of these various institutions was an effort by cities to gain respect through their cultural amenities.

74 Tomkins, *Merchants and Masterpieces*, 25.

75 Levine, *Highbrow, Lowbrow*, 146.

76 Tomkins, *Merchants and Masterpieces*, 25.

77 Levine, *Highbrow, Lowbrow*, 147.

78 Tomkins, *Merchants and Masterpieces*, 25–26.

79 Cantor, "Temples of the Arts," 331.

80 Tomkins, *Merchants and Masterpieces*, 23.

81 Cantor, "Temples of the Arts," 331.

82 Tomkins, *Merchants and Masterpieces*, 23.

83 Conn, *Do Museums Still Need Objects?*, 154–55.

84 Tomkins, *Merchants and Masterpieces*, 21.

85 Cantor, "Temples of the Arts," 331.

86 Conn, *Do Museums Still Need Objects?*, 174–75.

87 "Our Story," Philadelphia Museum of Art, www.philamuseum.org.

88 Bowlby, *Just Looking*, 6.

89 For helpful discussion of department store art galleries, see Whitaker, *World of Department Stores*, 55, 250.

90 Ibid., 249.

91 Ibid., 246, 249.

92 The Japanese department store Mitsukoshi had a stage and art gallery. Jordan Marsh of Boston started art galleries in 1894, although the works were for sale. Le Bon Marché, the French department store that Wanamaker saw as a model, began its gallery in 1874, earlier than Wanamaker. This gallery invited local artists to exhibit up to six weeks. Ibid.

93 Ibid., 7.

94 Art Misc., Box 126, Folder 7, WP.

95 Appel and Hodges, *Golden Book of Wanamaker Stores*, 249.

96 Ibid., 253.

97 Ibid., 80.

98 Ibid., 80, 265.

99 Ibid., 239.

100 *Wanamaker Herald* (1905), Folder 75, File 3, WP.

101 Appel and Hodges, *Golden Book of Wanamaker Stores*, 249.

102 Ibid.

103 Ibid., 253.

104 Gibbons, *John Wanamaker*, vol. 2, 80.

105 Folder 120, File 15, WP.

106 Duncan, *Civilizing Rituals*, 17.

107 Ibid.

108 Appel and Hodges, *Golden Book of Wanamaker Stores*, 249. The great exhibitions also suffered from overambitious attempts to display the most art possible in the available space.

109 Duncan, *Civilizing Rituals*, 10.

110 Art Inventories: Wanamaker Galleries, Box 49B, Folder 3, WP.

111 Ibid.

112 Duncan, *Civilizing Rituals*, 10.

113 The original Strasbourg clock resides inside the cathedral in Strasbourg, France. Jana Dolecki, "Strasbourg Cathedral," www.strasbourg.info. Wanamaker's model was one quarter the size of the original. Wanamaker's Strasbourg is now on display at the Franklin Institute in Philadelphia. Le Bon Marché also had a reproduction of the clock, which is no small coincidence given Wanamaker's frequent visits to the store for ideas.

114 Store Art Department, Pasquale Farina, "List of Paintings," Box 49a, Folder 17, WP. There are multiple inventories of Wanamaker's art in the archives and booklets showing the art.

115 Ibid.

116 Art Inventories: Wanamaker Galleries, Box 49B, Folder 3, WP.

117 Ibid.

118 From a twelve-page booklet introducing the painter Pierre Firtel's *The Conquerors*, produced by the John Wanamaker Store, Box 49, Folder 6, WP.

119 Clipping from *Wanamaker Herald*, 1905, Box 75, Folder 3, WP.

120 Morowitz, "Passion for Business," 184. Wanamaker and those who ran the business after him had the paintings on display in his Philadelphia store from 1911 to 1988.
121 *Christ on Golgotha* is sometimes called *Christ at Calvary*.
122 "Christ Before Pilate Sold," *New York Times*, February 10, 1887.
123 Morowitz, "Passion for Business," 185.
124 Morgan, *Protestants and Pictures*, 319.
125 Morowitz, "Passion for Business," 185.
126 Ibid., 190.
127 Ibid., 185..
128 Morowitz, "Passion for Business." *Christ before Pilate* measured 20 feet 8 inches long by 13 feet 6 inches wide; *Christ on Golgotha* is 23 feet 4 inches long by 14 feet 2 inches wide.
129 Nahshon, "Going against the Grain," 67–68.
130 Ibid., 74.
131 Ibid., 78. Whether it was murder, suicide, or an accident was difficult to determine, although authorities ruled it either an accident or suicide.
132 Morowitz, "Passion for Business."
133 Appel and Hodges, *Golden Book of Wanamaker Stores*, 261.
134 Rev. Henry Van Dyke quoted in "Christ on Calvary: The Painting by M. De Munkacsy," booklet, Box 240, WP.
135 Ferdinand L. French, "Two Great Pictures," typed essay, Box 49a, Folder 11, WP.
136 Clipping from *New York Times*, April 24, 1939, Box 49, Folder 10, WP.
137 Ibid.
138 Leach, *Land of Desire*.
139 Richard J. Beamish, "Wanamaker's Tomb Is Sealed as City Bows in Sad Rites," *Philadelphia Inquirer*, morning edition, December 15, 1922. In the spring of 2018, I was able to see Munkácsy's three paintings, "The Christ Trilogy," where they have been on display at the Deri Museum in Debrecen, Hungary. The color, size, movement, and power were startling to experience in person.
140 Marley, *Henry Ossawa Tanner*, 26.
141 Ibid., 23.
142 Gibbons, *John Wanamaker*, vol. 2, 80.
143 Marley, *Henry Ossawa Tanner*, 30. Tanner had not been to the Holy Land, but he had visited Chicago's Colombian Exposition in 1893, where he may have seen the Egyptian display and other Middle Eastern displays.
144 Gibbons, *John Wanamaker*, vol. 1, 53.
145 Marley, *Henry Ossawa Tanner*, 29.
146 Appel and Hodges, *Golden Book of Wanamaker Stores*, 254; Marley, *Henry Ossawa Tanner*, 37; Wilson, *Unofficial Statesman*, 175. Later, Wanamaker's trusted business partner Robert Ogden purchased Tanner's earlier paintings *The Bagpipe Lesson* and *The Banjo Lesson* for display at the Hampton Institute, hoping to inspire the students.

147 Marley, *Henry Ossawa Tanner*, 37.

148 Judith F. Dolkart, "The Life of Christ Comes to the 'Acropolis of Brooklyn,'" in *James Tissot: The Life of Christ, The Complete Set of 350 Watercolors*, ed. Judith F. Dolkart (New York: Merrell Publishers and Brooklyn Museum, 2009), 35–37.

149 Store advertisement clipping for Tissot Bible, Box 49, Folder 10, WP.

150 Duncan, *Civilizing Rituals*, 19.

151 Advertisement proof from the February 14, 1945, edition of the *Philadelphia Inquirer*, Box 49, Folder 10, WP.

152 Folder "Display Department: Correspondence W, 1938," WP.

153 Dunlap died in 1951. His brother sent the note in March 1953, which indicates that Dunlap wrote the piece several years earlier. There are other letters like it in the collection; see Box 49, Folder 1, WP.

154 William F. Hamill Jr. to John Raasch, president of the John Wanamaker Store, April 3, 1950, Box 49, Folder 10, WP.

155 John Raasch to William F. Hamill Jr., April 4, 1950, Box 49, Folder 10, WP.

156 Letter from the Reverend William Waide to Wanamaker Store, March 29, 1958, Box 49, Folder 1, WP.

157 Ibid.

158 An undated slip of paper in the Wanamaker Papers gives the talking points for the Munkácsy paintings by Evelyn B. Conner—not to be "used" without her permission (the slip is undated, although the paintings were not displayed in the Grand Court until 1928). There is evidence that Conner gave regular tours. One of the letters in the collection mentions listening to Conner's presentation on the paintings. Evelyn B. Conner, untitled notes, Box 49, Folder 10, WP.

159 Ibid.

160 Jean Shyrock to Wanamaker Store, May 4, 1965, Box 49, Folder 10, WP.

161 "Book on Luther," *New York Times*, February 10, 1907.

162 "Wanamaker Stables Burn," *New York Times*, July 22, 1907. In Herbert Ershkowitz's biography there is the story that the fires at Lindenhurst provided a large sum of insurance money at a time when Wanamaker was undergoing financial difficulty, raising a suspicion about the nature of the fire. Ershkowitz does not cite a source for this speculation and does not believe it is true, and no other sources mention the suspicion.

163 Gibbons, *John Wanamaker*, vol. 2, 78.

164 Schwain, *Signs of Grace*, 2.

165 Levine, *Highbrow, Lowbrow*, passim.

CHAPTER 5. CHRISTIAN INTERIORS

1 Appel and Hodges, *Golden Book of Wanamaker Stores*, 238.

2 Gibbons, *John Wanamaker*, vol. 2, 196.

3 Ibid. The Christmas hymn "O Little Town of Bethlehem" had extra meaning for Wanamaker. He was friends with its author, Phillip Brooks.

4 JW to RW, March 1, 1911 quoted in Gibbons, *John Wanamaker*, vol. 2, 186.

5 See Biswanger, *Music in the Marketplace*, 59–61. Biswanger's work is the only full-length well-researched historical account of the Great Organ and the store organists.

6 Gibbons, *John Wanamaker*, vol. 2, 189.

7 Appel and Hodges, *Golden Book of Wanamaker Stores*, 242.

8 Ibid.

9 Whitaker, *World of Department Stores*, 224.

10 Nostrum, *Economics of Retailing*, 199.

11 Appel and Hodges, *Golden Book of Wanamaker Stores*, 227.

12 Ibid., 228.

13 Ibid.

14 Ibid.

15 Ibid., 248.

16 Schaffer, *Daniel H. Burnham*, 166.

17 Ibid.

18 Ibid.

19 Biswanger, *Music in the Marketplace*, 57.

20 Appel and Hodges, *Golden Book of Wanamaker Stores*, 253.

21 Biswanger, *Music in the Marketplace*, 57.

22 *Grand Court Organ*, 1917 booklet, Box 75, Folder 7, WP.

23 *Employee Songbook*, Box 74, WP.

24 Ibid.

25 Ibid.

26 *Grand Court Organ*, 1917 booklet.

27 Biswanger, *Music in the Marketplace*, 43.

28 *Grand Court Organ*, 1917 booklet.

29 Vogt's career playing at Wanamaker's began long before her official position as store organist. She started working there at age twelve dusting baskets, and moved through the ranks, volunteering to play the organ when guest musicians failed to show. She became the permanent organist in 1917 and continued in that position until 1966. See Biswanger, *Music in the Marketplace*, 74, 48.

30 Biswanger, *Music in the Marketplace*, 43.

31 Ibid., 44–45.

32 Kilde, *When Church Became Theatre*, 123–28.

33 McDannell, *Christian Home in Victorian America*, 50.

34 The organ was sold after the fair, but the deal fell through, leaving it in limbo until Wanamaker's purchase. See Biswanger, *Music in the Marketplace*, 51.

35 A guarded secret, the purchase price of the organ is part of its myth. Biswanger found evidence that Wanamaker got an amazing deal, most probably buying the organ for less than 5 percent of what it cost to build. See ibid., 54.

36 Ibid., 56.

37 Ibid., 59.

38 Ibid., 65.

39 Biswanger discovered that the pipe count had long been padded to keep the organ ranked as the largest in the United States—and, pointedly, larger than its chief competitor in nearby Atlantic City. Certainly, this also helped with advertising. Whether Wanamaker knew of the padding is uncertain, but his son Rodman, who worked closely with the organ expansion long after his father's death, likely knew. The organ in the main auditorium of the Atlantic City Convention Hall (now Boardwalk Hall) was damaged in 1944 by a hurricane and again in 2012. It is considered the world's largest and loudest, with 33,114 pipes and 449 ranks. Since Wanamaker's organ is in working order and still performs regularly, it is often listed as the world's largest, fully operational organ. See ibid., 242.

40 Organ guidebooks were published every year and appeared to be popular. In contemporary times, the organ was entered on the National Registry of Historical Sites, and a group of boosters called Friends of the Wanamaker Organ formed in 1995 to protect and support the organ. *Grand Court Organ*, 1917 booklet.

41 For a deeper look at the role music served in department stores, see Tyler's incisive article, "'Commerce and Poetry Hand in Hand.'"

42 Ershkowitz, *John Wanamaker*, 155; and Schmidt, *Consumer Rites*, 159–69.

43 In over one hundred years at Wanamaker's, the organ has had only four organists, suggesting the pleasure of such a role.

44 *Grand Court Organ*, booklet, author's collection.

45 Russell later became the music director for the Philadelphia store. It is possible he met Wanamaker's son during Rodman's years at Princeton.

46 *Grand Court Organ*, booklet, author's collection.

47 Ibid.

48 Ibid.

49 Ibid.

50 Ibid.

51 Quoted in Biswanger, *Music in the Marketplace*, 62.

52 Tyler, "'Commerce and Poetry Hand in Hand,'" 76.

53 Ibid., 79.

54 Levine, *Highbrow, Lowbrow*.

55 Ibid., 80.

56 Ibid., 100.

57 Tyler, "'Commerce and Poetry Hand in Hand,'" 78.

58 For a full discussion of the evolution of American holidays in the commercial world, see Schmidt, *Consumer Rites*.

59 Clipping from *Examiner*, New York, December 28, 1893, Drawer 1, Appendix A, WP.

60 Clipping from *Watchman*, New York, December 27, 1894, Drawer 1, Appendix A, WP.

61 Lears, *No Place of Grace*, 184.

62 Franchot, *Roads to Rome*; and Kilde, *When Church Became Theatre*.

63 Rzeznik, *Church and Estate*, 90; and Addie Peyronnin, "'To Beautify His House': Rodman Wanamaker's Sacramental Silver Commissions" (M.A. thesis, University of Delaware, 2012), passim.

64 Biswanger, *Music in the Marketplace*, 80–81.

65 When the church moved from its Rue de Berri location to its current Gothic Revival building, the Tiffany windows were brought to the new sanctuary. France has declared the windows national treasures. Special thanks to the Reverend Scott Herr, senior minister of the American Church in Paris, for giving me a personal tour of the building and sharing the history of the church. He encouraged me to see Tiffany stained glass in a new way—up close. See "History, Architecture, & Tours," American Church in Paris website, www.acparis.org.

66 Peyronnin, "'To Beautify His House.'"

67 Rodman had three children—Fernanda W. Munn, Marie Louise Munn, and Captain John Wanamaker Jr.—as well as five grandchildren—Rodman Arturo Heeren, John Rodman Wanamaker, Fernanda Pauline Wanamaker, Gurnee Munn Jr., and Fernanda Munn.

68 Rzeznik, *Church and Estate*, 90.

69 Thomas H. Keels, *Philadelphia Graveyards and Cemeteries* (Mount Pleasant, SC: Arcadia, 2003), 61.

70 Schmidt, *Consumer Rites*, 162.

71 See Flag Heritage Foundation website, "The Wanamaker Collection," www.flagheritagefoundation.org (accessed August 19, 2017). The Flag Heritage Foundation purchased the Wanamaker flag collection in 1988. After restoration, the organization was not able to put the flags on display and decided to turn them over to various nonprofits for ongoing preservation and display. The Friends of the Wanamaker Organ received a large collection of the flags, which they put on display at Macy's department store, the current owner of the old Wanamaker store, while the Military History Museum in Vienna, Austria, received a collection of military flags.

72 Store advertisement, *Philadelphia Inquirer*, November 22, 1927.

73 Schmidt, *Consumer Rites*, 162.

74 While other department stores moved to a less "Christian" Christmas and Easter and filled their holiday displays with more innocuous gingerbread men, Santas, and Easter Bunnies, Wanamaker's religiously themed holidays persisted until the 1950s, long after his death.

75 Nelson, introduction to *American Sanctuary*, 10.

76 "1919 Christmas Carols in the Grand Court," Box 74, Folder 7, WP. The poem quoted is "Christmas Day" by John Keble.

77 Ibid.

78 See Klein, "Gospel of Wanamaker"; and Wasson, *History of the Bethany Presbyterian Church*, 10.

79 Store Records, Publications, Box 74, WP.

80 Schmidt, *Consumer Rites*, 205.

81 Store newspaper advertisement, *Philadelphia Inquirer*, March 18, 1936.

82 Schmidt, *Consumer Rites*, 205.

83 "Philadelphia Store News 1893," Drawer 1, Appendix A, WP.

84 Clipping, Box 120, Folder 16, WP.

85 Store photographs of "Tablets undated," Box 127, Folder 1, WP. The plaques remain in place and can be seen at Macy's, Center City as of 2017. There are also a series of state shields scattered among the columns in the same room.

86 Ibid.

87 Ibid.

88 Ibid.

89 *Wanamaker's Constitution Book* (1881), author's collection.

90 Store photographs of "Founder's Birthday memorial at the Eagle" celebrations from 1923–1933, Box 128, Folder 11, WP.

91 Dennis F. Crolly to John Wanamaker, March 21, 1922. Letter was retyped for a Gibbons research card. Gibbons Drawer 1, Appendix A, WP.

CONCLUSION

1 "Silent Tribute Paid Wanamaker by City," *Philadelphia Inquirer*, morning edition, December 15, 1922; and Richard J. Beamish, "Wanamaker's Tomb Is Sealed as City Bows in Sad Rites," *Philadelphia Inquirer*, morning edition, December 15, 1922.

2 Richard J. Beamish, "John Wanamaker Dies in Peaceful Passing from City He Loved," *Philadelphia Inquirer*, morning edition, December 13, 1922.

3 Mary "Minnie" Wanamaker Warburton married Barclay H. Warburton, a military man who served as the U.S. military attaché in London during World War I. The family traveled in aristocratic and royal circles, even meeting the Russian tsar's family. The youngest daughter, Elizabeth "Lillie" Wanamaker MacLeod, died in 1927 at the age of fifty-one. She had married Norman MacLeod.

4 Letters from Dwight L. Moody to John Wanamaker, Box 1, Folder 2, WP.

5 "The Wanamaker System: Its Place in Applied Economics," Wanamaker Papers, Box 75, Folder 3, Pennsylvania Historical Society. Also see Appel and Hodges, *Golden Book of Wanamaker Stores*, 160–77; and Smith, *The Search for Social Salvation*, passim.

6 Quoted in Ershkowitz, *John Wanamaker*, 56.

7 JW to unnamed correspondent, December 27, 1881, JW Letterbook, WP.

8 Bushman, *Refinement of America*, 232.

9 Ibid., 401.

10 Ibid., xv.

11 Ibid., 436.

12 See Boyer, *Urban Masses and Moral Order*, passim; and Lupkin, *Manhood Factories*, 5.

13 The Mart had been built to consolidate the Marshall Field store's wholesale business, but poor timing doomed the new venture. Construction completed in 1930 as the nation fell into the Great Depression. Kennedy had purchased the building in 1945 and returned the building to its wholesale roots.

14 See Garvey, "Merchandise Mart Hall of Fame," 156.

15 Ibid.

16 John Wanamaker, "Wanamaker Store Recognized as Stellar Philadelphia Attraction," *Christian Monitor*, May 21, 1958.

17 John Ruskin, *The Crown of Wild Olive: Four Lectures on Work, Traffic, War, and the Future of England*, reprint by Leopold Classic Library (New York: Thomas Y. Crowell, 1864), 60–61.

SELECTED BIBLIOGRAPHY

DOCUMENT COLLECTIONS

Bethany Presbyterian Church (Philadelphia, Pennsylvania), Records. Presbyterian Historical Society, Philadelphia.

John Wanamaker Collection, 1827–1987. Historical Society of Pennsylvania, Philadelphia. Series I, Personal records, 1850–1986; Series II, Store records, 1861–1987; Series III, Miscellaneous publications, 1827–1917, Series IV, Prints and photographs, 1861–1980; and Series V, Addendum.

Frederick M. Yost Collection on John Wanamaker's Department Store Publicity, 1861–1985. Historical Society of Pennsylvania, Philadelphia.

PUBLISHED SOURCES

Anderson, Benedict. *Imagined Communities: Reflections on the Origin and Spread of Nationalism*. Rev. ed. New York: Verso, 2006.

Appel, Joseph. *The Business Biography of John Wanamaker, Founder and Builder; America's Merchant Pioneer 1861–1922; with Glimpses of Rodman Wanamaker and Thomas B. Wanamaker*. New York: Macmillan, 1930.

Appel, Joseph Herbert, and Leigh Mitchell Hodges, comps. *Golden Book of Wanamaker Stores: Jubilee Year, 1861–1911*. Philadelphia: Self-published by John Wanamaker, 1911.

Arrigale, Lawrence M., and Thomas H. Keels. *Images of America: Philadelphia's Golden Age of Retail*. Charlestown, SC: Arcadia, 2012.

Bell, Marion L. *Crusade in the City: Revivalism in Nineteenth-Century Philadelphia*. Cranbury, NJ: Associated University Presses, 1977.

Benjamin, Walter. *The Arcades Project*. Translated by Howard Eiland and Kevin McLaughlin; prepared on the basis of the German volume edited by Rolf Tiedman. Cambridge: Belknap, 2002.

Benson, Susan Porter. "The Cinderella of Occupations: Managing the Work of Department Store Saleswomen, 1900–1940." *Business History Review* 55, no. 1 (Spring 1981): 1–25.

———. *Counter Cultures: Saleswomen, Managers, and Customers in American Department Stores, 1890–1940*. Champaign: University of Illinois Press, 1988.

Biswanger, Ray. *Music in the Marketplace: The Story of Philadelphia's Historic Wanamaker Organ, from John Wanamaker to Macy's*. Bryn Mawr, PA: Friends of the Wanamaker Organ, 1999.

Bjelopera, Jerome. *City of Clerks: Office and Sales Workers in Philadelphia, 1870–1920.* Champaign: University of Illinois Press, 2005.

———. "White Collars and Blackface: Race and Leisure among Clerical and Sales Workers in Early Twentieth-Century Philadelphia." *Pennsylvania Magazine of History and Biography* 126, no. 3 (July 2002): 471–90.

Bloom, Gordon F., F. Marion Fletcher, and Charles R. Perry. *Negro Employment in Retail Trade: A Study of Racial Policies in the Department, Drugstore, and Supermarket Industries.* Philadelphia: Industrial Research Unit, Wharton School of Finance and Commerce, University of Pennsylvania, 1972.

Blumin, Stuart M. *The Emergence of the Middle Class: Social Experience in the American City, 1760–1900.* New York: Cambridge University Press, 1989.

Bourdieu, Pierre. *Outline of a Theory of Practice.* Translated by Richard Nice. Cambridge: Cambridge University Press, 2007.

Bowlby, Rachel. *Just Looking: Consumer Culture in Dreiser, Gissing and Zola.* New York: Methuen, 1985.

Bowler, Kate. *Blessed: A History of the American Prosperity Gospel.* New York: Oxford University Press, 2013.

Bowman, Matthew. *The Urban Pulpit: New York City and the Fate of Liberal Evangelicalism.* New York: Oxford University Press, 2014.

Boyer, Paul. *Urban Masses and Moral Order in America, 1820–1920.* Cambridge: Harvard University Press, 1978.

Brewer, Franklin N. "Child Labor in the Department Store." *Annals of the American Academy of Political and Social Science* 20 (1902): 167–77.

Brown, Marianne. *Sunday-School Movements in America.* New York: Fleming H. Revell, 1901.

Brown, Peter. *The Rise of Western Christendom: Triumph and Diversity, A.D. 200–1000.* 2nd ed. Malden, MA: Blackwell, 2004.

Buck-Morss, Susan. *Dialectics of Seeing: Walter Benjamin and the Arcades Project.* London: MIT Press, 1989.

Buggeln, Gretchen, Crispin Paine, and S. Brent Plate, eds. *Religion in Museums: Global and Multidisciplinary Perspectives.* London: Bloomsbury, 2017.

Bushman, Richard L. *The Refinement of America: Persons, Houses, Cities.* New York: Vintage, 1993.

Callahan, Richard J., Jr., Kathryn Lofton, and Chad E. Seales. "Allegories of Progress: Industrial Religion in the United States." *Journal of the American Academy of Religion* 78, no. 1 (March 2010): 1–39.

Campbell, Colin. *The Romantic Ethic and the Spirit of Modern Consumerism.* 3rd ed. York, UK: Alcuin Academics, 2005.

Cantor, Jay. "Temples of the Arts: Museum Architecture in Nineteenth-Century America." *Metropolitan Museum of Art Bulletin* 28, no. 8 (April 1970): 331–54.

Carter, Heath. *Union Made: Working People and the Rise of Social Christianity in Chicago.* New York: Oxford University Press, 2015.

Clendenin, Malcolm. *Building Industrial Philadelphia*. Thematic Context Statement. Philadelphia: Preservation Alliance for Greater Philadelphia, 2009. Available at www.preservationalliance.com.

Conn, Steven. *Do Museums Still Need Objects?* Philadelphia: University of Pennsylvania Press, 2010.

Conwell, Russell. *Acres of Diamonds*. Reprinted by BN Online Publishing, 2007.

———. *The Romantic Rise of a Great American*. New York: Harper and Brothers, 1924.

Cooper, Patricia. "The Limits of Persuasion: Race Reformers and the Department Store Campaign in Philadelphia, 1945–1948." *Pennsylvania Magazine of History and Biography* 126, no. 1 (January 2002): 97–126.

Corrigan, John. *Business of the Heart: Religion and Emotion in the Nineteenth Century*. Berkeley: University of California Press, 2002.

Davis, John. "Catholic Envy: The Visual Culture of Protestant Desire." In *The Visual Culture of American Religions*, edited by David Morgan and Sally M. Promey. Berkeley: University of California Press, 2001.

Dorrien, Gary. *Social Ethics in the Making: Interpreting an American Tradition*. New York: John Wiley, 2011.

Douglass, Anne. *The Feminization of American Culture*. New York: Farrar, Straus and Giroux, 1977.

Du Bois, W. E. B. *The Philadelphia Negro: A Social Study*. Philadelphia: Published for the University, 1899.

Duncan, Carol. *Civilizing Rituals: Inside Public Art Museums*. New York: Routledge, 2010.

Engel, Kate. *Religion and Profit: Moravians in Early America*. Philadelphia: University of Pennsylvania Press, 2011.

Ershkowitz, Herbert. *John Wanamaker: Philadelphia Merchant*. Conshohocken, PA: Combined Publishing, 1999.

Evensen, Bruce J. *God's Man for the Gilded Age: D. L. Moody and the Rise of Modern Mass Evangelism*. New York: Oxford University Press, 2003.

———. "It's Harder Getting into the Depot Than Heaven: Moody, Mass Media and the Philadelphia Revival of 1875–76." *Pennsylvania History* 69, no. 2 (Spring 2002): 149–78.

Ferry, John William. *A History of the Department Store*. New York: Macmillan, 1960.

Finch, Martha. *Dissenting Bodies: Corporealities in Early New England*. New York: Columbia University Press, 2010.

Findlay, James F., Jr. *Dwight L. Moody: American Evangelist, 1837–1899*. Chicago: University of Chicago Press, 1969.

Fischer, Roger A. "'Holy John' Wanamaker: Cartoon Centerfold." *Pennsylvania Magazine of History and Biography* 115, no. 4 (1991): 455.

Fones-Wolf, Ken. *Trade Union Gospel: Christianity and Labor in Industrial Philadelphia, 1865–1915*. Philadelphia: Temple University Press, 1989.

Franchot, Jenny. *Roads to Rome: The Antebellum Protestant Encounter with Catholicism*. Berkeley: University of California Press, 1994.

Francis, Russell E. "The Religious Revival of 1858 in Philadelphia." *Pennsylvania Magazine of History and Biography* 70, no. 1 (January 1946): 52–77.

Garvey, Timothy J. "Merchandise Mart Hall of Fame." *Illinois Historical Journal* 88, no. 3 (Autumn 1995): 154–72.

Gibbons, Herbert Adam. *John Wanamaker.* Vols. 1 and 2. New York: Harper & Brothers, 1926.

Giggie, John M., and Diane Winston, eds. *Faith in the Market: Religion and the Rise of Urban Commercial Culture.* New Brunswick: Rutgers University Press, 2002.

Glass, William R. "Liberal Means to Conservative Ends: Bethany Presbyterian Church, John Wanamaker, and the Institutional Church Movement." *American Presbyterians* 68, no. 3 (Fall 1990): 181–92.

Gloege, Timothy E. W. *Guaranteed Pure: The Moody Bible Institute, Business, and the Making of Modern Evangelicalism.* Chapel Hill: University of North Carolina Press, 2015.

Greenhalgh, Paul. *Ephemeral Vistas: The Expositions Universelles, Great Exhibitions and World's Fairs, 1851–1939.* Manchester: Manchester University Press, 1988.

Griffith, R. Marie. *God's Daughters: Evangelical Women and the Power of Submission.* Berkeley: University of California Press, 2000.

Hall, David D. *Lived Religion in America: Toward a History of Practice.* Princeton: Princeton University Press, 1997.

Harris, Neil. *The Artist in American Society: The Formative Years, 1790–1860.* Chicago: University of Chicago Press, 1982.

———. *Cultural Excursions: Marketing Appetites and Cultural Tastes in Modern America.* Chicago: University of Chicago Press, 1990.

Hendrickson, Robert. *The Grand Emporiums: The Illustrated History of America's Great Department Stores.* New York: Stein and Day, 1980.

Hepp, John Henry, IV. *The Middle-Class City: Transforming Space and Time in Philadelphia, 1876–1926.* Philadelphia: University of Pennsylvania Press, 2003.

Higginson, Thomas Wentworth. "The Saints and Their Bodies." *Atlantic Monthly* 1, no. 5 (March 1858): 584–85.

Hines, Thomas S. *Burnham from Chicago: Architect and Planner.* Chicago: University of Chicago Press, 1979.

Hopkins, C. Howard. *History of the YMCA in North America.* New York: National Board of Young Men's Christian Associations Press, 1951.

Howe, Daniel Walker. *Making the American Self: Jonathan Edwards to Abraham Lincoln.* Cambridge: Harvard University Press, 1997.

Hudnut-Beumler, James. *In Pursuit of the Almighty's Dollar: A History of Protestants and Money.* Chapel Hill: University of North Carolina Press, 2007.

Huhndorf, Shari M. *Going Native: Indians in the American Cultural Imagination.* Ithaca: Cornell University Press, 2001.

Iarocci, Louisa M. "Spaces of Desire: The Department Store in America." PhD diss., Boston University, 2003.

———. *The Urban Department Store in America, 1850–1930.* Surrey: Ashgate, 2014.

John Wanamaker Store. *A Friendly Guide-Book to the Wanamaker Store, Philadelphia, 1916.* Facsimile edition by Friends of the Wanamaker Organ, 2002.

Kendi, Ibram X. *Stamped from the Beginning: The Definitive History of Racist Ideas in America.* New York: Nation Books, 2016.

Kilde, Jeanne Halgren. *When Church Became Theatre: The Transformation of Evangelical Architecture and Worship in Nineteenth-Century America.* New York: Oxford University Press, 2002.

Kirshenblatt-Gimblett, Barbara. *Destination Culture: Tourism, Museums, and Heritage.* Berkeley: University of California Press, 1998.

Klassen, Pamela. *Spirits of Protestantism: Medicine, Healing, and Liberal Christianity.* Berkeley: University of California Press, 2011.

Klein, Maury. "The Gospel of Wanamaker." *Audacity,* Summer 1996, 27–39.

Lambert, Frank. *"Pedlar in Divinity": George Whitefield and the Transatlantic Revivals.* Princeton: Princeton University Press, 1994.

Leach, William. *Land of Desire: Merchants, Power, and the Rise of a New American Culture.* New York: Vintage, 1993.

Lears, T. J. Jackson. *No Place of Grace: Antimodernism and the Transformation of American Culture, 1880–1920.* Chicago: University of Chicago Press, 1981.

Lefebvre, Henri. *The Production of Space.* Translated by Donald Nicholson-Smith. Malden, MA: Blackwell, 1991.

Levenstein, Harvey. *Seductive Journey: American Tourists in France from Jefferson to the Jazz Age.* Chicago: University of Chicago Press, 1998.

Levine, Lawrence W. *Highbrow, Lowbrow: The Emergence of Cultural Hierarchy in America.* Cambridge: Harvard University Press, 1988.

Lisicky, Michael J. *Wanamaker's: Meet Me at the Eagle.* Charleston, SC: History Press, 2010.

Long, Kathryn Teresa. *The Revival of 1857–58: Interpreting an American Religious Awakening.* New York: Oxford University Press, 1998.

Lupkin, Paula. *Manhood Factories: YMCA Architecture and the Making of Modern Urban Culture.* Minneapolis: University of Minnesota Press, 2010.

MacLeod, David I. *Building Character in the American Boy: The Boy Scouts, YMCA, and Their Forerunners, 1870–1920.* Madison: University of Wisconsin Press, 1983.

Maffly-Kipp, Laurie F., Leigh E. Schmidt, and Mark Valeri. *Practicing Protestants: Histories of Christian Life in America, 1630–1965.* Baltimore: Johns Hopkins University Press, 2010.

Marchand, Roland. *Creating the Corporate Soul: The Rise of Public Relations and Corporate Imagery in American Big Business.* Berkeley: University of California Press, 1998.

Marley, Anna O. *Henry Ossawa Tanner: Modern Spirit.* Philadelphia: Pennsylvania Academy of the Fine Arts, 2012.

McDannell, Colleen. *The Christian Home in Victorian Times, 1840–1900.* Bloomington: Indiana University Press, 1986.

———. *Material Christianity: Religion and Popular Culture in America.* New Haven: Yale University Press, 1995.

McGrane, Reginald. *The Panic of 1837: Some Financial Problems of the Jacksonian Era.* New York: Russell and Russell, 1965.

McKendrick, Neil, John Brewer, and J. H. Plumb. *The Birth of Consumer Society: The Commercialization of Eighteenth-Century England.* Bloomington: Indiana University Press, 1982.

Messenger, Troy. *Holy Leisure: Recreation and Religion in God's Square Mile.* Philadelphia: Temple University Press, 1999.

Miller, Michael B. *The Bon Marché: Bourgeois Culture and the Department Store, 1869–1920.* Princeton: Princeton University Press, 1981.

Moore, R. Laurence. *Selling God: American Religion in the Marketplace of Culture.* New York: Oxford University Press, 1994.

Morgan, David. *The Embodied Eye: Religious Visual Culture and the Social Life of Feeling.* Berkeley: University of California Press, 2012.

———. *Protestants and Pictures: Religion, Visual Culture, and the Age of American Mass Production.* New York: Oxford University Press, 1999.

Morgan, David, and Sally M. Promey, eds. *The Visual Culture of American Religions.* Berkeley: University of California Press, 2001.

Morowitz, Laura. "A Passion for Business: Wanamaker's, Munkácsy, and the Depiction of Christ." *Art Bulletin,* June 1, 2009, 184–206.

Nahshon, Edna. "Going against the Grain: Jews and Passion Plays on the American Mainstream Stage, 1879–1929." In *Jews and Theater in an Intercultural Context,* edited by Edna Nahshon. Boston: Brill, 2012.

Nasaw, David. *Children of the City: At Work and at Play.* New York: Anchor, 2012.

Nelson, Louis P. Introduction to *American Sanctuary: Understanding Sacred Spaces,* ed. Louis P. Nelson. Bloomington: Indiana University Press, 2006.

Noll, Mark, ed. *God and Mammon: Protestants, Money, and the Market, 1790–1860.* New York: Oxford University Press, 2002.

North, Douglass C. *The Economic Growth of the United States, 1790–1860.* Englewood Cliffs, NJ: Prentice Hall, 1961.

Nostrum, Paul. *The Economics of Retailing.* New York: Ronald Press, 1919.

Orsi, Robert A. *Between Heaven and Earth: The Religious Worlds People Make and the Scholars Who Study Them.* Princeton: Princeton University Press, 2005.

———. *Gods of the City: Religion and the American Urban Landscape.* Bloomington: Indiana University Press, 1999.

Pevsner, Nikolaus. *A History of Building Types: The A. W. Mellon Lectures in the Fine Arts, 1970.* Princeton: Princeton University Press, 1976.

Porterfield, Amanda, Darren E. Grem, and John Corrigan. *The Business Turn in American Religious History.* Oxford: Oxford University Press, 2017.

Promey, Sally M. "The Public Display of Religion." In *The Visual Culture of American Religions,* edited by David Morgan and Sally M. Promey, 27–48. Berkeley: University of California Press, 2001.

Putney, Clifford. *Muscular Christianity: Manhood and Sports in Protestant America, 1880–1920.* Cambridge: Harvard University Press, 2001.

Rice, Edwin Wilbur. *A History of the American Sunday-School Union and a Report of the Seventy-Fifth Anniversary at the Academy of Music, Philadelphia, May 24 and 25, 1899*. Philadelphia: American Sunday School Union, 1899.

Robert, Dana Lee. *Occupy until I Come: A. T. Pierson and the Evangelization of the World*. Grand Rapids, MI: Eerdmans, 2003.

Rydell, Robert W. *All the World's a Fair: Visions of Empire at American International Expositions, 1876–1916*. Chicago: University of Chicago Press, 1984.

Rzeznik, Thomas F. *Church and Estate: Religion and Wealth in Industrial-Era Philadelphia*. University Park: Pennsylvania State University Press, 2013.

Schaffer, Kristin. *Daniel H. Burnham: Visionary Architect and Planner*. New York: Rizzoli International, 2003.

Schlereth, Thomas J. *Victorian America: Transformations in Everyday Life, 1876–1915*. New York: Harper Perennial, 1991.

Schmidt, Leigh Eric. *Consumer Rites: The Buying and Selling of American Holidays*. Princeton: Princeton University Press, 1995.

Schwain, Kristin. *Signs of Grace: Religion and American Art in the Gilded Age*. Ithaca: Cornell University Press, 2008.

Selden, William K. *The Princeton Summer Camp, 1908–1975*. Princeton: Princeton University Printing Services, self-published, n.d.

Smith, Gary Scott. "Protestant Churches and Business in Gilded-Age America." *Theology Today*, October 2003, 311–31.

———. *The Search for Social Salvation: Social Christianity in America, 1880–1925*. Lanham, MD: Lexington Books, 2000.

Soucek, Gayle. *Marshall Field's: The Store That Helped Build Chicago*. Charleston, SC: History Press, 2010.

Stein, Roger B. *John Ruskin and Aesthetic Thought in America, 1840–1900*. Cambridge: Harvard University Press, 1967.

Tomkins, Calvin. *Merchants and Masterpieces: The Story of the Metropolitan Museum of Art*. New York: Dutton, 1970.

Trachtenberg, Alan. *The Incorporation of America: Culture and Society in the Gilded Age*. New York: Hill and Wang, 2007.

———. *Shades of Hiawatha: Staging Indians, Making Americans, 1880–1930*. New York: Hill and Wang, 2004.

Tweed, Thomas, ed. Retelling U.S. Religious History. Berkeley: University of California Press, 1997.

Tyler, Linda L. "'Commerce and Poetry Hand in Hand': Music in American Department Stores, 1880–1930." *Journal of American Musicological Society* 45, no. 1 (Spring 1992): 72–120.

Valeri, Mark. *Heavenly Merchandize: How Religion Shaped Commerce in Puritan America*. Princeton: Princeton University Press, 2010.

———. "Weber and Eighteenth-Century Religious Developments in America." In *Religion and the Marketplace in the United States*, edited by Jan Stievermann, Philip Goff, and Detlev Junker, 63–78. Oxford: Oxford University Press, 2015.

Van Slyck, Abigail A. *A Manufactured Wilderness: Summer Camps and the Shaping of American Youth, 1890–1960.* St. Paul: University of Minnesota Press, 2006.

Vásquez, Manuel A. *More Than Belief: A Materialist Theory of Religion.* New York: Oxford University Press, 2011.

Wagner, Charles. *My Impressions of America.* Translated by Mary Louise Hendee. London: McClure, Phillips, 1906.

———. *The Simple Life.* Translated by Mary Louise Hendee. New York: McClure, Phillips, 1903.

Walton, Jonathan. *Watch This! The Ethics and Aesthetics of Black Televangelism.* New York: New York University Press, 2009.

Wanamaker, John. "The John Wanamaker Commercial Institute—A Store School." *Annals of the American Academy of Political and Social Science*, 1909, 151–54.

Wasson, Samuel A., Jr., comp. *History of the Bethany Presbyterian Church and Sunday School, 1858–1958.* Philadelphia: Pennsylvania Historical Society, 1958.

Weinberg, H. Barbara. "Americans in Paris, 1860–1900" (October 2006). In *Heilbrunn Timeline of Art History.* New York: Metropolitan Museum of Art, 2000. Available at www.metmuseum.org.

Weisenfeld, Judith. *African American Women and Christian Activism: New York's Black YWCA, 1905–1945.* Cambridge: Harvard University Press, 1998.

Whitaker, Jan. *The World of Department Stores.* New York: Vendome, 2011.

White, Ronald, Jr., and C. Howard Hopkins. *The Social Gospel: Religion and Reform in Changing America.* Philadelphia: Temple University Press, 1990.

Wiebe, Robert H. *The Search for Order, 1877–1920.* New York: Hill and Wang, 1967.

Williams, Peter. "The Gospel of Wealth and the Gospel of Art: Episcopalians and Cultural Philanthropy from the Gilded Age to the Depression." *Anglican and Episcopal History* 75, no. 2 (2006): 173.

———. *Religion, Art, and Money: Episcopalians and American Culture from the Civil War to the Great Depression.* Chapel Hill: University of North Carolina Press, 2016.

Wilson, Philip Whitwell. *An Unofficial Statesman: Robert C. Ogden.* Garden City, NY: Doubleday, Page, 1924.

Winston, Diane. *Red-Hot and Righteous: The Urban Religion of the Salvation Army.* Cambridge: Harvard University Press, 1999.

Zola, Émile. *Ladies' Paradise.* Translated by Brian Nelson. New York: Oxford University Press, 1995.

Zulker, William Allen. *John Wanamaker: King of the Merchants.* Wayne, PA: Eaglecrest, 1993.

INDEX

A&P grocery, 204
abolitionists, 19, 110, 220n121
Academy of Music, 15, 47
Adams Dry Goods Company, 71
African Americans, 19, 96–99, 109–10,
112, 123, 152, 198, 202–3, 213n12, 216n22,
230n41; and black-owned businesses, 92;
employees at Wanamaker Store, 88, 91–92,
96, 109, 112, 120–22, 194, 200, 229n20. See
also minstrelsy; race; Robert Curtis Ogden
Association (RCOA)
Albert, Prince, 44
Alger, Horatio, 17, 215n6
Alms and Doepke Department Store, 227n87
American Art Association of Paris, 128, 152
American Missionary Association (AMA), 96
American Museum, 137
American Sunday School Union, 28–29
American University of Trade and Applied
Commerce. See John Wanamaker Com-
mercial Institute (JWCI)
Andrew and Phillip Brotherhood, 39
Anglicans, 175, 178
arcades, 52, 63–65, 225n19
architecture, 4, 7, 10–11, 44, 49, 61–62, 64–87,
126, 128, 130, 165, 175–77; and churches,
11–12, 31–32, 34–35, 177–78, 199, 206; and
Wanamaker's stores, 12, 50, 70–74, 77–87,
123, 165–66, 175, 182, 190–91, 197–98, 201–
4. See also art; class; taste
Armour, Philip, 5
Armstrong, Samuel Chapman, 96–97,
230n44
Armstrong Association, 92
art, 44–45, 50, 60, 163, 194, 199, 237n92;
displayed at Wanamaker Store, 4, 7, 43,
124–29, 133–36, 139–60, 172–73, 182, 186,
190–91, 202, 233n1, 235n31; and Protestant

aesthetics, 10–12, 129–33, 146–60, 175,
190–91, 197, 202; and the rise of muse-
ums, 137–42; See also architecture; class;
museums; taste
Arts and Crafts movement, 11, 103, 130
Art's True Mission in America (Duganne), 132
Atlantic City Convention Hall (Boardwalk
Hall), 241n39
Atlantic Monthly, 50, 110
A. T. Stewart's Emporium, 67–69, 215n5,
224n6, 227n85, 229n3
Au bonheur des dames/Ladies' Paradise
(Zola), 61, 224n3

Balzac, Honoré de, 171
Baptists, 15–16, 22, 35, 94
Barnum, P. T., 137
Behold the Bridegroom Cometh (Tanner),
144, 153
Beneficial Bank, 39
Benjamin, Walter, 45, 64
Bennett, Joseph N., 21–22, 41–43
Bethany Presbyterian Church (Bethany Col-
legiate Church), 4, 30, 54–56, 59–60, 81,
108, 118, 120, 129, 132–33, 159, 168–69, 193,
220n105, 221n150; architecture, 31–33, 74,
223n190; Bethany College, 40; social ser-
vices offered by, 37–40, 73; Sunday School
mission, 4, 30–34, 73, 93, 105, 151. See also
Friendly Inn; Penny Savings Bank
Biswanger, Ray, 240n5, 240n35, 241n39
Blauvelt, Augustus, 30
Blériot, Louis, 139
Bloomingdale's, 225n42
Bonaparte, Louis-Napoleon, 65–66
Booth, Evangeline, 194
Booth, William, 4, 105
Boucicaut, Aristide, 65–66, 224n6

ABOUT THE AUTHOR

Nicole C. Kirk is Frank and Alice Schulman Chair of Unitarian Universalist History and Assistant Professor at Meadville Lombard Theological School.

Printed and bound by CPI Group (UK) Ltd, Croydon, CR0 4YY

13/04/2025

14656574-0005